Representing African Music

Representing African Music
Postcolonial Notes, Queries, Positions

Kofi Agawu

ROUTLEDGE
NEW YORK AND LONDON

Published in 2003 by
Routledge
29 West 35th Street
New York, NY 10001
www.routledge-ny.com

Published in Great Britain by
Routledge
11 New Fetter Lane
London EC4P 4EE
www.routledge.co.uk

Routledge is an imprint of the Taylor & Francis Group.
Printed in the United States of America on acid-free paper.

10 9 8 7 6 5 4 3 2

Library of Congress Cataloging-in-Publication Data

Agawu, V. Kofi (Victor Kofi)
    Representing African music : postcolonial notes, queries, positions /
Kofi Agawu.
        p.   cm.
Includes bibliographical references (p.   ).
    ISBN 0-415-94389-2 (alk. paper) — ISBN 0-415-94390-6 (paperbound :
alk. paper)
    1. Music—Africa—History and criticism.   2. Postcolonialism—Africa.
I. Title.
    ML350 .A355 2003
    780' .67—dc21
                                                          2002153450

for Christie

Contents

Acknowledgments

I wish to acknowledge several friends and colleagues who read all or parts of the manuscript and offered much valuable feedback: Carolyn Abbate, Philip Bohlman, David Brackett, Meki Nzewi, Roger Parker, Ronald Radano, Paul Richards, Jonathan Stock, Ruth Solie, and Barbara White. I have also benefited from conversations with Kwasi Ampene, Kofi Anyidoho, Akin Euba, and Abiola Irele. Finally, I owe a considerable debt to two friends engaged in their own postcolonial adventures, Patrick Mensah and Olakunle George. As theorists in their own fields, they have helped me glimpse the larger enterprise in which we are all engaged; as my chief informants on matters postcolonial, they have been extremely generous. It goes without saying that I alone am responsible for what is published here.

Portions of this book have appeared or are forthcoming elsewhere: a version of chapter 1 will appear in the second volume of *L'Enciclopedia della Musica*, edited by Jean-Jacques Nattiez; chapter 3 appeared in the *Journal of the American Musicological Society* in 1995; chapter 5 is expanded from an article in *Research in African Literatures* 2001; and a short version of chapter 7 will appear in *The Cultural Study of Music*, edited by Martin Clayton, Richard Middleton, and Trevor Herbert. I am grateful to editors and publishers for permission to reuse this material.

Introduction

The music of Africa continues to draw converts, adherents, and enthusiasts. Concerts in parks, museums, school playgrounds, and community centers; workshops and clinics introducing African drumming to amateurs and neophytes; performances by celebrity singers, dancers, drummers, guitarists, and bandleaders; "musicking" at festivals, rituals, and at public and private gatherings; radio and TV broadcasts of World Beat: these and many more activities signal African music's continuing vitality at home and abroad.

What is the secret of African music? Some say that it is communal and inviting, drawing in a range of consumers young and old, skilled and unskilled. It allows for the spontaneous and authentic expression of emotion. It is integrated with social life rather than set apart, natural rather than artificial, and deeply human in its material significance. Its themes are topical and of sharp contemporary relevance, sometimes humorous and satirical, sometimes sad and affecting, often profound. Thoughtful observers celebrate the close affinities between language and music, marvel at the extraordinary intellectual acumen displayed by lead drummers, song crafters, and instrumentalists, call attention to musicians' clever use of iconic modes to signify, and, above all perhaps, proclaim the subtle and intricate domestication of a broad range of temporalities in African music—from the syllabic, speech mode employed by talking drummers to the mesmerizing, endless melody of mbira virtuosi. Obviously, then, little effort is required on the part of Africans to produce reasons for wanting to celebrate the extraordinary range and depth of their musical-artistic resources.

The spirit of African music is, however, not always manifest in the scholarship about it. There are several reasons for this. First, the community of scholars is diffuse, dispersed, and decentralized, a condition that has impeded the emergence of a viable, communally based critical practice. Second, the number of African scholars actively engaged in music research is relatively small. The field is dominated by foreigners whose ultimate allegiances are to the metropolis, not to Africa. Third, and related to this second point, much of the scholarship originating from the continent is directed outward, extraverted, as Paulin Hountondji has dubbed scholarly production oriented toward overseas markets.[1] Extraversion works to mute the sort of critical vibrancy that one observes—not without a certain amount of envy—in some Africa-based communities of philosophers, literary theorists, and social theorists. And fourth, African music, as a performing art in a predominantly oral tradition, poses uncommon challenges to those who seek to establish its texts and define its analyzable objects.

I do not mean to suggest that scholarly culture must somehow reproduce the dynamics of artistic culture in a one-to-one correspondence. Scholarship, after all, develops according to its own momentum, in response to institutional pressures and intellectual fashions, reflecting individual dispositions and abilities, and within the constraints of an academic market. There is, however, considerable potential for drawing lessons for scholarly practice from the kinds of affirmations and contentions that animate African musical performance. I'd like to think that these essays mimic its gestures and rhetoric: irreverent, playful, overstated where appropriate, always aiming to draw out the reader.

My aim, quite simply, is to stimulate debate about modes of knowledge production by offering a critique of discourse about African music. Who writes about it, how, and why? What assumptions and prejudices influence the presentation of ethnographic data? To what orders of authority do scholars appeal? What ethical considerations motivate individuals? How different is African music from other world musics, and how can we best construct difference? What obstacles are there to the emergence of a fruitful critical practice within Africa itself? What role has ethnomusicology played in promoting as well as inhibiting the development of African music? These are the sorts of questions that motivate the book's arguments.

Many people associate African music research with the discipline of ethnomusicology, and this is largely correct given the latter's traditional but by no means exclusive dedication to non-Western societies. But the ethnomusicological approach is only one among several. Earlier in the twentieth century, comparative musicology regularly invoked an explicit comparative framework by directly juxtaposing seemingly different musical practices. Erich von Hornbostel's seminal article of 1928, although focused on "African Negro Music," exemplifies some of the advantages of the comparative method.[2] In its metalanguage (antiphony, part-singing, organum, scale, interval, harmony, tonality, ostinato, form, and the relationship between speech tone and pure melody), its intra-African references (Wanixa, Wanyamwezi, Wasukuma, Luvemba, Mashona, Makua, Bateke, Bahutu, Kabure, Jao, Pangwe, Ewe), and its extra-African allusions (Middle Ages, Chinese, Melanesian, American Indian, Bach, Schumann), Hornbostel's study simultaneously engages African music directly while making it possible for later scholars to extend his insights, critique his assumptions, and build bridges to other musical traditions. Although comparative musicology has since been superseded by ethnomusicology, there are some who would wish to retain a carefully configured comparative impulse and to reject the solipsism of noncomparison that has become a permanent temptation for ethnomusicology.

The comparative impulse survives in reduced or alternate forms, of course, as in area studies, which feature research topics selected on the basis of geocultural conformity. Area studies journals like *Africa* (the journal of the International African Institute, the journal in which Hornbostel's essay appeared), *Présence Africaine, African Studies Review,* or the *Canadian Journal of African Studies* publish an occasional article on music alongside their regular fare from anthropology, economics, sociology, philosophy, folklore, and history. The journal *African Music,* the only one of its kind devoted to the subject, includes contributions from a broad range of individuals on a wide variety of subjects. Unlike ethnomusicology, area studies are not constrained by a relatively centralized methodology. *African Music,* for example, mixes anecdotal, informal, and even experimental ways of ordering knowledge with more formal styles of reportage to produce a far more interesting mix than the professional voice that emerges from the pages of *Ethnomusicology.*

African music, finally, has been an object contemplated by musicologists and music theorists. Although few in number, these contributions are nevertheless of the highest importance from a symbolic point of view. An exemplary work of musical organology such as Percival Kirby's *The Musical Instruments of the Native Races of South Africa* (1934) takes the written record seriously, provides a systematic description of various musical instruments, and transcribes into staff notation incipits and sample sounds to render them accessible to a wider musicological community.[3] Similarly, recent inquiries into African rhythmic structure by Jay Rahn, Jeff Pressing, and Willie Anku can be placed alongside any contemporary, quantitatively oriented work in music theory without creating the impression that the study of the structural properties of cycles, asymmetrical time lines, and master drum patterns is inappropriate or anachronistic.[4] Like their comparativist forbears, musicologists and music theorists have tended to approach African music through Western eyes and ears, so to speak. While some ethnomusicologists would wish to rescue African music from such impostors, we should point out that neither approach to African music— "Western" or "African"—is intrinsically good or bad. Much depends on one's purposes, terms of reference, and assumptions, and it will be an ongoing concern of mine in this book to encourage a more open, less tutored engagement with African music as a means to an end.

I have been using the term "African music" as if it possessed an agreed-upon provenance, but the term carries many different connotations. We must therefore pose the question: "What is African Music?"

Asked about the origins of his art, highlife musician Nana Ampadu once said, "If I say I will tell you where highlife started, then it means I am going to lie."[5] By the same token, if I say I'm going to define African music in a way that will satisfy all readers, it means I'm planning to fail. Still, the prospect of failure should not deter anyone who undertakes a project like this, so let me sketch a few ideas. African music is best understood not as a finite repertoire but as a potentiality. In terms of what now exists and has existed in the past, African music designates those numerous repertoires of song and instrumental music that originate in specific African communities, are performed regularly as part of play, ritual, and worship, and circulate mostly orally/aurally, within and across language, ethnic, and cultural boundaries. This potentially infinite set covers funeral dirges, children's game songs, recreational dances, music marking harvests, healing ceremonies, and court celebrations, among many, many genres of traditional music. "African music" also includes forms associated with urban life, such as highlife, jùjú, soukouss, makossa, afrobeat, mbaqanga, taarab, and fújì, among others. Enabled at a fundamental level by the recording industry, these forms represent an imaginative blend of European and African resources. Although some forms of African popular music have considerable currency in Europe and North America—they have to some extent "gone global"—their origin and most authentic performances lie deep in urban Africa. Then there is the tradition of so-called art music, consisting of folk operas, cantatas, orchestral compositions, choral works, and sonatas for various instruments, all of them normally written down by named literate men and women trained in the idiom and practices of European classical music. Performances, though infrequent, have been held in Lagos, Lomé, Nsukka, Nairobi, Kampala, Accra, Freetown, Kinshasa, and other places. Leading figures in this tradition—a tradition, incidentally, that has been mostly ignored by ethnomusicologists—include Fela Sowande (1905–

1987), T. K. Ekundayo Phillips (1884–1969), Ikoli Harcourt-Whyte (1905–1977), Akin Euba (b. 1935), Ayo Bankole (1935–1976), and Joshua Uzoigwe (b. 1946) (restricting mention to a few members of the Nigerian contingent for now).

Placing these vast repertoires into a simple tripartite scheme—traditional-popular-art—provides orientation only at the grossest level. Each type is in turn constituted by a wide range of expression, depending on contexts and purposes of music-making, performers' skills, and degree of integration with ritual. It is thus impossible to fit the entire range of products and processes into a single taxonomy. For our purposes, African music is best understood not only as encompassing these genres and repertoires but also as indicating a rich set of possibilities for artistic expression in musical language: markings, ultimately, of Africans' collective as well as individual genius.

Discourse about African music forms the target of critique in this book. By "discourse," I refer not only to specific utterances but also to an implicit framework for the production, dissemination, and consumption of knowledge. Such discourse is regularly encountered in books, monographs, and scholarly journals, as annotations to sound and visual recordings, and as oral texts in the form of conference papers, classroom lectures, and rehearsal or instructional talk. Like philosophy, literary criticism, or postcolonial studies, African musicology enshrines varying degrees of rigor in constituting or otherwise making sense of musical objects and (associated) practices.

And by "critique," I mean a network of interrogative practices: searching, questioning, probing, demystifying, laying bare. Critique is ongoing; ideally, it never ends. At the most basic level, a critique of discourse about African music will probe the conceptual schemes upon which knowledge of music rests. Although a critique in the spirit of a deconstruction surfaces from time to time in this book, I have sometimes found it necessary to curtail the unfolding of such a critique in order finally not to obscure certain political and pragmatic commitments. To say this is to acknowledge a potential conflict between the demands of an ideal critique and those of a more immediate political action. Embarking on critique without ever "landing" seems to me to be as problematic as rushing into political action on the basis of a limited engagement with the ironies, banalities, and contradictions inherent in the ways knowledge of African music has been engendered. But finding a suitable middle ground is more easily imagined than achieved.

Why is a critique of discourse about African music necessary? First, because, as pointed out earlier, there is a disjunction between the practice of African music and its scholarly representation. While such a disjunction is

in principle unavoidable, an attempt to minimize its effects may not be un-
desirable. A second, related reason stems from that part of the legacy of
modernity that concentrates increased awareness on the contingency of
our modes of knowledge production. V. Y. Mudimbe's hugely influential
book, *The Invention of Africa* (1988), made possible the kind of slate-clearing
exercise that the study of African music has long needed.[6] If you suspect
that there is no self-evident knowledge, that methodologies produce and
reproduce ideology, that it matters who we are and why we do what we do,
that conventional frameworks for reporting knowledge evince no invariant or a priori superiority to other frameworks, then it becomes difficult,
perhaps unconscionable, to proceed in the task of knowledge production
with little or no self-consciousness.

It would be inaccurate to say that African musicology has shown no
self-awareness so far. The writings of John Blacking, for example—vigorous, earnest, pointed, but also repetitive and occasionally overgeneral—
undermine such a claim. And so would a specific incident like that which
unfolded in the pages of the journal *African Music* during the mid-1970s.
Music theorist and composer Lazarus Ekwueme guest-edited a special
issue of the journal to which he himself contributed an analytical essay.
The essay included, among other things, an exhaustive intervallic account,
invocations of Schenker, and a strategic playing down of matters of context. Ekwueme's thumb-in-your-face declaration that we want to know
"*what* the African does musically, instead, merely, of *why* he does it"[7] provoked two strong reactions, one from Meki Nzewi, the other from Sam Akpabot. Nzewi found the analysis incomplete, and the suppression of
context unacceptable. Akpabot complained about the skimpy citations of
previous theoretical work (his own included, of course) and, more devas-
tatingly, of the author's intellectual orientation. According to him, Ekwueme was trying to "think white"; he, Akpabot, would prefer a white
person trying to "think black" any day.

Why did a Yale-trained African theorist's analysis of an Igbo song provoke such extreme reactions from two of his fellow countrymen? How
much contextual information should have been given? Where does African
thinking stop and Western thinking begin? Are those categories necessarily
synonymous with "thinking black" and "thinking white"? What has race
got to do with it? No doubt there exist other texts not available to readers
of the journal that might facilitate interpretation of this incident. Fascinating though it might be to examine the motives of this trio, we would be
flung too far afield trying to analyze the intricacies of that debate here. I
bring up the incident simply to show that passions have flared from time to
time in response to one or another approach to African musicology, and
that the characterization of African musicology as sleepy is not entirely ac-

curate. Still, the Akpabot-Ekwueme-Nzewi debate is the exception rather than the rule, for although *African Music* has occasionally encouraged discussion by publishing polemical reviews and articles, the journal could hardly be described as a site of terrifically vigorous debate about African music. Even less committed to such exchange is *Ethnomusicology,* whose African offerings, drenched in institutionally sanctioned methodology, leave little room for contestation.

There is, then, plenty of room for more critical discussion of the bases for knowledge production in African musicology, room for the relentless critique practiced by Martin Scherzinger in his advocacy of an empowering formalism for the analysis of Southern African music,[8] for Meki Nzewi's strident contestation of the myths and falsehoods that have delayed the emergence of an Africa-centered view of African music,[9] and for Philip Tagg's problematizing of "black music" and "white music" as essential categories.[10] There is room, too, for discussion of what may well be the most fundamental issue, conveyed in Klaus Wachsmann's remark that the word "ethnomusicology" is "an awkward one. . . . [It] offends many people,"[11] and in Akin Euba's firm belief that ethnomusicology is "unsuitable for African music studies" and, in fact, "irrelevant to African culture."[12] (Euba, a leading composer of African art music, is also a card-carrying ethnomusicologist.)

Critical discussion of these issues has been greatly facilitated in recent years by the emergence of postcolonial theory, one of whose central concerns is to unmask (or unveil, demystify, "lay bare") the enabling constructs of various knowledge systems. This theory serves as an overarching frame for the present study. As used here and with specific reference to Africa, postcolonial theory is understood as a constellation of critical practices drawn from philosophy, history, social theory, and literary criticism. It is committed to explicit thematization and theorization of the experiences of people whose identities are inflected by the metropolitan habits exported to Africa through British, French, Belgian, and Portuguese colonialism. Postcolonial theory encourages a new self-awareness, rewards the eagerness to lay bare the situatedness and precariousness of various frames of knowledge construction, and takes particular pleasure in relativizing and decentering European intellectual hegemony. Promiscuous in intellectual orientation and style, postcolonial theory is restless in spirit and vigilant about the play of power in shaping discourses. And there is often an implicit political program, ensuring that theory and aesthetics are not facilely privileged as domains that lie beyond politics. Writings by scholars such as Aijaz Ahmad, Gayatri Spivak, Edward Said, Homi Bhabha, Paul Gilroy, or, to move closer to home, V. Y. Mudimbe, Kwame Anthony Appiah, Kwasi Wiredu, Christopher Miller, Achille Mbembe, and Paulin

Hountondji, clear space for the acknowledgment, indeed celebration, of the incongruities, contradictions, antinomies, and hybridity of postcolonial culture and experience as necessary elements in the adequate theorization of contemporary Africa.[13]

I find this work inspiring principally because it offers grounds for the legitimization of apparently incoherent lived experiences. By incorporating a wide range of sociocultural experience, postcolonial theory returns a verdict of "normal" on lives that had hitherto been denied theoretical legitimacy, and honors them with attention and thought. People whose upbringing was irreducibly mixed, who partook of aspects of tradition as well as aspects of modernity, finally acquire unmarked status in the postcolonial critic's book. These are people who read Chaucer and Shakespeare, *Drum Magazine* and *Who Killed Lucy?*, Achebe and Ngugi, *The Students' Companion, Courtesy for Boys and Girls,* and the King James Bible. Although raised on tuo, fufu, eba, ugali, and gari, they have been known to eat shepherd's pie and spotted dick. They probably know more facts about the French Revolution or the Hundred Years' War than they do about the Songhay or Mali empires. The musicians among them may have played hymns and Mozart at the harmonium, danced to highlife, sung a chorus or two from *Messiah* as members of a church choir, and been assaulted by soul, reggae, and funk on radio. Some wear suits to work, cloth or agbada to funerals, and designer jeans to nightclubs.

To describe an individual molded within such a culture as hybrid, to invoke the metaphor of *métisse,* is to undercomplicate the dynamics of identity formation. For only an aggressive and largely irrational postulation of the purity of origins will sanction a description of such individuals and experiences in terms of deviations from what are in effect less-threatening norms. Postcolonial theory normalizes hybridity and thus makes possible a truer, more ethical mode of identity construction. In the hands of its most imaginative practitioners, postcolonial theory dramatizes the complex convergences as well as divergences that constitute African life.

The reader will forgive the cathartic mood of the last three paragraphs, but it seems important, in writing about African music, to proclaim the promise of postcolonial theory, because our field has up to now only indirectly engaged with its potentially fruitful and ethical ways of making sense of the (musical) world. This is not to imply that postcolonial theory is unified, that it does not have its critics, or that traces of its thinking do not already exist in the literature on African music. Indeed, a number of writings by Veit Erlmann, David Coplan, John Blacking, Christopher Ballantine, Louise Meintjes, Martin Scherzinger, and others are postcolonial in spirit. The fact that these writers all write about southern Africa is not accidental, for there the complex interaction of peoples, languages, and cultures raises analytical issues that have come to seem paradigmatic for postcolonial theory.

Among West Africanists, Christopher Waterman's writings often thematize the incongruities of postcolonial musical Africa. In a 1991 article that includes a critique of scholarship about African rhythm, for example, Waterman asks that scholars not dodge certain difficult questions:

> [T]he notion that ethnomusicology is the study of music "in context"—a phrase often invoked but rarely defined—has implicitly encouraged the reification of musical sound and the epistemological disjunction of music from the social and historical grounds of its existence. This has by and large allowed ethnomusicological discourse to bracket itself outside the very real world of colonialism, power relations, and the social production of knowledge.
>
> I would suggest that our understanding of sub-Saharan music has been conditioned by factors infrequently discussed in the literature: for example, the varied training and practical goals of investigators; the portrayal of similarity and differences between peoples of African and European descent; the invention of "traditional" or "tribal" musics under colonialism and since independence; and the variable, though always unequal, relationship of the scholarly subject to the human objects of his or her study. Africanist ethnomusicology has, with a few notable exceptions, lagged behind other branches of African studies in critically examining its own ideological "context."[14]

Waterman's list of issues may as well be adopted as a guide to the present study: music as sound versus music as context; the political implications of ethnomusicological discourse; notions of difference; power relations between researcher and researched; and self-awareness. Let me turn, then, to the specific concerns of the nine essays that follow.

I begin with a chapter baldly titled "Colonialism's Impact" in order to suggest that it is impossible to overestimate the extent to which colonialism has had an impact on African musical life and representation. Drawing on examples from twentieth-century Ghana, Nigeria, and the findings of Gerhard Kubik, I ask that we rethink the extent to which European influence has come to determine our construction of the "purest" of African musics, and to embrace the challenge of formulating a view of our creative activities not under the weight of a nostalgic look at the past but through a realistic look at the present. In chapter 2, I describe the body of texts that constitute the archive of African music, touching on issues such as language, orality, fieldwork, autobiography, and transcription. Chapters 3 and 4 are concerned with rhythm, perhaps the most sensationalized parameter in African music. Without denying that rhythm is imaginatively elaborated in African music, I question the motivation for its persistent thematization in Euro-American discourses, and I suggest that such emphasis may be part of a plot to deny that Africans can and do control the procedures within dimensions like harmony, melody, and form with comparable skill. Chapter 4 may be read as a technical supplement to chapter 3. In it, I examine in some detail notions such as polymeter, additive rhythm, and cross rhythm and argue that these are myths that have been reproduced in the literature on African music. In both chapters, I suggest that an eagerness to produce differences may explain the persistence of certain erroneous notions.

Chapter 5 extends the discussion of language begun in chapter 2. I begin by exploding the myths that African music cannot be merely listened to, and that the distribution of musics into functional and contemplative categories is useful. I then reflect upon certain aspects of the relationship between language and music: the usefulness of performance errors as sites of emergence of an indigenous discourse; tonemic transgression in metalanguage; singing in the throat; and modes of signification in drum music. Although these topics have all been written about before, my concern is to refine certain forms of understanding by rejecting some of the restrictions that certain disciplines have inadvertently placed on interpretation.

Chapter 6 deals with popular music, represented here by Ghanaian highlife. The bulk of the chapter is given over to a close reading of three highlife songs, the aim being to reinforce the point that African popular music is finally music, not social text or history. Unless we give due attention to the musical elements—the notes played or sung at specific moments, by means of specific articulations, and at specific levels of intensity—we cannot hope to develop a nuanced understanding of this most vibrant of African art forms.

Chapters 7 and 8 project certain positions. Chapter 7 interrogates the notion of difference as it has informed ethnomusicological writing about Africa. I remind the reader that difference is not real, that it is, like anything else, a construct rather than something given in nature, and that notions of difference have been employed by scholars seeking to exercise a certain form of power over African subjects. I propose that we rethink difference, that we put the accent on the material conditions that produce surface differences; I propose, therefore, that we reach for the more primal motivations—such as the need for music-making—that constrain all community-dwelling human beings. A strategic embrace of sameness may thus prove liberating. Notions of sameness enter into the discussion of music analysis in chapter 8, "How Not to Analyze African Music." As a performing art, music stakes a commanding claim to the present. All memories of music are formed from real or imagined performances. The performative essence of music in turn weakens the strictures of context, history, and authenticity. In this chapter, I argue for more analysis of African music, for the application of any and all methods: Schenkerian, set theoretical, semiotic, you name it. I aim, in short, to discourage African music analysis as the exclusive domain of ethnomusicologists; the insights of music theorists and musicologists are just as crucial to the development of a postcolonial musical analysis.

Finally, in chapter 9, I ask questions about the ethics of African music research. It is doubtful that one can find a grounding principle for ethical conduct beyond an ambitious and idealized desire to promote the common good; nevertheless, given our historical realities, a retreat from ethics might itself be unethical. Applying little theoretical pressure in this closing chapter, I present a series of anecdotes that might form the basis of theorization. Because these anecdotes concern the construction of ethnographies, the question as to whether the making of ethnography can ever be an ethical process remains. An epilogue reflects on the nature of the contradictions and antinomies that undergird my analyses and suggests that a postcolonial perspective is finally not reducible to a single, conflict-free stance.

With this last, I come to the end of my postcolonial notes, queries, and positions on African music. The issues are many and diverse; parts of the discussion are necessarily inconclusive and open. And referring to "African music" rather than to more local repertoires may irritate readers who do not see the disadvantages of excessive localization, or who are not alert to the possible gain in undercomplicating "Africa," treating it—as in the oppressor's mode—as a unity subtending diverse particulars. I hope that some of what follows will signal ways in which our critical responses can be freed of certain long-standing institutional prejudices so that we can do justice to the treasures of Africa's sound world.

A word about readership and the limits of what is attempted here: I have in mind primarily those who read and write about African music and who might (therefore) be interested in its politics of knowledge production. They include Africanist ethnomusicologists as well as nonethnomusicologists devoted to the continent's music. I hope especially to reach a few Africa-based readers who for various historical-material reasons have not had the opportunity to pursue the questions raised here in their own reading and writing. (That they are keenly aware of these issues goes without saying.) This particular ambition about readership may explain some of the discrepancies in tone and degree of background assumed in the book. There is simply no monolithic interpretive community out there when it comes to discourse about African music.

It should be obvious, too, that I lack the expertise to address the field of ethnomusicology as a whole. When I use the term "ethnomusicology," I am usually referring to what is embodied in writings about African music that are framed, designated, or packaged as ethnomusicological. Even then, I cannot hope to be comprehensive. Readers who feel that one or another aspect of ethnomusicological theory has been more productively formulated in other area studies will, I hope, forgive my inability to extend discussion into those areas.[15] Similarly, I should note that while a number of issues raised here are pertinent to other areas of musicological research (such as feminist musicology, gay-lesbian studies, and popular music research), I have not always sought such "outside" corroboration. The reason is that the specifics of the African condition need to be recognized for what they are, whether or not they are different or unique. The impulse to fold the book's critical concerns into a scheme operated by some sort of United Minorities League may seem natural in North America but it does not always serve Africa well. Therefore sacrificing the potential advantages of corroboration for a renewed focus on Africa's historical and sociocultural particulars seems to me to be a price worth paying.

1
Colonialism's Impact

Conquest

In the early 1400s, Portugal, a relatively small and not particularly well-endowed European nation, sent groups of explorers along the West African coast in search of opportunities to trade and to spread the Christian religion. Reaching Cape Bianco in 1441, the Portuguese proceeded to the Senegal River in 1444, Sierra Leone in 1460, Elmina in the Gold Coast in 1471, and finally farther south to the Cape of Good Hope in 1487. Within a hundred years, Portugal had consolidated its position as a significant imperial force in Africa, later counting among its possessions the coastal areas of Angola and Mozambique. It would not be long before other Europeans, notably the Dutch, British, Belgians, Germans, and French, motivated by similar imperial ambitions, joined the assault. Beginning in 1532 and extending into the second half of the nineteenth century, a massive trans-Atlantic slave trade, involving perhaps as many as 20 million Africans, provided a forum for the enactment of various forms of European ambitions for power and control. By the late nineteenth century, and as a result of agitation and conflicts between and among Africans and Europeans, the occupation of Africa could no longer be sustained as an unformalized arrangement. Hence, individual European powers met at the Berlin conference of 1884–1885 to partition the continent and to establish regulations that would protect their economic and political interests.[1]

The Berlin conference prepared the period of official colonial rule. Colonialism meant the usurpation of Africa's political sovereignty and independence. By 1914 all of Black Africa, with the exception of Liberia and Ethiopia, was under the rule of one or another European power. In time, however, the colonial presence began to be challenged by a not unexpected internal agitation for self-rule and by an increasing realization that maintaining an empire was a costly business. The tables turned in 1957 when the Gold Coast became the first Black African country to attain independence. Following in rapid succession were various colonies including Nigeria, Kenya, Uganda, Ivory Coast, Guinea, Senegal, Zaïre, and a host of others. Today, all of Africa is officially under indigenous rule, including the Republic of South Africa, where a long-standing institutional and systematic racism delayed the emergence of majority rule until 1994.

The five hundred or so years in which these events unfolded may not seem like a long time in the history of a continent many millions of years old, a continent credited with the origins of human life. But history is made not by time but by events, and it is in this sense that the European intrusion in Africa is properly understood. Colonialism had a profound effect on practically every aspect of African life: economic, political, social, and religious. Many historians regard this as a decisive phase in Africa's history. Basil Davidson describes "the arrival of Europeans [since the early 16th century]" as "the greatest calamity in [Africa's] history," while A. Adu Boahen calls colonialism an "extremely important" episode, one that "marks a clear watershed in the history of the continent."[2]

Our subject is music, but I have begun with a conventional outline of Africa's recent history in order to provide a context for understanding the specifically musical developments of the last one hundred years. For unlike political history, with its kingdoms and wars, migrations and inventions, music—an art of sound and a performing art in an oral culture—leaves different, more complex and elusive traces on the historical record, which may explain why historians of Africa have ignored its music. Kevin Shillington's widely used textbook *History of Africa* (1989) has nothing to say about African music; nor does John Reader's recent *Africa: A Biography of the Continent* (1998). The problem is even more acute in histories of precolonial Africa. While it is true that such histories have only recently begun to be authoritative on account of archaeological findings, themselves enabled by advances in technology, it is nevertheless striking that a volume like the *Encyclopedia of Pre-Colonial Africa* (1997), subtitled "Archaeology, History, Languages, Cultures, and Environments," has nothing to say about music. This systematic absence may well come as a surprise to those who regard music's role in Africa as basic and indispensable, and who therefore expect to find discussion of it in descriptions of African society. Such absence suggests that writing the history of a performing art poses unique challenges.[3]

The purpose of this chapter is to highlight salient aspects of the impact of colonialism on African music in order to prepare the postcolonial critique of subsequent chapters. What was the musical society like before the arrival of Europeans? How did contact with Europe affect musical practice? What sort of legacy is evident in the musical forms that circulate in postcolonial Africa? These are, of course, huge questions that require treatment in several monographs. Nevertheless, we can make a start by taking note of the most visible colonial traces.

Two qualifications need to be established from the outset. First, by "colonialism," I mean the broad range of European influences in Africa from the fifteenth century onward, rather than the narrower range of influences initiated during the 1880s. Strictly speaking, the colonial period began with the partitioning of Africa and ended at independence, roughly 1884 to 1957. To speak of colonialism is therefore to speak of events influenced by institutional practices and discourses put in place during this seventy-three-year period. But the formal partitioning was preceded by several centuries of European contact with initially coastal then later inland Africans, resulting in influences on religion, culture, and education. Speaking of colonialism in this expanded sense means overlooking differences in character between occupation after formal annexation and informal but power-based prior contact. While these differences are most pronounced in respect of sociopolitical life, they are less so in the area of musical practice, and so can be safely ignored. Second, this chapter cannot hope to provide a comprehensive account of its subject, detailing every trace of European colonial influence. Because my own experience is most complete with respect to Ghana, I will draw my main examples from there, incorporate others from the research of Gerhard Kubik and Michael Echeruo, and leave readers to supply analogous ones from other parts of Africa.

Precolonial Africa

Information about music in precolonial Africa is scanty. The earliest records stem from archaeological findings in which dance movements and musical instruments are featured. For example, in a 1956 expedition to the Sahara, Henri Llhote and a team of explorers discovered in the Tassili n'Ajjer at Sefar a rock painting featuring eight dancers (five women and three men). Experts think that the painting comes from the period 6,000–4,000 B.C. Gerhard Kubik, who cites this and other evidence in a discussion of "African music in history," draws on a theory of Helmut Günther's to suggest an affinity between the dance depicted in the rock painting and a contemporary Zulu stamping dance known as *indlamu*.[4] Whether or not the specific connection is valid is less important than that the bold dance gestures featuring the upper torso and the enhanced legs of the male dancers provide some indication of the antiquity of certain contemporary dance movements. Another musical finding, also a rock painting, depicts a solo musician playing a six-string harp. He is flanked by an auditor, a person of ostensibly high rank; both are seated on stools. This painting has been dated to the period ca. 800–700 B.C.[5] Its somewhat intimate setting suggests that contemplative music, that is, music composed to be listened to rather than danced to, is, contrary to popular opinion, not exactly unheard of in Africa's history.

With the Arab exploration of North Africa and the Sahara during the seventh through the twelfth centuries and the arrival of Europeans in the fifteenth, the written historical record becomes a bit more precise. Paintings and illustrations in books feature musical instruments and movement stances. For example, the second volume of Michael Praetorius's *Syntagma Musicum* (1620)—another piece of evidence cited by Kubik—is a work of organology in which is found an illustration of a seven-string harp of African origins. Kubik conjectures that this harp originated from Gabon, collected perhaps by a German consul.

By far the clearest imaginings of precolonial musical society come from the *written* accounts of various travelers, explorers, and missionaries. A number of writers have made intelligent use of these sources. Percival Kirby, for example, writing about the music of Africans in South Africa, includes a large number of prior references to musical instruments found in scholarly as well as nonscholarly sources.[6] Gerhard Kubik, likewise, seeking to untangle the knotted history of multipart singing in Africa, goes to some trouble to acknowledge what others have written on the subject, before adding his own discoveries and conjectures.[7] And, in a comprehensive portrait of Mande music, Eric Charry includes an appendix of "References Related to Mande Music in Historical Sources from the Eleventh to the Mid-Nineteenth Century."[8] In reading these reports, one must not underestimate the extent to which they are constructed, that is, woven together on the basis of observation, imagination, and prejudice.[9]

What, then, are some of the themes expressed in earlier writings? In a fascinating lecture describing the making of images of West Africans by medieval Arabs, John Owen Hunwick assembles a series of quotations from Arabic sources to illustrate the kinds of stereotypes that emerged during the ascendancy of Islam in North Africa and further south across the Sahara.[10] These include the African's gifts for music and poetry, his love of dancing and sensuousness, his laziness, and the modesty of his intellectual gifts. Africans were thought to be a cheerful people: "Cheerfulness was divided into ten parts; the blacks got nine parts, the rest of humanity one." From here it is but a short step to the association of cheerfulness with merrymaking, itself inevitably accompanied by music and dancing. Hunwick notes: "the stereotype of the African as the incorrigible dancer and instinctive rhythmist, [is] summed up in an epigrammatic Arabic saying: "If a black were to fall down from heaven he would surely fall down to a beat." The tenacity of these images in subsequent representations of Africa is striking. (We shall return to them in chapter 3.)

A more recent compilation by John McCall of references to African music in "early documents" reinforces contemporary views of the place of music in African society.[11] Starting with Hanno's *Periplus*, a Greek source dating from about 500 B.C., McCall combs works by well-known figures such as Mohammed ibn Abdullah ibn Battuta, William Bosman, and Sir Richard Burton, as well as those of lesser-known figures such as Al Bekri, the Abbé Proyart, and Archibald Schweinfurth, for musical references. There is information about instruments (their nature, construction, and the kind of music they make, whether pleasing or not) and about the contexts of music-making, including the ceremonies of royal persons, healing rituals, and recreation. One also finds references to drums and—more unusually—flutes as speech surrogates. Musical features mentioned include the relative brevity of musical phrases, the extensive use of repetition as an organizing principle, and various forms of vocal and instrumental polyphony. Ranging from the scientific to the condescending and racialist, McCall's references are remarkably consistent in highlighting the same basic aspects of African musical practice that feature in today's ethnographies. From this, one may be tempted to conclude that African musical practice has long remained static. Stable, perhaps, rather than static. The colonial moment introduced rapid, far-reaching change, however, change that has led to a dramatic reconfiguring of the earlier stability. In the last one hundred years, some aspects of tradition have remained intact, some have even intensified their authenticity, while others have metamorphosed into new traditions.

Transforming the Musical Language

The most obvious sign of colonial influence is the *material* presence of foreign musical instruments in Africa. It is true that Africa has long been the site of various forms of culture contact, contact that is not restricted to Europe. For example, the one-string fiddle or *goje* (it comes under a variety of regional names), prominent in the Sudan and in portions of the Islamic belt of West Africa, may well have come from the Middle East via North Africa. Similarly, the xylophone, which is widely distributed in East, Central, and Southern Africa, may, according to A. M. Jones, have come originally from Indonesia.[12] The *goje* and xylophone are today regarded as African, evidence that the assimilation and adaptation of "foreign" musical instruments have long been a facet of African culture. European instruments, however, not only outnumber other "foreign" instruments but also are symbolically more prominent in modern life. A partial inventory would include violins, violas, cellos, double basses (including the one-stringed bass), and harps. There are clarinets, oboes, flutes, saxophones, fifes, and piccolos. One also finds a whole slew of brass instruments including trumpets, horns, tubas, trombones, bugles, and euphoniums. Percussion instruments include the side and snare drums. Of special significance are keyboard instruments such as pipe organs, pianos, and harmoniums. And there is the ever-prominent guitar.[13]

The emergence of new institutions as a result of the encounter with Europe is responsible for the cultivation of certain types of music and musical instruments. Churches, the police, the army, and the entertainment industry provided opportunities for music-making. Bremen and Basel missionaries in the mid-1800s, for example, introduced the singing of hymns and anthems as well as the use of harmoniums and brass choirs to accompany congregational singing. In the Evangelical Presbyterian Church prominent in the Volta Region of Ghana, for example, a number of congregations (notably those at Amedzofe, Ho, Alavanyo, and Akpafu-Todzi) acquired brass instruments to enhance music-making during worship.[14] Although their repertoires were initially European, brass bands began to incorporate simple arrangements of African music. Elsewhere in Ghana, bands not affiliated with churches were formed in Agona-Swedru in 1905, in Kwanyaku in 1927, and in Yamoah's Trading House in Winneba in 1925. As the brass-band culture spread to other parts of the country, drawing in audiences as well as amateur performers, the repertoire expanded to include various forms of popular music, most prominent among which was highlife.[15]

The material presence of European musical instruments is ultimately of limited significance. More important and yet more elusive is the transformation of the musical language itself. Although the era of recorded sound does not allow us to begin our inquiry before the 1900s, it is nevertheless possible to extrapolate from present-day practices some sense of that transformation. To put the matter perhaps too directly: European music, in its most influential manifestations, colonized significant portions of the African musical landscape, taking over its body and leaving an African dress, transforming the musical background while allowing a few salient foreground features to indicate an African presence. In less-influential manifestations, the body remained African while sporting a European dress.

Let me illustrate one aspect of colonial influence by constructing a fictional narrative of the make-up of an individual African's musical imagination. The year is 1920, the place Cape Coast on the Gold Coast, one of the sites of earliest European contact with and subsequent presence in West Africa, an important center for both human and material trade, and home to some of the first churches and schools built in the country. Our protagonist is a young musician by the name Kwame. From hearing and overhearing the music played by Castle bands and various town bands, Kwame has internalized some of the idiomatic expressions of military band music. He knows a great many hymns from the Methodist Hymnal, being a regular churchgoer. He has been exposed to the music of *asafo* and *adowa* "traditional" ensembles, and he frequently listens to the songs sung by migrant Ga and Ewe fishermen. Occasionally he encounters a guitar-playing seaman from Liberia. As technical residue, Kwame's knowledge registers diatonic as opposed to chromatic melody, extensive repetition, frequent use of melodic ornamentation, modal scales, and, perhaps most important, certain closing formulas. He is also familiar with a number of rhythmic *topoi,* a set of distinctive and memorable rhythmic patterns associated with specific dances. These *topoi* are familiar to the man in the street as free-floating, interesting rhythms, not necessarily as the identifying rhythms of specific dances. Finally, Kwame's idea of harmony is guided by a preference for consonance at phrase ends (unison, octaves, or thirds, usually, but also fourths and fifths) and a polyphonic feeling based on streams of parallel thirds (or maybe fourths, based on what the Anlo-Ewe fishermen sing) and voice-crossing at cadences.

On the other hand, Kwame's store of knowledge of European music is marked by the diatonic melodies of his favorite hymns and of arrangements of sea-shanties that he hears the bands play. He tends to prefer major to minor mode; indeed, he has great difficulty singing melodic- and harmonic-minor scale segments in a few of the hymns that he encounters on Sundays. Kwame has developed a particular fondness for tonal harmony, in particular its reassuring points of punctuation, including ii6-V7-I and IV-V-I cadences articulated with great satisfaction by brass bands. Many times he hears the church organist play a 4–3 suspension over the final tonic in a perfect cadence, and he is struck by how long the organist withholds the note of resolution. He is aware that secondary dominants are very colorful, and that they make certain moments in his favorite hymns sweeter. He is also aware that too many secondary dominants spoil the hymns; he thinks that this is akin to putting too much meat in soup. Although Kwame has so internalized the expectations of diatonic harmony that he can improvise a bass line to a new hymn or anthem, he does not yet possess a long-term contrapuntal sense. He will often start a phrase with the correct harmony, sleepwalk his way through the intermediate harmonies, and then hit the final cadence with unerring accuracy and confidence.

Our hypothetical native of 1920 Cape Coast is not all that different from his grandchildren of today. The number of churches has multiplied considerably, of course, and the character of worship ranges widely. At the "high" end are Catholic and Anglican congregations, where one hears the intoning of psalms and the singing of Gregorian chant in the original Latin. In the middle are the Presbyterian and Methodist churches, which have retained the same form of worship from Kwame's day, but now boast a collection of indigenously inspired anthems, choruses, and local hymns. At the "low" end are numerous spiritual, charismatic, pentecostal churches. There, music-making is, as a rule, loud, rhythmically alive, geared to the present, and devoid of the fake solemnity of the "higher," orthodox churches. When Kwame's grandson attends the local Methodist church on Sunday, he looks for opportunities to embellish a phrase or two of his favorite hymn. He adopts the same hit-or-miss approach to improvising bass lines, and he never hesitates to liven things up rhythmically by singing ahead of the beat. He has never liked hymns with descants because they force him into the subordinate role of singing the hymn tune while the sopranos do something more interesting.[16]

Kwame's profile may seem particular to the urban experience, and it may be argued that outside urban centers there remain pockets of cultural expression that are not so obviously marked by European influence. This may be so within a limited understanding of markedness. Still, it is important to remind readers that individuals like Kwame actually *did* exist, and that, within the economy of contemporary cultural practices, their profiles possess as much—if not greater—symbolic power as those of ostensibly "pure" natives.

Tonal Harmony as Colonizing Force

There is no simple formula for determining the net result of Western and African musical influences, because there are affinities as well as differences. In terms of the three basic dimensions of European music—melody, rhythm, and harmony—we might say that the one with the greatest colonizing power is harmony. African melodies, especially those generated by the proto-musical essence of spoken language, are able sometimes to resist the blandness and squareness of certain European diatonic melodies. And African rhythms, given their sharp and characteristic edges, rarely sell their birthrights to Europe. But harmony is a different kettle of fish. Of all the musical influences spawned by the colonial encounter, that of tonal-functional harmony has been the most pervasive, the most far-reaching, and ultimately the most disastrous.

Listen, for a start, to the national anthems of various African countries and you will be struck by the "European" character of the harmonization. The Ghana national anthem is no exception. Composed by Philip Gbeho (1905–1976) in the months leading up to independence, the anthem originally concluded with a lively, dancelike appendix in the form of an "Osee Yee," a traditional cheer. Although not free of the diatonic harmony of the main anthem, the "Osee Yee" was nevertheless enlivened by simple polyphony and rhythmic variety. The textural uniformity of hymnlike harmony and the unchanging prosody of the English words of the main anthem were thus set into relief. Alas, the censors struck out the "Osee Yee" from the official version of the anthem. Did it seem too obviously "African," too different to mark the newly independent nation's entry in 1957 into the international league of nations?

Listen, too, to some of the popular music of the continent and you will be struck by its sometimes uncritical embrace of one or two idioms of tonal music, including the subdominant-dominant-tonic progression that is found in other popular musics of the world. The diatonic harmonic style of the popular South African group Ladysmith Black Mambazo, and indeed that of other exponents of the *Mbube* choral style, is so thoroughly ingrained and is produced so naturally and effortlessly that it seems very much beside the point to insist on its European origins. And listen, finally, to the art music of the continent, to, say, Fela Sowande's *African Suite*, with its diatonic foundations, Anthony Okelo's *Missa Mayot*, or to any of the numerous choral anthems composed by Ephraim Amu. Here, tonality in a restricted form provides the harmonic ground of composition. Only a handful of adventurous African composers have managed to imagine musical life in an atonal or nontonal world.[17]

What can be "disastrous" about the pervasiveness of functional harmony in Africa? Is not such a resource akin to a foreign or foreign-derived language (like English or French) that can serve as a convenient medium of communication, contributing a unifying effect in a linguistically heterogenous population? In one respect, users and consumers of functional harmony could be let off the hook if they simply acknowledged that they had *chosen* this "language" not because of its inherent superiority but for a pragmatic and purely practical reason, namely, to facilitate communication. There are, however, differences between musical and verbal languages. Musical language does not have the same primary communicative obligation in society that verbal language does. So, although one would not deny that music, as an aesthetic phenomenon, can be made to serve ideological and political purposes—that it can be made to bear the weight of a decipherable "content," a content that may be retrieved (incompletely and imperfectly, of course) through verbal language—one would nevertheless hesitate before endowing African musics and languages with comparable signifying potential. It might be argued, in fact, that the symbolic residue of musical language is greater than that of verbal language. Music is, in that sense, more *marked* than literature. Thus, ballroom dancing or the composing and performing of string quartets by Africans today would seem to be more marked cultural activities, "louder" in their legible significance, than the writing of poems, novels, or plays in English, French, or Portuguese.

The vast harmonic resources available in traditional African music, resources that include many viable alternatives to the Soprano-Alto-Tenor-Bass (SATB) texture of European hymns, for example, also remain underappreciated. The hierarchic SATB arrangement that churchgoers encounter on Sundays and that boys and girls are forced to endure as members of community and school choirs does not occur in traditional African music. Indigenous multipart singing is idiomatically quite varied, and there are some spectacular examples. Some of it is based on unison textures, some on a nonhierarchic polyphony (as heard, for example, among the BaAka of the Central African Republic), and some on a species of parallelism in which the consistency of texture—such as a stream of parallel thirds in a two-voice polyphony—is only apparent; the actual production of those thirds involves many voice crossings. Thus the negotiation of individual voices is much more interesting and complex from the performer's point of view than the "mere" resultant sonorities.[18]

These and numerous other indigenous harmonic/contrapuntal practices remain to be explored creatively and on a large scale. But such exploration is not likely to happen any time soon if, as too often happens, we remain deaf to local harmonic systems, refuse to standardize harmonic resources for compositional and pedagogical purposes, and succumb to the superficially intoxicating harmonies of European hymns and American pop songs. In conceding harmonic ground so readily, Africans unwittingly reinforce the impression that strongly implicative and cogent harmonic systems are simply not part of their traditional heritage. William Ward's claim, made at the end of a 1927 article surveying the basic elements of African music, that "if it could learn from Europe modern developments in form and harmony, African music should grow into an art more magnificent than the world has yet seen," is possible only against the background of such concession.[19] And yet, the number, variety, and intricacy of multipart techniques suggest that, contrary to what Ward imagined, Africa perhaps has a lot less—if at all—to learn from Europe in the house of harmony. Of the many legacies of colonialism, the consequences of an uncritical acceptance of a limited form of functional harmony have yet to be recognized, let alone resisted actively.

The Language of Church Music

The trade in musical ideas set in motion by the church dramatizes with particular force the effects of colonialism. Consider the activities of another fictional character, the Ghanaian musician Kwaku, who teaches music in a training college and is active in the Evangelical Presbyterian Church. On Sundays, he accompanies congregational singing on the harmonium, sometimes with the assistance of a brass band. He conducts the 30-member church choir in performances of anthems, some of them composed by him. He plays a voluntary at the close of each service. On special feast days, Kwaku provides other sorts of music. The "Dead March" is instantly recognized by many in his congregation even though few will know that it is excerpted from Handel's oratorio, *Saul* (1739). The "Wedding March" and its Bridal predecessor are in his repertory. However, like other organists, Kwaku has not quite mastered the wedding march, so he plays a truncated version, stopping as soon as the recession seems to be out of sight. At Christmas, Kwaku's choir combines with others to perform selected choruses from *Messiah,* including the ever-popular "Hallelujah Chorus." These choruses have been fitted with Ewe words to facilitate performance. The parts are taught by rote, memorized, and sung enthusiastically. You would not know from listening to them perform that none of the choir members actually reads music.

Other church activities blend European and African influences. Drumming and dancing, previously proscribed by Presbyterian authorities, are now incorporated into worship without any feeling of impropriety except among a few extremists. Kwaku's congregation nowadays sets aside some twenty minutes for "Praise" during each service. This interval is filled with vigorous drumming, dancing, and the shouting of appellations to God (for example, "Lord, you are Wonderful. My Lord, you are excellent!"). In congregations that are led by ministers who subscribe to the Africanization of Christianity, a talking drum may well announce the sermon while the preacher, in approaching the pulpit, is accompanied by a linguist (*Okyeame*) bearing the traditional linguist's staff.

Ambitious musico-dramatic experiments are also part of the church's musical history. Walter Blege, an educationist and prominent musician in the Evangelical Presbyterian Church, has composed a full-length opera entitled *Kristo.* The plot describes the first arrival of missionaries in Eweland, their battles with African chiefs, their eventual acceptance, and the creation of a new African Christianity that blends in equal measure African and European elements. The music of *Kristo* consists of a series of choruses interspersed with spoken dialogue and a small amount of sung dialogue. Blege, who wrote his own libretto, characterizes the African subjects with spirited dancing, drumming, and singing while the missionaries are represented by uninspired hymn-based singing with occasional extensions into the realm of virtuoso singing. The issue is not whether the opera is successful; developing appropriate criteria to measure success is not finally possible except as a highly provisional and strictly contextual measure. In any case, the fact that audiences seem to enjoy *Kristo* whenever it is performed is a sign of its positive reception. Rather, the issue is the fact of the opera's possibility: A bold creative effort in a genre that is more African than it might seem at first.[20]

Nineteenth-century Lagos

Lagos in the second half of the nineteenth century was a city bristling with life. With its diverse population, budding trade, and strong cultural and religious practices, Lagos epitomized the peculiar mix of influences that characterized the European and later colonial impact on Africa. Its musical life, too, was diverse. On the "traditional" side were drumming, dancing, praise singing, and the performance of masquerades. On the "modern" side were concerts organized by an emerging elite comprising missionaries, expatriate civil servants, the Brazilian community (made up of returnees from the New World), Sierra Leonians, and Liberians in government service or in pursuit of various professions, and, of course, educated Lagosians themselves.

In a fascinating portrait of what he calls "Victorian Lagos," Michael Echeruo draws on coverage in the Lagos press during the period 1863–1905 to show how the elite cultivated certain European musical habits.[21] Concerts were performed regularly in Lagos. Repertoire and modes of performance were directly imitative of European practice. In October 1882, a "Handel Festival" was produced by one Robert A. Coker, organist and pianist who later became a leading figure in the musical life of Lagos. On May 23, 1882, the Brazilian Dramatic Company, "under the patronage of the German consul, Heinrich Bey, performed a 'Grand Theatre' in honor of Queen Victoria's Jubilee." Note that this "multinational" event involved four nations: Brazil, Germany, Britain, and, of course, Nigeria. A performance of April 15, 1884, by the Lagos Melodramatic Society included songs, piano music, and comedy skits. August 1886 saw a performance of Gilbert and Sullivan's *Trial by Jury,* a work whose first performance had taken place in England only eleven years earlier. In addition, there were many choral performances by school-based choirs such as the choir of St. Gregory's Grammar School in 1887 and the Ibadan Choral Society. To think that these events were taking place not in Lisbon, Paris, or London but in Lagos, Nigeria, is to gain some sense of the deep imprint of "Europe" on the coastal African soundscape.

The Lagos press, as Echeruo makes clear, was more interested in covering high society activities such as these than traditional music performances, so one must not suppose that all of Lagos attended piano recitals, choral concerts, and the staging of operettas every week. Performances of traditional music took place in the relevant segments of society. What we see, then, is a coexistence of musical traditions of diverse provenance. It is this state of affairs, consolidated during the colonial period, that has become a paradigm for contemporary African urban musical life. Images of dancing Africa, an Africa in the grip of ancient customs and musical practices represent at best only *one* aspect of African musical life. While perpetuators of such images (including many ethnomusicologists) may not be in a hurry to acknowledge pockets of "Westernized" Africa, no one can deny their existence.

The elite musical practices of Victorian Lagos resemble those observed in other colonial institutions, notably the Christian church and various educational institutions. We have already mentioned some aspects of church musical activity, but it is important not to underestimate the influence of Christianity in Africa. There are many Africans today whose affective investment in "What a friend we have in Jesus," "Courage, brother, do not stumble," "Thy way not mine, O Lord," "Lead kindly light amid the encircling gloom," "Abide with me, fast falls the eventide," "O perfect love all human thought transcending," or "Love divine all loves excelling" is far greater—deeper and more sincere—than anything that might be awakened by a traditional funeral dirge or hunter's chant. The lineage of this investment begins, predictably, with the introduction of hymns into worship as part of missionary proselytizing in the 1840s. In time, entire hymn books were translated into the vernacular so that both English and non–English-speaking Africans could enjoy the tunes, harmonies, and sentiments expressed in the words, in particular texts that give hope and comfort to those in pain or distress. Hymn-singing has by now become second nature to many church-going Africans, some of whom can readily improvise parts to a hymn melody they've never heard before. We should not underestimate the potency of the hymn in the African reception of European music.

Achimota School, Ghana

Educational institutions, too, have become important sites for the cultivation of European or Europeanized music. Consider, for example, Achimota School in Ghana. Founded in 1925 as the Prince of Wales College, Achimota is one of the premier schools in West Africa, and a leading center for the study and performance of music. Indeed, the school's logo consists of a segment of a piano keyboard whose black and white keys symbolize harmony between Africans (blacks) and Europeans (whites). Many prominent Ghanaian musicians have been associated with Achimota. One was Philip Gbeho, composer of the Ghana national anthem, one time conductor of the National Symphony Orchestra, and an influential teacher of traditional and European music. Another was Dr. Ephraim Amu (1899–1995), a leading composer of anthems and choral works and a self-conscious African by virtue of dress, lifestyle, and talk. Both taught for some years at Achimota. Generations of past students owe their love of music to what they heard and played as students there.[22]

When I attended Achimota in the early 1970s, the musical ambience was very much in keeping with what its founders had envisioned. There was a music school complete with twelve practice rooms, each equipped with an upright piano. Upstairs was a small recital hall with a seven-foot Steinway for rehearsals, lectures, performances, and examinations. The music staff alone numbered five full- and several part-timers, most of them trained in part in Europe and sporting an impressive range of expertise in performance, composition, and theoretical work. A modest chamber orchestra rehearsed once a week, working up a repertory for performances in both school and on national television. Every Christmas, the Aggrey Chapel Choir—whose members were required to audition for placement—put on a Festival of Nine Lessons and Carols modeled on the original service associated with King's College, Cambridge. And every other year, staff and students joined together in a production of a Gilbert and Sullivan opera (*Mikado* in 1971, *The Pirates of Penzance* in 1973). In addition, a biennial interhouse Singing Competition provided an opportunity for students to assemble and train choirs, and, in some cases, to compose a new work or arrange an existing one for immediate performance. Finally, the school's music curriculum prepared students for Ordinary and Advanced Level Certificate Examinations as administered by the London Board of Education. Set works were selected from the standard repertory. Students offering music for the Ordinary Level examinations in 1972 were expected to know Ravel's String Quartet, Act 1 of *The Marriage of Figaro*, and the opening movement of Beethoven's First Symphony. For the Advanced Level examinations two years later, the set works were Shostakovich's Eighth Symphony and Schumann's Piano Quintet, op. 44. In addition, the Associated Board of the Royal Schools of Music sent an examiner every year from the United Kingdom to various African countries (Sierra Leone, Ghana, Nigeria, South Africa) to examine students in various practical subjects.[23]

There were two other prominent avenues for creative musical expression at Achimota. One was the Pop Chain competition, which brought together bands from various schools to perform a variety of pop musics. Achimota school regularly featured one or two four- or five-member bands in this student-initiated competition. The other involved traditional music. Every year, Achimota School held a Founders' Day celebration. Various traditional chants and ritual dances accompanied this celebration, which culminated in a mock procession by ethnic groups and their respective chiefs, queenmothers, and subjects. The occasion provided an opportunity for students to enact "African" traditions by singing African songs, beating African drums, and dancing African dances. The self-consciousness with which these African students performed African traditions was no different from the self-awareness with which they played Bach on the violin or sang Vivaldi's "Gloria." The very ground of their cultural being did not correspond to some pristine, uncontaminated African essence, one that might be said to be innocent of "outside" influences. No, their origins were irreducibly mixed, hybrid, syncretic, in-between, impure. And this is one of the enduring effects of colonialism.

Popular Music, Art Music

Perhaps the most decisive musical consequence of colonialism was the emergence of two traditions of music, one socially prominent, the other less so, both conceived as active responses to Europe. The first is the tradition of popular music, the other the tradition of so-called art music. In Ghana, interethnic popular music such as highlife originated from the diversions required by elite populations of the coastal areas to pass their leisure hours. Helped along by technological innovations—radio, recording, amplification—and active trade with Europe and America, popular music found enthusiastic audiences in urban populations whose daily routines now allowed ample time for its consumption. Although no one could have predicted its fate at its inception in the early decades of the twentieth century, the extent to which African popular music has become a global phenomenon is astonishing. Insofar as the importation of "Western" technology made possible its rapid development, African popular music may be understood historically as a direct outgrowth of colonialism.

Highlife, a supreme example of West African popular music, is based on a distinctive and danceable beat. Its melodies are singable and easily remembered, although some, notably those influenced by Islamic singing styles, are not free of elaborate ornamentation. More important, the words of songs, when well crafted, often capture an aspect of present or past experience in language that sticks even after a single hearing. These texts are aggressively relevant to the here-and-now. Drawing upon the kinds of conversations that take place in buses, drinking bars, churches, entertainment halls, schools, at football matches, and on the streets, highlife texts in turn provide matter for conversation among factory workers, market women, laborers, civil servants, crooks, and layabouts. Composers invoke aspects of tradition to code a series of reflections on the modern African experience. Highlife texts make fascinating reading. They celebrate love, tease jilted lovers, poke fun at the disabled, criticize modern women, rehearse money troubles, react to death, warn politicans in power about a coming coup d'état, ponder some of life's enigmas, and recount the activities of jùjú men and women. Taken as a whole, these imaginatively composed texts provide a window onto the contemporary African mind.[24]

There is, then, an aspect of African popular music that is accessible only to cultural insiders. And yet the particular triumph of this music stems from its dissemination across ethnic or national borders. Nigerian *jùjú*, *fújì*, or Afrobeat, Zaïrean *soukouss* or *rumba*, Cameroonian *makossa*, and South African *mbube*—recordings of these and numerous other varieties of popular music circulate widely in Europe, America, and throughout the world. Without seeking to mystify its content, one may still describe the best popular music as grounded in "deep" values.[25] African popular music may be conceptualized as a layered phenomenon, a repository of musical idioms of diverse origins (African, Afro-Cuban, European, African-American, Islamic) arranged in such a way that a dominant element or group of elements conveys a "message" to listeners of different social, linguistic, and musical backgrounds. As far as we know there was no precolonial popular music of comparable standing, although recreational genres existed. Nor is it easy to imagine such music spreading rapidly across the continent without the technological props that we take for granted today, including cassettes, compact discs, videos, radio, television, and the Internet.

African art music stands as another significant but much less visible response to colonialism. Just as creative writers like Ngugi, Achebe, Armah, and Soyinka drew on European traditions of poetry and the novel, using a "European" language albeit one inflected by various African languages, so composers like Ayo Bankole (Nigeria), Cyprien Rugamba (Rwanda), Nicholas Z. Nayo (Ghana), and Justinian Tamusuza (Uganda), among many others, have sought to write "classical" music for nonparticipating audiences, music that might be regarded as the African equivalent of Bach, Beethoven, and Brahms. In the catalogue assembled by Akin Euba of archival holdings of modern African music housed at the Iwalewa-Haus, University of Bayreuth, Germany, over one hundred groups and composers are listed in the first section on "Christian Religious Music" alone, some of them credited with only a handful of scores, others with several. A section entitled "Art Music and Music Theatre" lists over forty composers and nearly 300 scores. Genres include opera, sonata, suite, ballet, concerto, and symphony; works are scored for chamber orchestra, violin and piano, clarinet and piano, bamboo flutes, synthesizers, and, in the case of sung works, SATB or voice and piano.[26] The piano in particular has engendered a subgenre named by Euba "African Pianism" comprising works by African composers and their descendants in the diaspora. Euba's catalogue is necessarily incomplete, but read in conjunction with the program for a 1995 festival of African chamber music organized by the Hochschule für Musik in Würzburg, and with the initiatives pursued in the United States by the St. Louis African Chorus to promote performances of African music, one gains a strong sense of a musical tradition that was bound to emerge in Africa and that has lately made significant inroads into the metropolis.

Like African literature, African art music does not consist solely of imitative products. There is a vast range of works, from exercises in composition based on various European models to fully worked out compositions in an original language. Among the more forward-looking works are those that seek to appropriate European *and* African instruments and modes of expression at a first or natural level, not with quotation marks—as if the composer were a ventriloquist. Akin Euba's *Four Pieces* for flute, bassoon, piano, and Nigerian drums (1964) are strikingly effective in their (modernist) exploitation of the less-traveled registers of his instruments, and in their use of a series of apparently disjointed musical gestures. The resulting language grows in consistency as the work unfolds, so that the listener is not drawn into a guessing game about the "European" or "African" origins of the work's ideas and orchestration. Similarly, Joshua Uzoigwe's imaginative *Masquerade* for *iyailu* drum and piano (1980) explores the common percussive core of the two instruments as well as their melo-rhythmic properties, using imitation, ostinati, and a semi-improvised manner to create a subtle and impressive work of chamber music. Euba and Uzoigwe are among the few African composers who have experimented with other systems of pitch organization. Portrayals of African art music as elitist, as needlessly cerebral, and as ultimately un-African in its apparent suppression of spontaneity reveal at best a very partial acquaintance with what, in reality, is a wide-ranging and aesthetically plural set of practices. In the end, it is not the number of composers or compositions that is of interest; rather, it is the fact that Africa's engagement with modernity serves as a condition of possibility for such creative practices.

Inventing Traditional Music

Less obvious but no less important is the impact of colonialism on "traditional" music. Here there are two opposing tendencies, one involving transformation, the other involving a consolidation and redefinition of that practice. It is the latter that I wish to comment upon. The impulse to protect that which is yours in the face of manifestly foreign influences is a common and understandable reflex. It is therefore not surprising that in postindependence Africa, one frequently encounters the most self-conscious attempts to hold up certain cultural products as quintessentially "African." In communities that are not faced with any significant outside threat, artistic innovation may proceed according to a natural, inner dynamic. There is no Other to make you anxious about codifying the dimensions of Self. In the more dramatic European encounters with Africa, however,

African self-awareness has dictated a fresh viewing of myth, ritual, music, dance, play, and modes of worship.

Consider, for example, the situation in nineteenth-century Lagos discussed earlier, where such an encounter forced some traditional leaders to think about the role of drumming in their communities. At one point, complaints were lodged by various residents about the level of noise emanating from all-night drumming. The governor sought to limit the hours of drumming or in some cases ban it altogether. A meeting of Lagos chiefs with the governor and the commissioner of police in late 1903 gave the chiefs an opportunity to reiterate the significance of drumming in their lives and culture. Hence the document "Native Grievances: The Drumming Question" that appeared in the Lagos newspaper *Record* of January 2, 1904, and which is quoted extensively by Echeruo.[27]

A Chief Obanikoro outlined the utility of drumming: "[It] is very good, it heartens soldiers for war, it sings praises of our fathers, it brings back to recollection the great men of past times, it rejoices our hearts." Another, Kasumu Giva, noted that "[a] town without a sound of the drum is like a city of the dead," while a third, Chief Aromire, reinforced the common view about Africans' appetite for music: "We all like to hear the sound of the drum." The document as a whole establishes the following: Chiefs keep drummers to play for them on occasions; there are professional drummers who depend on drumming for their livelihood; some drummers are entrusted with the task of maintaining the historical record; drumming often accompanies activities like marriage ceremonies; drumming is sometimes used to prepare soldiers (psychologically) for war; and finally, Muslims frequently use drums to wake worshippers up during Ramadan. Thus the threat of a ban forced the chiefs of Lagos to construct an account of what drumming meant in their communities. To speak of this as a "construction" is not to imply that the chiefs lied. (In any case, cultural insiders—or those who adopt their manners—are not allowed to say that chiefs lied even if they did!) It is rather to underline the *motivated* nature of the truths they told. Such motivation lies at the heart of African inventions of traditions.

The impulse to justify an aspect of tradition begets another, namely, to preserve a newly invented tradition. Precolonial African cultures were predominantly oral cultures whose poetry, dance, and song resided in the memories of performers and audiences. Each occasion of performance provided an opportunity to retrieve what had been stored and to display it afresh. But creativity in the functioning of human memory meant that each poem, dance, or song was configured as irreducibly multiple. When European colonialism brought a written culture and alternative means of preserving both aural and visual data, it forced a reconfiguration of cultural products. One could now speak in a concrete sense of an archive of African materials. (The archive will form our object of discussion in chapter 2.) But it is misleading to define as categorical the difference between oral and written, for that which is enshrined in a sound recording, for example, is only one among several possible renditions. What finally undercomplicates the dynamics of the oral-written encounter is the failure to give a proper account of the invariant supplementary knowledge without which no poem, dance, or song can be brought to life in performance.

Beginning in the 1960s, musical tradition was invented in Ghana through the establishment of the Arts Council of Ghana, the creation of a National Dance Ensemble, and the formation across the country of many so-called cultural troupes. These associations brought together drummers, singers, and dancers from different ethnic groups to learn and perform their most popular or most prominent dances (including *Kpanlogo, Adowa, Atsiagbekor, Bawa,* and *Damba-Takai*). The result would be the establishment of a transethnic canon, a classic collection of cultural artifacts. Public concerts featured a selection of these dances for nonparticipating audiences. The idea was to preserve the authenticity of each dance by reifying certain dance steps, body movements, costumes, and styles of singing and drumming. In constructing edifices to serve as foundations, sites of authenticity, primordial sources, and markers of African difference, this invention of tradition engendered a range of responses. On one hand, traditional culture was understood as a rebirth through a kind of *Sankofa* ("go back and retrieve") philosophy. On the other, traditional culture was interpreted as new, as the result of fresh initiatives that, although marked by a thematic relation to "old" or rural Africa, nevertheless represented bold, new ventures. Herein lies one of the paradoxes of postcolonial African life.

A special place must be reserved for a group calling itself the Pan-African Orchestra. Formed in 1988 and led by Nana Danso Abiam, this Ghanaian ensemble has taken the notion of artistic renaissance to one inspiring extreme. The musicians play "traditional" instruments including xylophones, bells, rattles, *Atenteben* (Bamboo) flutes, *Wia* (notched) flutes, *Gyile* (xylophones), *Kora* (harp lutes), *Gonje* (African violins), *fontomfrom* (and other) drums, and horns. Unlike cultural troupes that originated in the 1960s, however, the orchestra also includes a significant number of instruments from other parts of Africa—hence the designation "pan-African." More important, musicians in the orchestra read from carefully notated scores, producing a sound that seems so authentically traditional that it immediately betrays its origins in the effort to model tradition rather than to express ideas from within it at a first level of articulation. The remarkable ingenuity and inventiveness demonstrated by the leader of the group and his musicians is on par with the best composers of art music. And yet, whereas the products of art music are generally understood as having been created by an individual composer, the works of the Pan-African Orchestra achieve such a thorough communality that they may be easily mistaken for transcriptions or arrangements of traditional music. It is testimony to the power and uniqueness of this music that it forces us to reexamine our basic taxonomical categories.[28]

Transforming Discourse about Music

I have saved for last what is perhaps the most profound aspect of the impact of colonialism, namely, the transformation of the terms of discourse about African music. This book is written in English by a Ghanaian whose first language, Siwu (spoken by the Akpafu people), is not a written language; whose first written language, Ewe, has no currency as a medium of scholarly exchange in Europe or America; and whose schooling facilitated familiarity with French as well as two other Ghanaian languages, Twi and Ga. This little genealogy may serve as an indication of the complex linguistic paths that many postcolonial scholars have had to follow, and of the necessarily fragmented and registrally marked fluency that they attain in both indigenous and colonial languages. It will also suggest that the ground upon which thought and discourse about African music are nurtured is complex, necessarily "contaminated," and irreducibly plural. Colonialism gave rise to a layering of strands of discourse, an intricate configuration reminiscent of the Tower of Babel. The difference, though, may be that African discourses are mediated—sometimes in a heavy-handed way—by one European language or another.[29]

African oral histories have so far not been shown to be repositories of an overwhelming vocabulary for discourse about music. And yet, as research has shown, and as we shall see in chapter 5, there is plenty of subtle and precise expression around performance traditions that could facilitate the development of modern critical discourses. The trouble is that the traces left by a performing art are performances, and because performances typically engage the present rather than the past or future, their evaluation is likely also to be aimed at the present, with no ambitions for an unspecified future. Only in the age of recording and writing has there arisen the possibility and need to preserve a certain critical vocabulary, to accumulate material marked by its pastness for present or future use. The corollary desire to model criticism on a putative precolonial practice betrays an extraordinary confidence in—and arrogance about—the authenticity of old Africa's modes of expression. Still, the need to understand African musicians on their own terms and in their own languages, and to attempt to excise layers of European assumptions that might have impeded our understanding of African musical practice, remains pressing.

No ethnotheorist can claim ignorance of the broad contours of European conceptions of music. In one sense, then, ethnotheories represent attempts to steer clear of European-sounding conceptions of African musical structure and performance. Writers are liable to stress not the parallels in conception but the differences. For example, many African languages are said to lack words for "music" and "rhythm" while terms associated with performance almost always have multiple meanings. Thus, the Kpelle term *pêle* describes a multivalent music event, the Akan term agorɔ indexes a range of behaviors associated with "play," while the Igbo term *egwu*, which also means "play," connotes music, dance, song, and visual design.[30] European vocabulary is portrayed as clinical, atomized, cold, and scientific, whereas African vocabularies are natural, spontaneous, and index spiritual dimensions. That these binaries hide as much as they reveal is obvious, for not only are "music" and "rhythm" in the European conception also polysemic—marked, that is, by an excess of signifieds over signifiers—but informal or folk discussions manifest a more complex profile. If the information unearthed by ethnotheorists is thus motivated, if authorial plots betray the tendencies just attributed to them, then evaluating a given ethnotheory could benefit from a fuller awareness of the temptations of such difference-seeking plots.

A more balanced view of African thought about music would acknowledge parallels as well as divergences at a number of levels. Constructing such a view would mean rejecting the restrictive binary framework in which European items are compared directly with African ones. It would mean developing an ethnographically grounded comparative framework that allows students to move readily from Kpelle to Dan to Vai to Akan to Yoruba cultures, across to Luo, Shona, Zulu, and Gogo worlds, and back again to Hausa, Wolof, Fon, and Dagomba territories. The effort would not overlook interethnic historical contact but would explore the ramifications of such contact for the building of a coherent theory. Our theorist would also acknowledge the pervasive and by now naturalized European influence on certain African conceptions of musical reality, investing most heavily in what thoughts are possible (in African languages) rather than in what is recorded as having been thought on some occasion. By shifting the emphasis from what happened to what could happen, from events to the possibility of certain happenings, this newer, truer, and—yes—more authentic discourse would accept the diverse conceptual worlds that currently circulate in Africa as mutually determining, enabling, perhaps even inspiring, not as independent streams to be sorted out into things "African" and things "European." "Musical discourse" as used here embraces everything from performance instructions (including the reading of notation) through aesthetic or critical evaluation to the most precise structural description. It is motivated by, and in turn motivates, composition, performance, reception, and analysis. Such a discourse cannot, of course, develop independently of broader patterns in society at large.

Conclusion

Colonialism has produced a complex musical society in Africa. As the foregoing sketch of schools, churches, hymns, bands, art music, popular music, and talk about music has shown, contemporary Africa is shaped by a bewildering diversity of inter- and intracontinental musical influences. "Foreign" modes of expression sometimes retain their original forms in the new environment, sometimes transform indigenous forms, and sometimes have no impact at all on the indigenous forms, merely coexisting with them. Postcolonial Africa is thus best characterized as a *constellation* of musical practices. To say this is not to imply that Africa is different from postcolonial India or Latin America, as if Africa's critical burden was, by definition, to establish difference in order to be taken seriously. Nor does the idea of a constellation deny that individual or group perceptions of the place of music in a given society are shaped by real or imagined hierarchies. The challenge is to remain vigilant in ensuring that no perceived hierarchy is facilely interpreted as corresponding to a fixed reality.

Understanding the impact of colonialism has sometimes been approached with nostalgia for a lost, if little-known African past. It is as if the faint traces of Africa's ancient musical history point to a magnificent era now permanently inaccessible, an era to be desired, invented, and reinvented as often as is necessary. It is also as if the far-reaching stimulus provided by Europe since the fifteenth century and by America since the nineteenth, a stimulus that has in turn produced some of the most significant African music, indexes a lack, an absence, an inadequacy. But why cling to the origins of musical instruments, idioms, and styles? Why not turn attention, instead, to their subsequent lives, to the extraordinarily fertile conditions that have nurtured various musics on the African continent during the last one hundred years? No one should, of course, be denied the opportunity to lament Africa's losses, to brood over an imagined past, to dream about a future rendered impossible by colonialism. But more of us should begin to be fired by the complex and contradictory reality of contemporary Africa to pursue a future in which the vastness and potency of our collective musical resources inspires composers and performers to aim even higher for excellence in creativity.

2
The Archive

This chapter provides a critical introduction to the archive of knowledge about African music. My desire to reach Africa-based readers in addition to the usual cosmopolitan ones runs into a little difficulty here, for surely Euro-American students who routinely consult *The New Grove Dictionary of Music and Musicians*, the Africa volume of *The Garland Encyclopedia of World Music*, or the German language *Die Musik in Geschichte und Gegenwart*, do not need an introduction to the archive. Nor do they need to be told about journals like *African Music, World of Music, Ethnomusicology*, scores of academic monographs published by major university presses, and, in recent times, dozens of websites featuring information on African music. The contrast with Africa-based students and scholars, however, is immense. While a few well-placed readers in Lagos, Accra, Kinshasa, or Nairobi (leaving aside the generally better situation in some South African cities) may have access to some of these sources, many will find them generally inaccessible. In general African students are not aware of the holdings abroad in such locations as the Library of Congress in Washington D.C., the New York Public Library, the British Library, or the Musée de l'homme in Paris. Few have seen an exhibit of African musical instruments at the Museum of Natural History in New York, the Museo Pigorini in Rome, or the Musée Royal de l'Afrique Centrale in Tervuren, Belgium, and fewer still have had the opportunity to visit the Herskovits Library in Evanston, Illinois, the International Library of African Music in Rhodestown, South Africa, or the Phonogramm-Archiv in Berlin. In other words, Africa-based scholars have little idea of the cumulative resources available for study of their own music. Nor is it clear that the ethnomusicologists and curators who manage these resources are sufficiently exercised by the disparity to want to close the gap.

It will be necessary, then, to speak at different levels in order to reach our diverse interpretive community. Following some preliminary comments on the nature of the oral versus the written, I discuss the coverage of Africa in a standard musicological reference work, *The New Grove Dictionary* (1980), and follow that with an assessment of the most comprehensive bibliography of writings on African music, John Gray's 1991 book, *African Music: A Bibliographical Guide to the Traditional, Popular, Art, and Liturgical Musics of Sub-Saharan Africa*. Critical comments on the idea of archive are then offered under four subheadings: language, fieldwork, the autobiographical turn, and finally, transcription. My aim is to lay bare the factors that privilege some of our professional habits by questioning their self-evidence, drawing attention to the biases they subtend, and, in general, urging greater self-consciousness among scholars.

In ordinary usage, the word "archive" denotes "a place in which records or documents of interest to a government, institution, family, etc. are preserved." It also refers to "the material so preserved."[1] I will be using the term in something like the latter sense to denote the vast body of existing knowledge about African music. Our archive includes written as well as oral sources. Books, articles, as well as Internet repositories constitute the written part of the archive, but audio and video recordings are vital, too. Oral sources include pedagogical schemes, repertoires, and critical discourses that reside in the memories of individuals or collectives and are recalled, invoked, reinvented, or simply constructed as occasions demand. The archive is bounded only in principle; in actuality, it is an ever-expanding store, because it includes not only the artifacts themselves but the factors that make possible their particular modes of knowledge organization.[2]

The Oral versus the Written

The inclusion of oral sources in an archive may prompt some skepticism. Oral sources matter, however, because African cultures remain largely oral. (I leave out of consideration the very real possibility that, for all the historical advantages claimed through writing, Euro-American cultures in the age of TV, telephones, and portable CD and cassette players are by and large oral, too.) Critical appreciation of the arts, for example, takes the form of vibrant oral exchanges at funerals and in community parks, beer bars, taxis, schools, churches, and government offices. It follows then that a definition of the archive that excludes untranscribed oral data necessarily bars large numbers of knowledgeable Africans from participating. The knowledge possessed by musicians who make music daily, who have internalized grammatical constraints and performance practices, and who, either by word or more often deed, bring various traditions to life in ritual and entertainment cannot be discounted simply because it does not (yet) exist in written form. The oral portion of the archive thus needs to be included to ensure the participation of significant numbers of indigenous African critics.

In reality, the line separating written (or recorded) from oral is not as categorical as it may seem. At first sight, written sources seem ontologically concrete and immune to individual distortion at a basic level of retrieval, whereas oral sources seem nebulous, subjectively constituted. Oral sources seem dependent on the sharpness of an individual memory (as when ritual prayers recite elaborate genealogies), or on creativity in the enactment of the source (as when a historical record is invoked to ground a praise song for a paying patron). Sometimes, too, local pressures may condition what is or is not appropriate to say, and thus redefine truth for the occasion. Written sources frequently require oral knowledge to come alive, however. Without this necessary supplement, the written text cannot exist. Moreover, some oral texts have acquired a certain contextual fixity as a result of repeated performance; they are texts in more than a metaphorical sense. Neither orality nor literacy carries intrinsic value. The written is not better than the oral in itself. Rather, oral and written accrue value within a larger economy of knowledge contestation.[3]

The fact that most of the *recognized* texts in the archive of African music are written rather than oral reflects a European bias in the institutional ordering of knowledge. Thus, ethnomusicologists' description of rituals, musical instruments, performance sites; their fantasies about the relationship between musical structure and social structure; or their interpretation of the "hotness" of African rhythm all are privileged forms of knowledge that take the form of written texts in books and articles. But we know that many expert drummers, poets, chiefs' linguists or spokespersons, and praise singers carry in their heads large volumes of oral text. And these texts are constituted within (sometimes elaborate) schemes that must not be violated in performance. The African artist is, in other words, equipped to manipulate both language and metalanguage within the oral milieu. Paradoxically, texts carried by individuals like Desmond Tay, Alhaji Abdulai Ibrahim, and Godwin Agbeli—highly knowledgeable insiders (or "informants," or, nowadays, "research associates," among other euphemisms)—acquired value in the Euro-American academy precisely at the moment of transcription, the moment when they crossed over from the oral into the written realm, when they were *reduced* to writing and could be packaged and sold as commodities.[4]

The move from traditional societies into cosmopolitan spaces engenders a reevaluation of the oral against the written and assigns privilege to one. Enabled by late capitalist modes of communication, written texts win out against oral ones because they are thought to be precise, easy and efficient to duplicate and disseminate, and stable in content over long periods. Communication theorists would probably wish to qualify these attributions, but it is beyond our purposes here to enter into such debates. Working from the metropolis fully armed with the power of literacy, it is easy to wax eloquent about the spontaneity, liveliness, and suppleness of oral traditions. I believe that African musicology is better off with a pragmatic attitude, one that recognizes that, despite the great store of archival knowledge in our oral and performing traditions, the way of the material world undervalues orality. Therefore the road to empowerment is one that embraces the challenge of written representation and gives urgent—but not exclusive—priority to textual production. If, under other circumstances, or at a later historical conjuncture, orality regains its privileged status, we can shift our priorities accordingly.

The *New Grove* Africa

It was a happy occasion in 1980 when the *New Grove Dictionary of Music and Musicians,* the most comprehensive English-language reference work on music, appeared in its sixth edition with extensive and largely unprecedented coverage of Africa. The previous edition (1954) did not feature an article on "Africa"; what little information there was consisted of an occasional reference in other articles. For example, in the article "primitive music," Percival Kirby, speculating on "the musical practices of prehistoric man," cited such things as the close relationship between speech and song, the exploitation of the harmonic series discovered in the musical bow, and the emergence of a pentatonic pitch space among South African Bushmen, Venda, Hottentots, and others. The reliance on an evolutionary paradigm was not unusual then, as witness Marius Schneider's 1957 article on "Primitive music" (which of course includes Africa) in the first volume of the *Oxford History of Music* devoted to Ancient and Oriental Music.[5] The 1950s also saw the emergence of the discipline of ethnomusicology. Ethnomusicology drew productively from anthropology and ethnology, and very selectively from Kirby's and Schneider's brand of comparative musicology, in general avoiding approaches that enshrine an a priori valuation of one music over another. By 1980, ethnomusicology had been in business for some time, consolidated its methodology, engaged a whole slew of fieldworkers, and facilitated forms of exchange between African musicians and Euro-American scholars. By 1980, it was possible, and not just in a token sense, to reduce the level of ignorance about African music. Thus James Koetting spoke for many when he enthusiastically welcomed the *New*

Grove Africa. According to him, the sixty-five or so entries by thirty-nine different authors filling some 176 pages with photographs, transcriptions, text, and maps made the dictionary "the best single source of printed data of African music."[6]

In 2001, a new edition of the *New Grove* appeared. Coverage of Africa now included biographies of composer-performers of popular music and composers of art music. In assessing the dictionary's representation of Africa, however, I focus on the 1980 edition for a number of reasons. First is its historical and symbolic importance: The 1980 edition marked the most significant metropolitan affirmation of Africa's musicological existence. Second, the mode of coverage in the 2001 edition closely follows that of the former. Third, although there is a quantitative advance (as measured by the number of words written about African music), the extent to which one can speak of a qualitative improvement is not at all clear. (Compare the articles on "Africa" and "Nigeria" in the two editions, for example, and you will see difference but not necessarily improvement.) Fourth, for various economic reasons, very few Black African institutions could afford the 1980 *New Grove* (fewer still can afford the 2001 *Revised New Grove*). What follows may thus serve as report and critique.

The *New Grove* includes the following country entries: Algeria, Angola, Benin, Botswana, Burkina Faso, Burundi, Cameroon, Central African Republic, Chad, Congo, Egypt, Ethiopia, Gabon, The Gambia, Ghana, Guinea, Ivory Coast, Kenya, Lesotho, Liberia, Malagasy Republic, Malawi, Mali, Mauritania, Morocco, Mozambique, Niger, Nigeria, Rwanda, Senegal, Sierra Leone, Somalia, South Africa, Sudan, Tanzania, Togo, Uganda, Zaïre, Zambia, and Zimbabwe.

Entries for ethnic groups include Arab Music, Bushman Music, Fulani Music, Hausa Music, Hottentot Music, Igbo Music, Nguni Music, Pygmy Music, Songhay Music, Tuareg Music, Venda Music, and Yoruba Music.

Separate entries exist for styles of music such as Congolese music, Highlife, and Kwela. Then there are entries for specific musical instruments such as Marimba, Goge, Kora, Hourglass drum, and Mvet. And of course there is an article on Africa as a whole, as well as a few regional studies, notably "North Africa."

Collectively, these entries bear witness to the vastness of the geocultural space we call "Africa." The coverage is uneven, however. About the tiny French-speaking West African country of Togo, for example, we are told that "no comprehensive study of the music of Togo has been made." Readers are then referred to the article on Ghana, which includes information on the Ewe, an ethnic group that straddles Ghana, Togo, and Benin. Again, the article on Chad declares: "Knowledge of the music is superficial since there have been few specialized studies." The focus is thus shifted to "the

organological aspect of the traditional music of Chad." Again, the un-
signed article on Niger, noting that its principal ethnic groups are found in
neighboring countries, sends readers to Hausa music, Fulani music, Songhay music, and Tuareg music.

Nigeria, by contrast, and perhaps befitting its status as a giant in Africa,
is represented by a substantial entry, some seven and a half printed pages
long, featuring photographs of instruments and playing techniques, transcriptions of songs and instrumental music, and a text that covers history
and culture, including passing mention of composers of art music. Even
longer is the entry on Uganda, distinguished by its emphasis on musical instruments, and by the inclusion of a separate section on the kingdom of
Baganda. Ghana, too, fares well. Its six pages include four photographs and
two brief transcriptions, and the text manages to achieve a fine balance between structural description and stylistic characterization.

Ultimately, the unevenness in coverage could not have been helped, for
large portions of Africa remain terra incognito to many. Nor was the research enterprise centralized anywhere in Europe to ensure that Gabon
and Guinea were given comparable attention, or that Zaïre and Zimbabwe
were examined within similar parameters. Articles were assigned mostly
(but not exclusively) to metropolitan scholars who could boast periods of
fieldwork in Africa. Thus Simha Arom was well placed to write about the
Central African Republic because he had spent several years there, while
John Blacking could draw on his twenty-two months' fieldwork to write
authoritatively about the Venda. Gerhard Kubik, perhaps the single most
devoted field researcher in African music active today, brought his exper-
tise to bear in the entries on Cameroon, Malawi, and Angola, while Hugo
Zemp, author of one of the best ethnographies of West African music,
Musique Dan, prepared the article on the Ivory Coast. The main article on
"Africa" was written jointly by two senior scholars, Klaus Wachsmann and
Peter Cooke, both of them sporting years of research in East and southern
Africa.

Although some editorial guidelines must have been issued to individual
authors (it is no accident that many entries begin with a geographical-
cum-historical orientation and end with a section on "modern developments"), the priorities enshrined in the articles differ, ultimately reflecting
the skills, interests, and vision of individual scholars. Ruth Stone's
"Liberia" entry, for example, is rich in linguistic matters (indigenous expressions for music, play, and performance are duly noted), revealing her
knowledge of Kpelle and her alertness to metalinguistic codes. A similar
interest in indigenous thinking is evident in some of Kubik's entries (Angola, Malawi, Cameroon), and in Zemp's article on Ivory Coast. Mwesa
Mapoma's background as a musician and composer shapes the article on

Zambia, which includes transcriptions with timelines that immediately align south Central Africa with West Africa, thus facilitating comparison along the lines initiated by A. M. Jones's *Studies in African Music,* a book that also brings West Africa (Ghana) and southern Africa (Zambia) into the same orbit. And Kazadi wa Mukuna draws on performing experience to convey essential aspects of the structure of Congolese music.

Again, the organological interests of writers as diverse as Monique Brandily and Klaus Wachsmann are in evidence in the articles on Chad and Uganda, respectively. Then, too, there is a writer like Arom, whose life-long commitment to explicating the organizational principles of African music has left a mark on the article on the Central African Republic. Several authoritative statements of a music-theoretical kind set this entry apart. There is a historical depth to some of the articles as well, including Nketia's on Ghana, Pierre Sallée's tracing of migration patterns in the Gabon article, Alan Merriam's on Zaïre (Democratic Republic of the Congo), and several of Kubik's. Merriam's interest in previous scholarship leads him to cite and criticize previously published views of Zaïrean music.

As ethnographers, many of these authors researched musical life in specific African communities, not in a comprehensive, stock-taking manner based on the nation state. The latter kind of task—surveys compiled from commissioned regional reports—is normally carried out by government organizations like Ministries of Culture. Unlike ethnographers, government officials are compelled to accept the physical constraints imposed by national borders and to aim—at least in principle—for representative coverage. Had the editors of the *New Grove* worked more closely with such in-country personnel in order to incorporate their official accounts, the profiles of some of the entries would have been significantly different.

The contrast between a profile based on country and one based on ethnic group serves as a reminder of the oft-remarked illogic of colonial boundaries, and points to the increasingly urgent need to think beyond borders. Akan-speaking peoples in Ghana such as the Ashanti have strong musicolinguistic ties with the Baule of Ivory Coast; Hausa is spread across northern Nigeria, northern Togo, northern Ghana, and Niger; there is a diffuse Mande cluster in West Africa encompassing Guinea, The Gambia, Ivory Coast, Burkina Faso, Mali, and Senegal. Nonadjacent connections, such as the existence of instruments in far-flung locations also abound. Rouget links the Abomey Court in Benin with the Baule of Ivory Coast,[7] while Kubik posits numerous connections among East, southern, Central, and West African groups on the basis of organological and stylistic affinities.[8] While it is by now not productive to continue to lament the self-serving ways in which Africa was partitioned at the end of the nineteenth century by British, French, Belgians, Portuguese, and Germans, it is worth reminding ourselves that one unfortunate effect of such partitioning and subsequent firming up of boundaries at independence is a hardening of political allegiances that, in turn, discourages scholars from undertaking intercountry projects.

Consider as an example the Ewe-speaking people of Ghana, Togo, and Benin. To date, there has been no comprehensive study of their music across national borders. Part of the problem is practical: working in English- and French-speaking Africa among peoples with marked dialectic differences and by now striking surface differences in musical idiom poses huge challenges. And yet, the work of linguist Hounkpati Capo on so-called "Gbe" languages, which cuts across the borders of nation-states, suggests that there is an underlying coherence to the diverse manifestations of Ewe or Ewe-related languages, and that an Ur-Gbe or proto-Gbe, an original language belonging to the pre-divided Ewe state, might have once existed.[9] Might an analogous Ur-Ha (*ha* = Ewe word for song), a primordial song linking the various Ewe peoples in West Africa, be a possibility? Of course, it would be too much to expect a reference work like the *New Grove* to give priority to the search for such coherence, because the knowledge it promulgates is in the first instance knowledge about Africa for Euro-Americans. The search for such coherence must come from within the African community itself, and would represent a quest for historical self-definition that on some level escapes the European gaze and promises no immediate pecuniary benefit.

A recurring theme in the *New Grove,* indeed one that comes close to being invoked as a formula, is *diversity.* About Chad, Brandily notes that its inhabitants:

> live in areas of great climactic and geographical contrast. Since they are in addition descended from different ethnic groups, it is not surprising that their ways of life and socio-religious traditions vary considerably, as do their musical traditions, which are bound to these cultures.

Arom writes that "the remarkable ethnographic and linguistic variety [in the Central African Republic] is reflected by diverse musical styles." Pierre Sallée remarks upon "the great ethnic and linguistic diversity of Gabon," even though he folds this diversity into "a relatively homogenous cultural unit." Hugo Zemp identifies "60 different peoples" in the Ivory Coast "whose diversity of culture and language is reflected in their music." Sierra Leone is said to have "a rich variety of music," and Zambia "a diversity of music because of the diversity of contexts in which it is used and of ethnic groups which perform it." According to Washington Omondi, "there are great differences between the music of [the various regions of Kenya], and to talk of Kenyan music as a homogenous entity is inaccurate." And about Africa as a whole, Wachsmann and Cooke write:

It is customary in the Western world for people to use the term "African music" as if it were a single clearly identifiable phenomenon. Yet when one considers the size of the continent (the second largest in the world), the enormous differences in climate and terrain producing contrasting ways of life across the land mass, and, above all, its extreme multilingualism (more than 1000 different languages have been identified), one should not be surprised at the diversity of music and the difficulty of isolating distinctly African features common to the whole continent. Besides, the study of the music did not proceed everywhere with equal thoroughness, insight or purpose.

Thus, spoken languages, religions, musical idioms, genres, compositional processes, aesthetic ideals, instrumental resources, performance practices, audience roles and behaviors, and other dimensions of African musical·life are said to differ widely. Faced with so much diversity, it is tempting to deny the coherence of African music at a deep level, tempting to say, with Kubik, that "there is no African music, rather many types of African music."[10] Yet, when placed in the context of other world musics, the distinctiveness of African music is often immediately apparent, which is why Meki Nzewi insists:

Incontrovertibly, there is an African (south of the Sahara) field of musical sound. Furthermore, there are distinguishing Bantu, Sudanese etc. musical sounds. And when verbal language is encoded in song, musical speech or drum language of any intention, it helps to determine ethnic musical peculiarities such as Igbo, Akan, Bemba, Xhosa, etc. When closer attention is focused on the Igbo (population about 15 million), for example, there are phonic criteria determining whether a piece is Northern, Western, Eastern, Central or Riverine Igbo. Further discriminations of phonic properties enable us to detect typologies and styles of music within or across communities.[11]

Obviously, there is a place for studies committed to constructing African music as a unified practice. And equally obviously, there is a place for studies that do not ride roughshod over the particularities of individual expressive forms. Finding imaginative ways of negotiating the continuing dialectic between the particular and the general ranks high among the challenges of representing African music.

The New Grove appeared in 1980, and although it gave rise to a number of spin-off publications—studies of individuals or small groups of composers, separate dictionaries on opera, musical instruments, and jazz—the collective writings on Africa were never assembled as a separate publication. This is a pity in a way, for taken together, they provide a picture of far greater complexity and accuracy than what one encounters in the single-author introductory texts by Francis Bebey, Kwabena Nketia, and Monique Brandily.[12] Nor is it clear in what sense one might speak of an advance in subsequent competing publications like *MGG* (1994–) and *The Garland Encyclopedia of World Music: Africa* (1998). Even more sobering is the fact that coverage of Africa in the revised *New Grove Dictionary* published in 2001, although more extensive—Togo, for example, now has a substantial article, and nearly twenty African art-music composers are given individual biographies—cannot be said to present an unequivocal qualitative advance. (This may explain, in part, my own focus here on the 1980 edition). The main entry on Africa, for example, now written by Kubik, includes more empirical data as one would expect, but its positions are more readily identified with Kubik's own research than the comparable entry in the 1980 edition, which, because it relied less fully on Wachsmann's and Cooke's research, conveyed numerous other opinions about African music, including unresolved internal dissonances. The principal advance since 1980 has come in a series of monographs offering additional data, alternative perspectives, and more concentrated studies of individual communities not to replace but to augment the *New Grove* offerings.[13]

Reviewing all of this scholarship here is beyond my capability, but we should affirm the continuing usefulness of dictionaries and encyclopedias, in particular those that are sensitive to the language character of our music, that take orthography seriously and do not routinely misspell African names, that seek a coverage that is truly representative of contemporary Africa rather than of an Africa invented by Europe, and that—therefore—incorporate, indeed privilege the thinking and writing of African musicians and scholars. There is room, too, for imaginative reconstructions of various aspects of African music in history, including various forms of regional or interethnic coherence.

Material Disparities

The written part of the archive we have been discussing exists mainly in Euro-American libraries, not in Africa. And this disparity requires that we comment briefly on the material realities that have shaped and continue to shape the archive of African music.

The plight of individual music scholars in Africa does not make for a happy tale. A senior lecturer (the rough equivalent of a tenured professor in the United States), who earns the equivalent of $150 a month, has a wife and four children, and any number of relatives knocking on his door regularly, will have his hands full keeping body together—soul is another matter altogether. The thought that he might be able to afford a visit to the British Library, the Library of Congress, the UCLA Ethnomusicology Archive, or the Archives of Traditional Music at Indiana should be dispensed with immediately; airfare alone would consume half a year's salary, and if you add the cost of food and accommodation for even a short research trip, you might as well forgo the full year's earnings. Nor is it likely that our lecturer can afford a regular subscription to journals like *The World of Music, African Music,* or *Ethnomusicology.* Kind friends, relatives, or colleagues abroad may send xeroxed copies of articles from time to time, but even if they arrive in the mail—and one cannot take this for granted since the postal workers, too, must "eat," as we say—they are unlikely to provide the kind of stable ecology that will support an active scholarly life. However gifted, knowledgeable, or hardworking, our Africa-based colleague simply cannot participate meaningfully in our self-styled "global" conversation about African music.

African music scholarship belongs to the rich, or at least to the well-to-do. This may come across as a gross exaggeration, an unnecessary provocation. Being rich is a matter of context, it will be said. But I know of no method of reckoning that would undermine the claim that a significant gap in earnings separates Africa-based scholars from their Euro-American counterparts. This should not make metropolitan ethnomusicologists defensive. These disparities exist, are reflected in the conduct of scholarship, and account in part for the skewed distribution of the archive's contents. Acknowledging such disparities in more than a token way would introduce a badly needed ethical dimension into Africanist scholarship.

Distribution of recorded materials provides further illustration of material disparities. Alan Lomax's 1968 description of Africa as "the best-recorded of continents"[14] may come as a surprise to those not accustomed to seeing Africa in first place in global competitions other than those dealing with genocide, famine, or the spread of AIDS. Yet, if you compare the modest holdings of schools, universities, independent archives, and radio stations on the continent to their counterparts in Europe and America, you will see that there is simply no comparison. Published discographies and videographies confirm that, as with books and articles, the majority of ethnographic recordings are found outside the continent.

There are exceptions, however. One of the most remarkable collections of recordings of traditional African music is that of the International Library of African Music (ILAM) in Rhodestown, South Africa. Begun by Hugh Tracey in 1954 and continued by his son Andrew after his death in 1977, the ILAM collection stands as a comprehensive coverage of music from eastern, southern, and Central Africa, a remarkable testimony to the spectacular range and diversity of styles of African music. For economic and political reasons, however, this collection has not been easily available to scholars working elsewhere on the African continent. And although items from the ILAM collection are now being rereleased in CD format, the price of individual CDs will be prohibitive to ordinary music scholars in Africa. (A CD on average costs $17, which is what it would take to feed a family of four for three days in an urban setting in Ghana, say. Given a choice between feeding your family and acquiring a luxury item such as a CD of "old" (traditional) music, there is no ambiguity about which way the decision will go.)

On a much smaller scale are the Archives of Recorded Sound at the Institute of African Studies, Legon, Ghana. This valuable resource, made up of field recordings dating back to the 1950s, as well as early recordings of popular music, existed in Legon for a number of years, underused to be sure, until Wolfgang Bender and his team managed to copy the entire collection and have it deposited at the Johannes Gutenberg University in Mainz, Germany.[15] While it is gratifying to see Mainz build its collection of material on African music for use by scholars from around the world, it is sad to note that, once again, activity on the African continent has been more or less declared impossible. Certainly working in Mainz is from the point of view of creature comforts and accessibility easier than working at Legon, where the archivist may not be seen for days, where the playback equipment, although visibly displayed, does not work, and where a request for a copy of this or that recording may be greeted by the suspicion that the scholar is going to make money with it. (How strange that the archivist and his staff have not sought to make money with these recordings all these years.) Then follows the invention of any number of excuses why a copy would be hard to make. (Dangling your wallet can work wonders on such occasions.) The archives are, in a sense, a microcosm of the difficulties that enshroud institutions in postcolonial Africa, difficulties that have led to a profound undervaluing of treasures that lie under our very noses. It is hard not to feel that the lifting of the Legon materials out of Africa liberates them for more liberal use elsewhere—a form of poetic justice, perhaps.

Even a work as basic as *The Garland Encyclopedia of World Music: Africa,* edited by Ruth Stone, the first ever "encyclopedia" devoted to African music, is beyond the budgets of most African libraries. At its current price of $250, the book would require an individual lecturer to give up more than a month's salary, or a town library to give up a sizable portion of its annual budget. Why publish books that cost so much, anyway? Is it ethical to publish books about African music that few employed Africans can afford? These are naive questions, of course. Whoever thought that Euro-

American publishers had African economies and consumers in mind when it came to books on their music?

These preliminary remarks—the anecdotes could be multiplied, of course—will serve to remind us that scholarly practice is enabled by a set of material conditions. It seems strange to have to say something so obvious, but there is a tendency, I believe, to underplay the significance of material disparities in contemporary African music scholarship. And unless its canons are radically redefined, productive scholarship, it would seem, cannot be done on the African continent, or in African libraries and archives at the present time; indeed, a precondition for significant and authentic contribution to scholarship may well be that the individual scholar leave Africa, if only temporarily. The archive of African music must therefore necessarily exist outside the continent's geographical and perhaps psychical boundaries. It must exist overwhelmingly in the hands of others, not Africans.

Making Sense of the Archive: John Gray's Bibliography

Turning now to the archive itself instead of the circumstances of production: how does one make sense of the body of materials produced? Different authors go about this differently; there is no one, correct way. But it would be helpful to open up the issues by turning to John Gray's *African Music: A Bibliographical Guide to the Traditional, Popular, Art, and Liturgical Musics of Sub-Saharan Africa*. Published in 1991, this source lists well over 5,000 items of research in books, articles, and recordings. Gray was not the first to produce such a compilation. Douglas H. Varley, A. P. Merriam, D. L. Thieme and L. J. P. Gaskin, and C. Lems-Dworkin, among others, had published bibliographies of materials relating to African music before. Gray's is, however, numerically superior. He recognizes four central genres of African music, "Traditional," "Popular," "Art," and "Church," and devotes a chapter to each. There is an introductory section on "Cultural History and the Arts," and a separate chapter labeled "Ethnomusicology." The author generously provides three separate appendices listing reference works, archives and research centers, and a discography.

How to index this unwieldy and heterogenous material? Gray elects to produce not one but four indexes so that readers can access the bibliography by ethnic group, subject, artist, and author. As always with classification systems, categories are chosen, not given; each category subtends important decisions about how knowledge is produced, owned, and disseminated. Indexing by author, for example, seems perfectly logical and standard in societies in which individuals sign articles, or take credit for musical works as composers or performers. But it works less well where knowledge is communally rather than individually owned. Multiple authorship of ritual texts or ceremonial musics, for example, does not lend itself to neat classification. Indexing by ethnic group also seems perfectly natural, but readers will want to understand the origins of ethnic boundaries, their invention, in fact, by colonial governments, and some of the politics that constrain identity formation based on ethnicity. A subject index is no less problematic. A separate category of "aesthetics," whose contents are diffusely distributed, is not as watertight as, say, "highlife," because where the latter is definable in respect of a specific historical moment, specific people, and a recorded legacy, the former is more elusive even though it presumably exists where and whenever music is made. But this is a matter of degree, because the highlife style, too, has seeped into other genres, producing in-betweens like gospel-highlife, highlife-rock, and hip-life. Categories, in short, are neither transparent nor self-evidently pertinent.

None of this is to suggest that Gray's classification has severe limitations. Librarians and catalogers are faced with these sorts of problems all the time, and often adopt pragmatic solutions. The fact that Gray's bibliography has proved immensely useful to students should, however, not hide the fact that alternative orderings are conceivable. For example, Gray is notably ambivalent about disciplinary orientations. Thus he recognizes one separate discipline, "ethnomusicology," but not "musicology" or "music theory." And while it is true that the discipline of ethnomusicology has been the traditional home for work on African music, it is also the case that some work does not fit under that rubric comfortably. (For example, work that expresses value judgments about different sorts of music is *not* admitted to ethnomusicology, because the discipline *notionally* presumes the equality of all musics.) One may also wonder why "ethnomusicology" has to be set aside from research into "traditional music"? Presumably, the reasoning here is simply one of disciplinary methodology: Ethnomusicology calls for a specific fieldwork-enabled methodology, whereas writing about traditional music can take many forms. The tension here is between ethnomusicology and so-called area studies, the latter being more flexible with regard to methodology.

We might speculate on other ways of ordering research writing, ways that would reveal other agendas. Items could be ordered chronologically, from the earliest to the most recent. This would show the growth and decay in numbers of publications and facilitate comparative study of research priorities in different epochs. Correlations between political events and the building or destroying of archives will be easier to make. A whimsical analogy might even be drawn between the age of an article and its significance, bending perversely the African respect for old age. One might also—and more controversially—divide the bibliography into outsider and insider contributions, African authors and their Euro-American counterparts. Such a classification would grate against the antiessentializing impulses that self-styled "progressive" scholars are being required to acquire these days, but it could still capture at a simple numerical level the geographical origins of authors. Some would argue that research is research, that it attains a level of autonomy once it is out there. Others might question the definitions of the very terms "insider" and "outsider." How does one classify a scholar of African origins whose intellectual orientation is (said to be) Western? And what about an American scholar whose writing about, say, a Cameroonian community takes its intellectual orientation from the Cameroonians themselves? If it is possible to lose or acquire the more privileged "insider" status, then both scholars will surely wish to be accurately represented.

There is an undeniable anxiety—marked, perhaps, among American ethnomusicologists—about acquiring insider status, and with that, the authority of authenticity. We will discuss this matter more fully when we turn to fieldwork, but let me stress here the extent to which one or another version of the outsider-insider distinction constrains what we do as scholars of African music. Look, for example, at the cover of David Locke's analytical study of Kpegisu, a Southern Ewe dance, and you will find a prominent picture of his long-time collaborator, the late Godwin Agbeli.[16] You may even be forgiven for thinking that the well-dressed African displayed in that portrait is either the author or the subject of the book. Here, the pressures of framing come from outside, from an unspoken suspicion that the outsider can never truly penetrate the indigenous culture. Thus Locke, whose understanding of African music is deep, is forced to signal authenticity by putting the "wrong" picture on the cover.

Again, the U.S.-based journal, *The Black Perspective in Music*, under the editorship of its founder, Eileen Southern, actually identified those of their contributors who were African American: "It is germane to the purpose of this journal to identify black-American writers. Accordingly, the symbol (+) is used for such identification." Few editors of musicological publications today can afford to be this honest, realistic, or brave. Although none, I feel sure, will want to deny flatly that historically situated differences— black versus white, African versus non-African, insider versus outsider— still play a part in the way scholarship is conducted, few will have a clear-headed way of acknowledging them. The fear of seeming politically incorrect, patronizing, essentialist, racialist, or racist leads them to adopt the deadliest of all positions: indifference.

We have traveled a long way from Gray's work. As a bibliography, it certainly minimizes—in principle—the interpretive element. Its task is to inform by documenting knowledge, not to enter into the ideologies of knowledge construction. And yet, as we have seen, its lists are ordered, and thus demand to be minimally interpreted. These ostensibly minimal interpretations could have decisive consequences on the work of understanding. Even the most apparently transparent categories already enshrine alternatives insofar as they are propped up by certain presuppositions. Gray's valuable work thus raises important conceptual issues.[17]

Language

Language is basic to research because it dominates our conceptual apparatus. Beyond its ordinary communicative role, language as idea, as song, and as agent for aesthetic and ethical discoursing is prevalently expressed in a vast range of musicoverbal genres throughout Africa. Intuitively, at least, many Africans understand the power and significance of the word. Yet, although there are over 2,000 languages in Africa, and although their oral literatures harbor musical data, the written archive is dominated by English and French. (There is some research in Portuguese, German, and Italian, as well.) This situation reflects our colonial past, of course, but its ramifications are yet to be fully explored.

Given that the written archive is in European languages, the oral archive in African languages, it is not surprising that the field is dominated by outsiders, and that scholarly production is oriented more to foreign markets than to local ones. Such a regime forces African scholars to function on other people's terms, learn other people's languages, parcel out their research using other people's frameworks, and in the end, lose out by achieving partial rather than full control over the protocols of other people's scholarly careers. Partial control arises not because Africans are incapable of acquiring native fluency in any language but because the institutional arrangement in postcolonial Africa compels individuals to divide their efforts among many competing tasks, to wear many hats, to risk becoming jacks-of-all-trades. For if the production of a certain kind of written text is what finally counts, then unless our professional priorities cumulatively reinforce the acquisition of such skill, we will always seem to need to have the bar lowered for us. What a great pity it is that we have not woken up to the urgent need to reformulate the very mechanism of assessment.

Linguistic colonization need not be as total as it appears to be in certain parts of Africa. Indic musicology, for example, although strongly marked by English, is aided in its resistance by the existence of a distinguished tradition of indigenous writing and notating. So why does Africa seem so porous, so welcoming of Western influence, so uneager to resist? Although some would see this simply—and naively—as a case of a stronger culture dominating a weaker one, the real reason may lie elsewhere. Perhaps it is the deep compatibility between Africa's musicolinguistic cultures and those of Europe that is unsettling. Perhaps we are more alike than the

West would be willing to grant. Perhaps, then, the association of Western-influenced education with Euro-American traditions of ordering knowledge reflects only a surface, and ultimately untenable, incompatibility.

Multilingualism provides a good illustration of individuals' partial competencies and of the fact that the power in the accumulation of such partialities remains to be realized and profited from. Consider the situation in Ghana, where there are said to be forty-four languages.[18] In the 1960s, the news on Ghana Broadcasting Corporation was read successively in six principal languages: Twi, Ga, Ewe, Ga-Adangbe, Dagbani, and Nzema. There was some virtue in repetition, because some listeners in time acquired a modest vocabulary from these daily broadcasts and were put in a more vivid frame of mind about the reality of the new nation-state. Most schooled Ghanaians are at least bilingual, some trilingual, and a few quadrolingual. The languages they speak occupy different social registers, of course. English is used in school, the civil service, and political life (as when the Prince of Wales or the president of the United States visits Ghana). Twi, Fanti, Ga, or Ewe may be associated with church, market, domestic situations, entertainment, and significant segments of social life. Not all forty-four languages can boast a written literature, and it is often the case that many individuals speak Twi, Ga, or Ewe but can neither read nor write any of them. In other cases, reading in indigenous languages is confined to the Bible and hymn books, perhaps an occasional short story; all other reading is done in one or another metropolitan language. Thus the greater control that comes from a combination of speaking, reading, and writing—from exploring language in different, mutually reinforcing modes of articulation—is denied us. Still, the fact of being able to move among these language worlds facilitates certain analogical ways of thinking that could significantly enrich humanistic scholarship.

It has been long known that African music and language are closely related. According to Kubik, African music is "closely connected with language, to an extent that it is hardly possible today to study it without the necessary background in African languages."[19] For the music scholar, knowledge of African languages is called upon when you need to translate a song text, interpret drum language, or reconstruct native modes of conceptualization. There is also a more elusive sensible dimension, often highlighted in performance, but ultimately inaccessible to those who do not understand the particular musicodramatic language or its supplementary critical language. This is not to say that Akan or Yoruba drumming cannot be understood by those who do not speak Akan or Yoruba. Understanding, after all, exists at different levels. It is rather to claim that the depth of an Akan or a Yoruba worldview, to which music alone provides access, is harder to retrieve or reconstruct if one does not enter into the linguistic and hence philosophical worlds of those cultures.

It goes without saying, however, that the archive of African music contains research produced by individuals who do not possess what Kubik calls "the necessary background in African languages." This is neither a virtue nor a vice; it is simply the fact of the matter. For certain kinds of research, linguistic competence is not immediately relevant; for others, it is crucial. A lot then depends on which aspect of African music the individual researcher is studying. This ostensibly balanced view, however, hides a troubling asymmetry. It is hard to imagine histories of German, Russian, or French music written by individuals with no competence in those languages. Africa, however, is there to be had by whomever pleases; after all, given the pervasiveness of colonial languages, one can always rely on interpreters. The potential for altering the canons of scholarship by originating research questions from within the indigenous culture is thus lost. One could, of course, argue that origins do not matter, that only the final product does. To this one may answer by pointing out that different theories of origins privilege different groups, so that from a political point of view, origins do matter. Certainly the population of insiders would be curtailed, while that of outsiders would diminish considerably, if a requirement for the production of an ethnography was also that it be written in the indigenous language.

One of the amusing but at the same time tragic signs that African languages are undervalued is the near-hysteria that greets Europeans who have some fluency in an African language. As children, we used to marvel at German missionaries who preached the sermon in Ewe. Of course, they sounded funny (although the Evangelical Presbyterian Church did not encourage outright laughter during services), frequently got the speech tones wrong, and generally came across as stiff and proper, as if they had written the entire sermon by looking up words in Diedrich Westermann's 1928 dictionary.[20] But we were impressed, perhaps even moved by this, because of the thought that a white man (complete with all the symbolic capital that he carried) had actually managed to learn our language, stooped to our level. Similarly, in more recent times—and I rely here on anecdotal evidence—much is made of prominent metropolitan ethnomusicologists, anthropologists, and literary scholars who speak Fon, Yoruba, Kpelle, Igbo, Nango, or Twi. It is not the fact of their possessing superior knowledge that is admired; it is the mere fact that they are heard speaking these languages. A native Fon's acquisition of English would not be as marked as a native Englishman's fluency in Fon, even where the period and circumstances of exposure to the other language are comparable. Thus the Euro-American's ordinariness is figured differently by Africans. Instead of taking pride in our infinitely greater understanding of our own languages, instead of focusing on our gifts of multilingualism, we devote our energies to celebrating our historical oppressors' mediocrity.

The core difficulty remains the absence of a vigorous critical discourse in response to a well-identified problematic originating from and situated primarily in the African world, and carried out by individuals or groups fired by the exigencies of our historical situation to pursue strategies of mental emancipation. Beyond token acknowledgment of the need to acquire "the necessary background in African languages," metropolitan scholars are unlikely to institutionalize modes of study that would prevent individuals who do not care about our languages from being certified as competent in our music. If African languages are going to be properly valued, the initiative, as always, must come from within Africa itself. And until that happens, the wealth of our multilingualism will remain at the level of potential, not achievement. For music scholarship, interpretation and understanding will be impoverished as a result.

Fieldwork

A significant portion of the archive of African music is the fruit of ethnographic research. Fieldwork or on-site research, the first stage in the making of an ethnography—the second being reportage[21]—lies at the heart of ethnomusicological research. Typically, an individual scholar selects a site for research based on any number of factors: curiosity stimulated by a prior encounter with a given culture; the advice of friends, teachers, or acquaintances; the relative safety of the location; fascination with the music, dance, or performance tradition; or simply the desire, at a certain stage in life, to do something different. The prospective researcher then embarks on preparatory reading, study of the country or region or ethnic group, listening to whatever recordings are available, or, in a few cases, undergoing a formal training methodology (such as Alan Lomax's cantometrics course). Then he or she packs bags, travels to the field, spends a year or two in the field (depending on the grant), and returns to the metropolis. Analysis of the data follows, the results are assembled as a dissertation, book, or article, and in time the individual acquires a reputation as an expert. Expertise could be of a genre, a tradition, the dynamics of gender, instruments, a specific geocultural space, or simply theory. The expert is invited to speak at conferences and on campuses, to referee articles for professional journals and presses, and to evaluate dossiers for the promotion of junior colleagues.

Since the 1950s at least, the production of written knowledge about African music has been based for the most part on fieldwork. And yet this master narrative entails many beliefs and moves that are not transparent and that therefore need to be interrogated. Some of this interrogation is already part of the intellectual histories of anthropology and ethnomusicology, and so need not be recapitulated here.[22] My own interest stems from the fact that a number of African scholars are ambivalent about fieldwork, or at least the kind of fieldwork sanctioned by the ethnomusicological establishment. This fieldwork is sponsored in a recognized way, and the framing of sponsorship is a crucial part of the presentation of research results. Knowledge acquired informally and over long periods occupies a lower rung on the ladder. Only if it can be framed as sponsored, as intentionally acquired within a circumscribed period, and paid for by a recognized body, does such knowledge begin to accrue value. Almost by definition, then, many Africans are written out of the fieldwork-enabled arena; definitionally, they are turned into informants. This is not to deny that some African graduate students in Europe and America return home to collect data, or that Africa-based scholars do not shun dedicated periods of work with knowledgeable culture exponents. It is rather to remark upon the extraordinary premium placed on a certain kind of intentional but often hurried search for certain forms of knowledge and the corollary dismissal of others.

That fieldwork is important, indeed central to the construction of knowledge about African music, is evident from the care that writers take to announce how much of it they have actually done. "How much" is a quantitative measure indexing length of time spent in the field; it obviously does not refer to the nature or quality of the experience. In the acknowledgments to his *Venda Children's Songs,* John Blacking writes: "in all I spent twenty-two months in the field."[23] When later he gave the set of popular lectures published as *How Musical Is Man?,* the biographical note reckoned the period of fieldwork not in months but in years: "During 1956–58 he undertook fieldwork among the Venda of the Northern Transvaal."[24] And on one occasion, when forced to defend his approach to transcription, Blacking crossed over from the quantitative to the qualitative realm: "The transcriptions are performing scores derived from detailed transcriptions of recordings. During twenty-two months' *intimate contact with Venda music,* I learned to distinguish what is musically significant" (my emphasis).[25] These small but telling mutations bespeak an anxiety over fieldwork, the ultimate source of authority, it would seem, for a certain kind of ethnomusicologist.

Creativity in informing readers of one's fieldwork credentials can be helpful. Michelle Kisliuk describes her book, *Seize the Dance,* as spanning "field research in Centrafrique over nine years (1986–95)."[26] By this she does not mean nine continuous years, or indeed that she was resident there for nine years while taking an occasional trip abroad. She means, rather, that nine years span her first and last visits there as of the writing. She explains that the nine-year span includes a two-year stay, and that between 1992 and 1995, she undertook "five short-term spans of follow-up research." Had she, like Blacking, told us the actual number of years she spent in Centrafrique, the number nine would have been halved. Repeated visits have a great advantage, of course, for you can observe change, incorporate a diachronic dimension into your story if you so please, search for answers to questions that may have arisen in the course of analysis, bring in a comparative perspective, and, overall, maximize the normative functions of collecting during fieldwork and cogitating outside the field. Kisliuk's book shows this cumulative advantage. I mention her phrase "over nine years" only because some inattentive readers may credit her with having spent more actual time in the field than she did.

In a different but related vein is the need to inform readers about one's practical experience with African music. David Locke, in an important article on rhythmic practices associated with southern Ewe music, lets readers understand that he is no armchair theorist but one who has studied drumming both in the field and at home:

> My performance training includes: 1969 (Columbia University), Eve music and dance with Alfred Ladzekpo and Nicholas England; 1971–1975 (Wesleyan University), repertory of the Ghana National Dance Ensemble with Abraham Adzinyah; 1972–1975 (Wesleyan University) Eve music and dance with Freeman Donkor; 1975–1977 (Institute of African Studies, Legon) Akan drumming with Kwasi Adei, Eve drumming and dance with Gideon Foli Alorwoyie, 1975–1977 (Art Council of Ghana Folkloric Company, Accra), Eve drumming and dance with Godwin Agbeli, Dagomba music and dance with Abubakari Lunna; 1975–1977 (Volta Region, Ghana), the music and dance of Atsiagbeko with dance clubs from the towns of Afiadenyigba, Aflao and Anyako.[27]

In a relatively transparent culture like that of the United States, Locke's acknowledgments might be read on face value as providing basic information and expressing gratitude to former teachers. Postcolonial readers, however, may detect some strain in this mode of informing.

Not every writer is anxious about establishing his or her fieldwork credentials. After an initial visit in 1963, Simha Arom later spent four years in the Central African Republic, returning there subsequently. You would have to look hard, however, to find traces of anxiety about fieldwork anywhere in his publications. Fieldwork for him was a means to an end, and so emphasis was put on the end and not the means. And A. M. Jones, who spent over two decades in Zambia, does not introduce his magnum opus, *Studies in African Music*, by claiming near-authenticity based on length of time spent in the field.

Thematizations of fieldwork are generally not pronounced in the work of African scholars. Nketia, Nzewi, Euba, Fiagbedzi, and Mensah rarely fret about doing time in the field. Anxiety over fieldwork therefore seems to be an outsider's problem. Nor is it common for African scholars to devote entire conferences or significant portions thereof to discussing the problematics of fieldwork. At their conferences, Africans worry about education, the standardization of textbooks, incorporating African texts into the curriculum, church music, teaching children to play instruments, compositional idioms, and above all, resources. This is not to say that no existential matters are broached. But the urgency of material and practical concerns renders guilt-ridden discussions of soft existential issues like ethics and authenticity a luxury.

The dichotomy is striking, though not altogether surprising. It suggests that the kind of knowledge produced by people who are anxious about fieldwork may bear traces of that anxiety. Certainly the eagerness to inform about length of time spent in the field is one such sign. (More is always better, it seems.) Then also the packaging of research results to emphasize differences rather than similarities (a topic addressed more fully in chapter 7) may reflect a similar anxiety. Relatively short periods in the field (such as a two-year stay, which, ironically, is often regarded as more than adequate for knowing a musical culture), based on expectations already prepared, do not normally inspire the production of sameness-stories. Difference-stories have greater market potential.

Fieldwork-enabled knowledge is normally constrained by the language and intellectual traditions of the scholar and by the interpretive community to which the ethnography is addressed. Ethnographic knowledge is in this sense not discovered but deliberately choreographed. Even material objects like musical instruments, which seem to have an objective, measurable existence, and which can therefore be described more or less accurately, betray ways of naming that the researcher brings to his or her work. To describe a drum as a "membranophone" is to use a term that Africans do not normally use. A drum may be a sacred object, a god, an ancestor with a deep voice, or the kid brother in the family.[28] My point here is not that there is no use for the term "membranophone"—the visceral satisfaction of employing "big" or polysyllabic words as markers of erudition is, thanks to colonial education, still very much with us—but that placing it in a wider pool of descriptive terms, rather than giving it a priori significance in practically every standard work, might enhance its usefulness and lessen its alienating effect.

It is ultimately a moot point whether certain kinds of fieldwork produce better knowledge. Perhaps some do, though coming up with criteria for distinguishing superior knowledge is not always easy. Nor has it been possible to prescribe a practical way of doing fieldwork that would guarantee such knowledge. What matters exists at the level of performance. In other words, where you go, how long you spend there, and what you do are not as important as the kind of story you end up telling and to whom you do so. If you are blessed with expository or descriptive skills, if you can break into poetry from time to time as you recount your field experience, you will appeal to a certain kind of reader. If you are patient, and describe everything from power outages and goat sacrifices to synchronized canceling of stamps at a post office and tapping of feet in a bar, if you adopt the typical outsider's pose of feigning surprise at everything you see, you may well win over a metropolitan readership hungry for such tales. It is not the nature of the experience, not the authenticity of the field experience, but the power of the writing—that is what determines the success or failure of an ethnography.[29]

Claims for the authenticity of the field experience are further compromised by the fact that reportage, the second stage of ethnographic construction, usually takes place outside the field, not within it. The reasons are often practical: Writing a book while living in an African village is difficult. A condition, therefore, for the production of ethnographic research is something resembling what Johannes Fabian describes in terms of a "*denial of coevalness,*" that is, "*a persistent and systematic tendency to place the referent(s) of anthropology in a Time other than the present of the producer of anthropological discourse*" (author's emphasis).[30] If you have to move out of the place and time frame of your informants in order to represent them, then such placing of the referents of ethnomusicological research in a different time frame becomes a condition, not merely a by-product, of the production of knowledge. In other words, the disjunction between researcher's world and that of the researched is not fortuitous; it is necessary, along with the asymmetry of power that such a disjunction implies. Successful fieldworkers are not those who make token or pious gestures toward undermining the asymmetry but those who treat it openly as a condition for knowledge production.

If getting out of the field is a practical as well as a logical condition for producing an ethnography, then we should be able to imagine ethnomusicological research that is not based on the normal kind of fieldwork. Analytical or theoretical work is a case in point. Think of the vast archive of recorded African music, and consider the unstated orthodoxy in ethnomusicology that, although you may use other people's recordings in teaching, say, World Music surveys, or for your own edification and amusement, you generally do not base your research on them; you collect your own. And collecting your own invariably entails a trip abroad. This position will be more fully contested in chapter 8, but I want to suggest here that we reject the exclusivity granted fieldwork and embrace any and all activities that promote the advancement of knowledge about African music. Whatever the "field" was in its classical formulation, it is no longer fixed. The field is an idea of place, not a specific or specifiable space. It may migrate freely, frequently, or not at all, shrink, or expand; its subjects may be few or many, relatively uniform or varied, more or less reticent about divulging information about their culture. The field, in other words, is unstable and amorphous, an assembly of fragments, not a unified or unifiable whole.

This formulation, although entirely consistent with some existing research, has the advantage of encouraging more experimental kinds of work. It rejects the a priori privilege accorded to those who have been there—including, I fear, native scholars—and bases judgments of value on the nature of the musical or scholarly product. The tradition of bringing native musicians to the metropolis, for example, will continue, while research that scrutinizes recordings will receive a new boost. Demystifying fieldwork may well bring to light work by nonconforming scholars whose insights are nevertheless acute. Above all, this reconfiguration of fieldwork will foreground the role played by the imagination in the construction of ideas about African music.

The Autobiographical Turn

One potential obstacle to the construction of an Africa-oriented archive is the autobiographical mode that is increasingly employed in reportage. At one level, the presence of the writer in the text provides precise information. It helps to situate limits by specifying where, when, with whom, and how long the ethnographer has been. In place of all-encompassing or impersonal locutions, in place of an omniscient authorial voice, the ethnographer adopts a mode of discourse that seems friendly, honest, and modest. Autobiography brings a human dimension to the writing, drawing the reader into an experience with real people and actual places, rather than conveying a sense of detachment. Autobiographical narratives serve as valuable vehicles for self-reflexivity. Texts no longer hide the fact, for example, that the ethnographer, too, has feelings about his or her day-to-day experiences in the field, and that these feelings need not be suppressed.[31]

Without disputing the importance of this humanizing tendency, one might nevertheless note the following asymmetry: African scholars of music have so far not shown much interest in exploiting or exploring the autobiographical mode *in this phase of their collective project*. (When, however, they leave the continent and join the postcolonial fray in its American incarnation, and realize that there is money to be made from telling stories about their childhood and the relatives who stayed behind, things change.)

Anxieties about fieldwork, identity, authenticity, and voice are not as marked as one finds among metropolitan scholars. This is not to suggest that there is anything obscure about individual scholarly voices or manners. Nzewi's relentless struggles to resist English assimilation of the peculiar shapes of Igbo concepts and realities, Nketia's considerable powers of synthesis, Euba's disarming and penetrating directness, or Mensah's lightly worn erudition: these differing profiles are available to anyone who cares to look. To the extent that they steer clear of personal testimony, they are united in their difference from a certain metropolitan stance.

The reticence about talking about oneself may have something to do with conventions of scholarship, but it may also be influenced by the scholar's relationship to the people studied. Autobiography can index arrogance; the writer may be accused of being self-serving or perhaps even obscenely narcissistic, rewriting the purpose of fieldwork to coincide with a search for self rather than a selfless representation of other cultural practices. The responsibilities placed on whomever would speak for members of an African community can sometimes be considerable; because every word spoken/written or, especially, not spoken/not written touches a person, clan, or whole village in some elemental way, getting it right is of the essence. To substitute for this imperative of accurate or—and this complicates it—favorable representation a self-indulgent play with one's own subjectivity, one's sense of alienation, the intricacies of one's personal identity, and so on, would seem irreverent as well as exploitative. Here we may well be faced with a clash of cultures in that, because ethnography is the metropolitan scholar's ultimate passport to professional status, he or she may not wish to be deterred from reaching that goal by succumbing to the supposed sensitivities of this or that ethnic group in faraway Africa.

There is a sense in which all writing is autobiographical. Every ethnography contains an autobiographical sediment, whether or not aspects of self are thematized explicitly. Therefore the claim that this or that writer is writing from experience is limited, if not a tautology. Is Arom not writing from experience when he offers detailed structuralist charts of the music of the Banda-Linda? Or is "experience" limited to inhaling a dream-inducing powder in the compound of a Tumbuka healer, or playing bass guitar at an Ariya ceremony in Yorubaland? Our modes of discourse are unavoidably marked, however subliminally, by something we might call experience, which is in turn mediated by a conventional form of communication. So the significant distinction is not between those who write from experience and those who do not, but between those who *say* they are writing from experience and those who simply get on with it.

We cannot in any case confer an a priori value on any writing that is advertised as autobiographical, self-reflexive, or emanating from experience.

Because all such narratives are designed for consumers, they circulate as commodities and are subject to the vagaries of the market. What if my story, although true, is not sensational enough, not moving enough, not particularly interesting? What if it is not well written by conventional standards? Does that lessen its value as a window onto a truth that I believe and feel deeply? Also, depending on the social climate, some things make better stories than others. An Ivorian in Tanzania who learns Kiswahili for the purposes of fieldwork is not as much of a sensation as a (white) Brit who studies Yoruba in order to write about their oral poetry. Similarly, stories about a Jewish-American male who has been made chief of a Yoruba village, or an Irish-American woman who has been enstooled as queen-mother in a village in Northern Ghana, have high commodity value in the United States at present because of their frankly exotic nature. Once we accept the commodity status of any representation—including, and especially, self-representation—we must disabuse ourselves of any illusions regarding its truth or authenticity. Ethnographic narratives are performances. And since performance is an accentuation, a re-presentation, a rhetorical exertion, a rendition, it betrays the ultimate untruth of every principled departure from the ordinary temporal realm. Its authenticity lies precisely in its inauthenticity.

Perhaps that last claim is a little exaggerated, because isn't there some virtue in the personal point of view? The point is not to deny a place for self-reflexive writing about African music. My concern rather is to point out the potentially exploitative nature of such storytelling, and to suggest that in invoking the Other merely as a pretext for talking about self, the metropolitan scholar indirectly demeans African subjects. On this point, too, positive change from the African point of view must be initiated by Africans themselves. And thinking about fieldwork as a potential source of empowerment may help in enacting the counteroffensive.

Transcription

An important, if nowadays undervalued, part of the archive of African music is the body of transcriptions of various repertoires. There is a long history of writing down African music in "Western" notation; however, the most extensive and influential transcriptions have been produced during the last century. I will not be repeating that history here, not only because it is available elsewhere[32] but also because having to rehearse such a history is oppressive to the African scholar. A detour is necessary to elaborate briefly on this.

We relate to the European tradition at an angle, so to speak. We joined it in midstream. We are therefore at liberty to deny any or all aspects of its prehistory, as we please, and to establish origins where they matter to us.

This strident countermove would thus replay something that Europeans have taught us in the familiar if apocryphal story about them arriving on the shores of an African country, stepping off the boat, and planting a flag to claim the land. Just like that! Likewise, we should plant a few flags by claiming or denying certain terrains within certain metropolitan intellectual histories. For if, as a condition for formulating thoughts about African practices, we are obliged to absorb Western histories and techniques that developed without the slightest sympathy for anything that might vaguely be called an African point of view, then chances of accelerating the process by which we attain deep self-knowledge are small. This, presumably, remains a challenge for postcolonial theorists.

After a century of active practice in the transcription of African music, it is possible to observe the play of ideologies, the development of alternatives, and the impact of transcription on performance and theorization. It is possible, in other words, to constitute a viable history of practice. But to require African scholars to control the entire history of transcriptional practice as a precondition for registering their own views is to ask them to do double duty, to go twice the distance. Such a requirement is grossly unfair, although dissertation advisers, program chairs, and journal editors seem blissfully unaware, always hiding behind a reading of the ostensibly conventional to keep African students in the slow or marginal tracks. Fairer would be to endorse a radical selectivity in the appropriation of things European. This, in turn, entails relativizing Europe, speaking "it" where necessary as a kind of pidgin, alongside the African pidgin. Two pidgins make a whole—or so it appears in the post-colony.

Although there are significant alternatives, the predominant mode of transcribing African music is via staff notation. If we add together the body of transcriptions made by comparative musicologists and amateurs beginning in the 1920s, ethnomusicologists from the 1950s, and African scholars from the 1960s, we have a sizable body of work that constitutes a valuable portion of the archive. As with other parts of the written archive, however, this one is diffuse, making it difficult for scholars to reap the full benefits of a centralized resource.

It would have been nice to be able to take for granted the important role that an archive of musical transcriptions can play in the scientific project of African musicology. Many African scholars include transcriptions in their work not primarily to establish credentials but to facilitate precise and concrete talk about music. According to Ter Ellingson, "by the late 20th century, changing emphases in ethnomusicological theory and method make it possible to ask whether transcription has not at least declined in importance, or even become a peripheral or anachronistic remnant of outmoded ideas and methods."[33] This may be so for other culture areas, but not for Africa, where the practice is sporadic and diffuse, and has therefore not benefited from its potential cumulative impact. Moreover, not all scholars are alert to the pragmatic benefits of certain modes of musical scholarship, have hands-on skills in transcription, and see that transcription can aid the global cultivation of African music. And so doubts continue to be raised about the value of transcriptions by individuals who do not necessarily have Africa at heart.

A transcription is a translation into musical symbols of a sound reality. The reality might be a perception by an individual or, where the acoustic rather than the musical element is given priority, a set of "mechanical vibrations or pressure oscillations of various sorts."[34] Making a transcription is subject to various interferences, and reading one demands recourse to the conventions of interpretation particular to a given interpretive community. There are, in other words, universal as well as particular aspects of every transcription.

To choose a tiny example: Ghanaian musicians brought up under the influence of Ephraim Amu's and Kwabena Nketia's scores tend to align themselves with either subtradition as 2/4 (Amu) or 6/8 (Nketia). These competing ways of representing meter—which, as far as I can tell, exist only at the notational level and not at the level of realization—are in turn appropriated from compositional practice. An outsider ignorant of this tradition, or one unwilling to grant that although Africans did not invent staff notation, enclaves of thinking musicians have established meaningful conventions of notational practice that have been working well for them for many decades, may fail to grasp the intertextual world within which the African scholar's transcription makes sense.

I will be returning to matters of notation and transcription in subsequent chapters, but let me rapidly take stock of some significant contributions. In the 1920s Hornbostel transcribed various melodies and rhythms based on close listening to recordings of music by the Pangwe, Ewe, Bateke, Babutu, Luvemba, Makua, Mashona, Nyamwezi, and others.[35] These are descriptive but with potential prescriptive and conceptual benefits. (I'm using Ellingson's terms here.) Then there are the conceptual transcriptions of Nketia, starting with Akan funeral dirges (1955) and continuing through various Ghanaian repertoires (for example, *Akan Drumming,* 1963), including the 1963 volume, *Folk Songs of Ghana,* to culminate in notations of compositions from different parts of the continent published in his widely used textbook, *The Music of Africa* (1974). Rose Brandel, in the 1950s and 1960s, produced, strictly by ear, a series of transcriptions of African music, most notably her monograph *The Music of Central Africa: An Ethnomusicological Study* (1961). Most extensive are the transcriptions of A. M. Jones, the second volume of whose *Studies in African Music,* published in 1959, consists of scores of Ghanaian and Zambian repertoires.

These transcriptions include full dance pieces, thus providing counterevidence to the enduring prejudice that African music is merely repetitious and therefore not worth transcribing in full. David Locke, the principal heir to Jones, has worked with Dagbamba and Ewe repertoires and published transcriptions in extenso in such books as *Drum Damba: Talking Drum Lessons* (1990) and *Drum Gahu: A Systematic Method for an African Percussion Piece* (1987). Akin Euba's magisterial study of *dùndún* drumming (*Yoruba Drumming: The Dùndún Tradition* [1991]) is laced with transcriptions, as are various studies of Nigerian repertoires by Anthony King, Meki Nzewi, and Joshua Uzoigwe. And from Ghana in recent times have appeared the contributions of Willie Anku (*Structural Set Analysis: Adowa*, 1992) and Kongo Zabana (*African Drum Music Series: Kpanlogo, Agbekor, Adowa*, 1997).

Other scholars have used a modified form of staff notation. They include Kubik, whose work deals with eastern, southern, and Central African music (see, for example, *Theory of African Music*, 1994), and perhaps most important, Simha Arom, whose *African Polyphony and Polyrhythm* published first in French in 1985 and in English translation in 1991 is the single most extensive documentation of Central African Republic music in notation. Important, too, are Gilbert Rouget's recently published book on music at the court of King Gbefa of Benin (1996), and Trevor Wiggins's essays on drumming and xylophone music in the northern territories of Ghana published in a 1999 volume, *Composing the Music of Africa*, edited by Malcolm Floyd. This list could be greatly extended to take in equally significant work on other regions of Africa, but what has been mentioned should convince skeptics that a comprehensive and critical account of the library of transcriptions of African music is not only possible but potentially interesting and revealing.

The archive of African music would be greatly impoverished without the labors of these workers. Showing us what African musicians do puts us in a better position to understand how they do it. This is not to pretend that the "what" is expressible only in one kind of medium, or that it is knowable without remainders; the point, rather, is that there is no substitute for the pursuit of that "what," whatever it is. One reason for skepticism about transcriptions is the often careless claim that African music cannot be adequately transcribed into European notation. I will return to this in chapter 3, but it is well here to lament the fact that the transcriptions mentioned in the previous paragraph remain underused by scholars. They have not (yet) formed the basis of a critical discussion of African music. For example, Akin Euba's extensive transcriptions of Yoruba *dùndún* drumming, Pierre Sallée's detailed study of music from Gabon, Nketia's collection of Akan folk songs, Marcos Branda-Lacerda's analyses of bata and *dùndún* repertoires from Benin, and other studies are infrequently visited. As with certain ethnographies, transcriptions are sometimes aligned too closely with individuals, instead of being seen as documents "out there" for study and debate.

It is noteworthy that the debate about the appropriateness of staff notation for African music is a subject of particular interest to outsiders, not insiders. African scholars from Kyagambiddwa to Kongo have for the most part accepted the conventions—and limitations—of staff notation and gone on to produce transcriptions in order to inform and to make possible a higher level of discussion and debate. None of this is to suggest that they do not see the limitations of staff notation. But why have they postponed philosophical analysis of such limitations? There is a simple and pragmatic reason, which I believe stems from the reality of our postcolonial situation. As indicated in chapter 1, the "language" spoken by many schooled musicians is a language with roots in European practices and assumptions. Having considered the affinities between European and a putative African notation, some have decided that, although it distorts some aspect of African musical realities—which notational system doesn't?—staff notation is nevertheless adequate for getting things off the ground. Just as creative writers use English or French to express African realities, so musicians use staff notation to express African musical "realities." It is highly doubtful that there are any ultimately unique and untranslatable African realities, instead of idiomatic preferences shaped by tradition, convention, material circumstances, and cultivated sensibilities. If no African qualities refuse translation, we are better off putting our energies toward building a basic library—with all its imperfections—that can enable an informed rather than impressionistic discussion of the actual notes, rhythms, and timbres that African musicians play and sing.

There is, then, a pressing need to consolidate this aspect of the African archive. There is a need to key transcriptions to specific performances—as Locke, Branda-Lacerda, and Rouget, among others, have done—so that we can debate specific texts. Just as our philosophers debate Placide Tempels's *Bantu Philosophy,* our artists scrutinize "Man on a Bicycle" or the coffins shaped as cars, drums, fish, or other objects figured as metonymic with the dead, and our men of letters pore over Achebe's *Things Fall Apart,* so music theorists ought eventually to be able to discuss the metrical, formal, or semiotic properties of E. T. Mensah's "School Girl," Fela's "Lady," or Ladysmith Black Mambazo's "Paulina." And the existence of texts, even those that are essentially fictional (which texts are ultimately not?), would greatly facilitate such debate. We need, then, to reject as unpragmatic calls for new notations for African music. For if part of the burden of postcoloniality is a search for imaginative ways of inserting ourselves into a global space, where difference and sameness can be negotiated in cunning ways and with a view to altering the balance of power, then running African music through the old notational sieves may help to foreground certain features; it may even help to inflect what was previously considered canonical by showing how ineffectively it responds to African idioms.

I should stress, again, that none of these recommendations, which, although unsubtle, may well achieve political results that more subtle deliberations may not, is meant to discourage careful reflection on the imagined particularities of African musical thought and experience. My concern is simply that we not put the cart before the horse. Too often, African scholars have inherited problems created by others, causing them to expend energies on acts that do not serve their purposes. For example, because their discipline is founded on the construction of differences, ethnomusicologists are more likely to encourage the representation of African music in new, unconventional notations than in standard staff notation. Yet the use of standard notation has a way of facilitating comparison, thus enabling a keener appreciation of differences. The ethnomusicological interest in new notations should be seen as their problem, not ours.

Conclusion

This chapter has urged greater self-awareness in making and evaluating the contents of the vast archive of written, recorded, and oral texts. I have suggested that no accurate assessment of the order of knowledge about African music can afford to overlook the material grounds that sustain scholarly practice. I have emphasized that language is of utmost importance, fieldwork is not unproblematic, autobiographical writing is not beyond criticism, and transcriptions are indispensable. Stated so plainly, these politically motivated remarks could either provoke controversy or be summarily dismissed as naive. But the complex worlds of theory and practice in African music, the wide dispersion of actors and consumers, enjoin us to evaluate musicological claims with more than casual attention to the immediate as well as delayed benefits that will accrue to specific individuals or groups at specific historical moments. Probing the ideologies of practice makes us aware of the darker side of knowledge ordering. I hope that my attempts to point to a few of these has provided a stimulus to further discussion of the archive. In subsequent chapters, we will consider aspects of this practice, starting with the invention of African rhythm.

3
The Invention
of "African Rhythm"

Inventing African Rhythm

That the distinctive quality of African music lies in its rhythmic structure is a notion so persistently thematized that it has by now assumed the status of a commonplace, a topos. And so it is with related ideas that African rhythms are complex, that Africans possess a unique rhythmic sensibility, and that this rhythmic disposition marks them as ultimately different from us.

Consider a few of these characterizations. The eleventh-century Christian physician and theologian, Ibn Butlan, in a tract entitled "On how to buy slaves and how to detect bodily defects," claimed that "If a black were to fall from the sky to the earth, he would fall in rhythm."[1] In other words, even while facing certain death—speaking as metaphorically as Butlan did—blacks (especially black women) continued to exhibit an essential and irreducible rhythmic disposition. The association of dancing with death, the racialist conferral of particular sensibilities on particular groups of people, and the construction of African rhythm as complex, superior, yet ultimately incomprehensible: these and other implications of Ibn Butlan's casual remark are found reproduced in diverse ways and with diverse accents throughout the history of discourse about African music.[2]

On the behavioral aspects of African music, John Ogilby wrote in 1670 that Gold Coast Africans

> have great inclinations to Dancing; so that when they hear a Drum or other Instrument, they cannot stand quiet, but must show their skill. . . . The women in the Kingdom of ARDER, at the east of the

Gold Coast are so addicted to Dancing, that they cannot forbear upon the hearing of any instrument, though they be loaden with one Child in their Belly, and another at their Backs, where they commonly carry them.[3]

In 1759, Michel Adanson, a correspondent for the Royal Academy of Science in Paris, described music-making in Senegal:

The Negroes do not dance a step, but every member of their body, every joint, and even the head itself, expresseth a different motion, always keeping time, let it be never so quick. And it is in the exact proportioning of this infinite number of motions, that the Negroes' dexterity in dancing chiefly consists: none but those that are as supple as they, can possibly imitate their agility. Notwithstanding the violence of this exercise, it lasted a good part of the night, during which they drank off several pots of a very strong sort of beer made of millet.[4]

Thomas Bowdich wrote in 1819 that "the wild music of the (Ashantee) people is scarcely to be brought within the regular rules of harmony,"[5] and Richard Freeman in 1898 referred to the "irregular rhythms" and "incoherence" of African music.[6] Colonel Northcott, a colonial officer, wrote somewhat bemusedly in 1899 that

Iteration and reiteration of the same airs never seem to weary the West Africa. His chief musical treat, however, is the tom-tom. In season and out of season, all day and all night, he is prepared to abandon himself to the delight of a noisy demonstration on this instrument of torture, and it is more often exhaustion on the part of the performers than boredom by the audience that puts a period to the deafening and monotonous noise.[7]

In many twentieth-century accounts, the emphasis on dance and the constancy of music-making are retained while rhythm as a separate dimension is singled out for special mention.[8] Erich von Hornbostel describes a piece of African xylophone music in which he found one of the parts "syncopated past our comprehension."[9] William E. F. Ward, writing in 1927, states that "if European music is specially marked by the rich variety of its forms and the splendor of its harmonies, African music is similarly marked by the fascination of its rhythms." According to him, "the basis of African rhythm . . . [is] so completely different from that of Europeans that the European system of bar lines is foreign to African music." (Incidentally, the use of bar lines remains one of the most contested issues in transcriptions of African music.) Echoing the medieval Arabic writer quoted earlier, Ward further claimed that "Africans have not merely cultivated their sense of rhythm far beyond ours, but must have started with a superior sense of rhythm."[10] Richard A. Waterman opens his study "'Hot' Rhythm in Negro Music" with the claim that "those who have had opportunity to listen to Negro music in Africa or the New World have been almost unanimous in agreeing that its most striking aspect is its rhythm."[11] And A. M. Jones, writing with characteristic enthusiasm and confidence in 1949, declares that "if anyone were to ask, 'What is the outstanding characteristic of African music?,' the answer is, 'A highly developed rhythm.'" Furthermore, "the African is far more skilled at drumming rhythms than we are—in fact our banal pom, pom, pom on the drums is mere child's play compared with the complicated and delicate interplay of rhythms in African drumming."[12]

Any suspicion that these are simply "older" characterizations of African music (they were all written before 1950) is quickly laid to rest by the continuing reproduction, in slightly—but only slightly—sanitized form, of the same motif. According to Alan Merriam, "the importance of rhythm in the music of Africa is an unquestioned principle: in fact, it bulks so large that African music could perhaps be set off as a musical culture area dominated by this concept and opposed to other equally large musical culture areas."[13] Helen Myers writes in a reference article that "rhythmic complexity is the hallmark of African music."[14] Among the "pervasive principles" of sub-Saharan musical style recognized by Bruno Nettl, "complex development of rhythm" is judged to be "most prominent."[15] Francis Bebey identifies "an instinct for rhythm" among Africans, while Philip Gbeho, like Ward, believes that "where rhythm is concerned, the African is ahead of the European."[16] Henry Weman, in a book entitled *African Music and the Church in Africa*, states that "the African is supreme in his mastery of rhythm; we might even begin to speak about contrapuntal rhythm in this connection, since independent voices appear as rhythmic lines and weave a strange pattern of rhythmic excitement and vigour."[17] Léopold Senghor, principal architect of the *négritude* movement, devoted several publications to demonstrating a specific and uniquely black rhythmic sensibility. He identifies "imagery and rhythm [as] the two fundamental characteristics of the African-Negro Style," arguing that "nowhere else has rhythm reigned as despotically [as in Black Africa]."[18] Again, in a set of guidelines for adjudicating music festivals in Africa, judges were told that "complexity of rhythm is often a fair guide to the authenticity of an African song."[19] A review by the Reverend Dr. Brian Kingslake of A. M. Jones's *Studies in African Music* includes a colorful description of African rhythm as strange and complex:

> [Jones's book] introduces us into a strange enchanted world of pure sound, made up almost entirely of complex patterns of drum and

gong taps. To call these "complex" is an understatement; the very thought of them makes one dizzy! Imagine two drummers playing together in cross rhythm, 3 against 2. Now stagger them so that they are out of phase. Now add two other drummers, and a singer, and clap accompaniment, all rhythmically at cross purposes and out of phase with one another.[20]

Finally, Kwabena Nketia, the most prominent African scholar of African music, justifies the apparent poverty of other dimensional behaviors in African music by appealing to the predominance of percussive textures: "since African music is predisposed towards percussion and percussive textures, there is an understandable emphasis on rhythm, for rhythmic interest often compensates for the absence of melody or the lack of melodic sophistication."[21] And there are literally hundreds of such statements scattered throughout the literature. African rhythm, in short, is always already complex.[22]

At first sight, these would seem to be mainly the views of outsiders, non-Africans responding enthusiastically to the unfamiliar intricacies of African ensemble playing. But this is not quite so. The notion of an irreducibly complex African rhythm has been promulgated by *both* Western and African scholars: Hornbostel, Jones, and Weman are of European origin; Nketia, Bebey, and Gbeho are African. It is therefore not simply a case of Westerners (mis)representing African music—although, given the political and economic realities that have shaped the construction of the written archive of African music, and given the blatant asymmetries of power that the colonial encounter has produced, there are solid grounds for indulging in the politics of blame. What we have, rather, are the views of a group of scholars operating within a field of discourse, an intellectual space defined by Euro-American traditions of ordering knowledge. It is difficult to overestimate the determining influence of this scholarly tradition on the representation of African music.

Resisting African Rhythm

Not everyone has been swept along by this tide. Among dissenting voices are those of scholars who have questioned rather than actively countered the portrayal of African music as an essentially rhythmic phenomenon. Introducing Ugandan and Ghanaian music to his American readers, James Koetting refers to "our fixation on African rhythm" while Wachsmann identified "a Western fantasy about African rhythm" in some of the decisions that have influenced the making of sound recordings of African music.[23] And David Rycroft, in an otherwise favorable review of John Miller Chernoff's book, *African Rhythm and African Sensibility,* expressed skepticism about the applicability of the author's conclusions, arrived at from a study of drumming in two Ghanaian communities (Ewe and Dagomba), to areas in eastern and southern Africa:

> Chernoff seems to be a compulsive continentaliser (like my colleague the late A. M. Jones). Many of his claims just *are not* acceptable as pan-African, either to someone who (like me) was born and bred in a quite different corner of the continent where they have musical bows and no drums, and dance to their own slow polyphonic singing, or to anyone familiar with other quite big sections of Africa where the lyre is the dominant instrument, or the xylophone, or the *mbira*. To return to my earlier analogy: why set yourself up as an expert on European cookery when all you have tried is Dutch?[24]

Indeed, as soon as we recall that some styles in Senegal, Mali, The Gambia, Tanzania, or Nigeria are strongly marked by Arabic or Islamic influence, and that, as Rycroft notes, there are East and southern African cultures dominated by xylophones and mbiras, as soon as we move outside the purview of the few symbolically powerful groups that have come to represent African musical/rhythmic structure, claims for rhythm's predominance become a good deal more fragile.

The first problem in these characterizations, then, is the putative claim that African music constitutes a homogenous body. Our complex and diverse continent is virtually unrecognizable in the unanimist constructions employed by some researchers. In his pathbreaking assessment of the nature of knowledge about Africa, V. Y. Mudimbe provides a sustained interrogation of the very idea of "Africa," showing it to be a construction of European discourse.[25] Beyond its relative stability as a geographical pointer, "Africa" is not readily ontologized from within an imagined African worldview; nor is it easily graspable either as a unified cultural phenomenon or as a fruitful epistemological referent. Kwame Anthony Appiah similarly argues that "the very invention of Africa (as something more than a geographical entity) must be understood, ultimately, as an outgrowth of European racialism."[26]

That Africa is a continent rather than a country, that crossing national borders is not—in terms of restrictions—like going from one American state to the next, that a greater portion of it is French- rather than English-speaking, that its numerous languages are not mutually comprehensible dialects of a few languages: knowledge of these and other "facts" cannot yet be taken for granted. Indeed, it is possible to discern an ongoing resistance to knowing about Africa. Why should we bother to learn the strange and often unpronounceable names of people in remote places practicing weird customs when we can simply use the all-purpose term "Africa"? There is, I suggest, an unwillingness to lift the veil that now enshrouds Africa, a fear that doing so might have a civilizing effect on the discourse of the West, thus depriving its practitioners of one of their most cherished sources of fantasy and imaginative play.

The problem of unanimism is a relatively trivial one, however, for seen in the context of the history of European and American constructions of Africa, the continued use of the phrase "African music" when one's authority is an African village, town, or region reproduces the metonymic fallacy—the part representing the whole—faced by most writers on Africa. While "Nigerian music" is African music, "African music" is more than "Nigerian music." To grant the former equation, however, is to undermine the force of the antiunanimism argument, for it might be claimed that, with few exceptions, no writer pretends to be representing the continent as a whole. In that sense, global titles such as *Studies in African Music, African Polyphony and Polyrhythm,* and *African Rhythm and African Sensibility* are no more or less misleading than the regional *Musique Dan, Drum Gahu,* or *Venda Children's Songs.* At any rate, this part-whole problem is a product of European and postcolonial discourse. A model of simple alterity, however, obscures the fact that the lines of connection, influence, and affiliation in the construction of Africanist discourses are too complex to submit to an explanation enabled by a simple binarism.

David Rycroft's insistence that other parts of Africa be brought into the picture in evaluating the claims of any self-styled study of "African rhythm" brings us to the second, less trivial, problem contained in these characterizations, namely, the retreat from comparison. All of the remarks quoted earlier presuppose a comparative framework: "African rhythm" is "complex" presumably in contrast to a relatively simple "European rhythm" or "American rhythm." To "set [Africa] off as a musical culture area dominated by [the] concept [of rhythm]," as A. M. Jones has suggested we do,[27] is necessarily to imagine other culture areas in which rhythm plays a less decisive or less significant role. But there is a downside to Father Jones's benediction, for it easily leads to a reciprocal attribution of deficiencies. Nketia's surprising remark that "rhythmic interest often compensates for the absence of melody or the lack of melodic sophistication" is the kind of mythology that has allowed some Europeans to claim harmony and deny it to the Africans, or some Asians to claim elaborate melody and deny it to the Africans.[28] For such comparisons to have force we need to do more than casually allude to the other term in the binary framework. In practice, however, a comparative framework, although logically presupposed, rarely leads to explicit comparison. Instead, one side of the opposition is given short shrift, conveniently silenced, suppressed, ensuring that writers' initial prejudices reemerge as their conclusions.

Even the occasional exception to the tendency to retreat from comparison encounters problems at the level of framing. For example, Chernoff's effort to show what is different between "our music" and "African music" invokes the opening four bars of Beethoven's Sonatina in G Major (Kinsky-Halm Anh. 5).[29] But the choice is already problematic, for Chernoff was writing during the late 1970s, at a time when "our music," which presumably means European and American music, could scarcely be configured without—choosing more or less at random—Brahms, Bartók, Carter, Reich, Stravinsky, or without Hungarian, Bulgarian, or Scottish folk songs. Whether it is appropriate to compare, for example, Stravinsky's *Rite of Spring* (with its acknowledged challenges to, and extensions of, conventions of metrical articulation) or Steve Reich's *Music for Pieces of Wood* (with its undisguised appropriation of the identifying rhythm of a Southern Ewe dance) with African music, or whether it is proper to juxtapose Akan funeral dirges with Karelian laments, is for our purposes less important than the fact that such comparisons are, in principle, possible. The choice of an appropriate comparative frame is already ideological. Indeed, a determined researcher could easily show that the sum of isolated experiments in rhythmic organization found in so-called Western music produces a picture of far greater complexity than anything that Africans have produced so far either singly or collectively. One could, in short, quite easily invent "European rhythm."

Allied to the retreat from comparison is a retreat from critical evaluation of African musical practice. The pious dignifying of all performances as if they were equally good, of all instruments as if they were tuned in an "interesting" way rather than simply being out of tune, of all informants as if a number of them did not practice systematic deception, and of the missed entries and resulting heterophony in dirge singing as if they did not result from inattentiveness or drunkenness: these are acts of mystification designed to ensure that the discourse about African music continues to lack the one thing that would give it scientific and hence universal status, namely, a *critical* element. As with other disciplinary practices (one thinks of African literature and especially African philosophy), African musicology desperately needs critical searchlights if it is to become more than a colorful but decidedly marginal spot on a multidisciplinary map. It is, however, unlikely that such a critical practice can emerge if it is not fired by the day-to-day aesthetic and critical concerns of continental Africans themselves. If contemporary research continues to be outwardly directed, designed mainly for export, the attainment of a relevant and authentic critical practice may elude us for a while yet.

"African rhythm," in short, is an invention, a construction, a fiction, a myth, ultimately a lie. In that sense, it is not unlike a number of inventions that postcolonial theorists have brought to our attention recently: the invention of tradition (Hobsbawn and Ranger), tribalism (Ranger), Africa (Mudimbe, Appiah), women (Oyewumi), and "'traditional' or 'tribal' musics under colonialism and since independence" (Waterman).[30] Every invention has a purpose, and so analysis or critique must enter as fully as possible into the contexts of production and reception, and their dynamics of power. My purpose here is partly to acknowledge the fact of and psychological need for inventing, and then try to understand the terms of this particular invention by speculating on the motivations and impulses of scholars. Attributing impulses is a dangerous undertaking, but since institutional and professional pressures constrain what and how we think and write about Africa, a little self-examination may not be entirely inappropriate. Following, then, are three instances of the invention of African rhythm.

Interrogating a Lexical Gap

It seems remarkable that it never occurred to A. M. Jones— or if it did that he did not mention it—in the course of writing some 533 printed pages mainly on the rhythmic structure of African music, in particular that of the Southern Ewe people, to ask his "native" informant, Mr. Desmond Tay, whether the Ewe have a word for rhythm or a concept of rhythm.[31] Had he done so, Jones might have met with a blank stare or a puzzled look. And had he pursued the point, he would almost certainly have been led down a strange (I use this "orientalism" advisedly) and picturesque terrain of overlapping words, concepts, and ideas.

There is no single word for rhythm in the Ewe language. If you look in Diedrich Westermann's dictionary or *Gbesela* of 1930, for example, you will find the consecutive entries "rhinoceros," "rhyme," "rib," "ribbon;" the absence of an entry for "rhythm" between "rhyme" and "rib" is glaring.[32] Could it be that Westermann was somehow unaware of the popular constructions of Africans as rhythmic people, or that in seeing Africans make music on a daily basis he remained unstruck by its rhythmic character? Perhaps lexicons are meant to record only what is verbalized, not to mirror patterns of behavior.

Indeed, if you look at other vocabularies for talking about music in West Africa, you will be struck by a similar absence. According to Charles Keil, the word *rhythm* "really has no single equivalent in Tiv" (nor, incidentally, is there an equivalent for the word *music*). Lester Monts finds "no equivalent of the word rhythm" in the Vai language spoken in western Liberia. David Ames and Anthony King include no entry for *rhythm* in their work on the Hausa, the most widely spoken sub-Saharan African language. And

Eric Charry, writing about the Mande, says that he has "not come across an extensive Mande vocabulary related to rhythm."[33] Such a consistent and widespread absence may come as a surprise to those for whom "African music" and "African rhythm" have always seemed synonymous, and who had expected to find rhythm represented in African vocabularies.

It is, of course, an old critical move to attempt to undermine an ethnographer's findings by showing that the people studied do not have a word for something attributed to them. (The boringly famous example is the supposedly large number of words by which Eskimo refer to "snow.") But what can we learn from such an absence? In the case of African rhythm—and here I retreat into the relative security of my own work among the Northern Ewe—although the equivalent of a single word meaning "rhythm" is not to be found in Ewe, related concepts of stress, duration, and periodicity do in fact register in subtle ways in Ewe discourse. What this suggests is that the semantic field of rhythm is not a single, unified, or coherent field but rather one that is widely and asymmetrically distributed, permanently entangled, if you like, with other dimensions that discourse about Western music has balkanized into separate domains. Ewe conceptions of rhythm often imply a binding together of different dimensional processes, a joining rather than a separating, an across-the-dimensions rather than a within-the-dimensions phenomenon. Rhythm, in other words, is always already connected.[34]

Jones could have recovered some of this genealogy either by asking his informant(s) directly, or better, by eavesdropping on conversations among Ewe musicians during rehearsals or performances. Whenever things went wrong, for example, Jones would almost certainly have heard remarks dealing with, or at least alluding to, rhythm. But this way of doing fieldwork—striving to attain an invisible status in order not to eliminate but to minimize the harmful effects of interference caused by the (white) ethnographer's presence, would not have appealed to Jones. "The African," as he was fond of saying, was an informant, not a theorist. The African "is utterly unconscious of any organized theory behind his music. He makes his music quite spontaneously."[35] Africans (such as Desmond Tay) provided the data with which Jones manufactured his theories, theories designed not only for the local market but also for export back to the colonies. For him, the complexity of African rhythm was emblematic of the otherness of African peoples, their essential difference from us.[36]

The view that Africans are essentially different, and therefore that African music is essentially different from Western music, still endures. It is a view that has limited validity, however, for without difference we cannot formulate thoughts or speak meaningfully. But while granting the importance of making sense through difference, we might also note that difference, depending on how it is utilized, can obscure certain realities and impose extraneous qualities. (Chapter 7 will address these matters more fully.) Even the ostensibly neutral tags used to identify African subjects are already freighted. Hornbostel frequently refers to "them," Jones and Weman to "the African," Blacking to "the Venda," Monts to "informants," Nketia to "African societies," and Chernoff to "African associates." Such totalizing descriptions have a nominal identifying function, but it is not hard to see that they are already dedicated to the construction of difference.[37] When was the last time an ethnomusicologist went out to hunt for sameness rather than difference? When did we last encourage our students to go and do fieldwork not in order to come back and paint the picture of a different Africa, but of an Africa that, after all the necessary adjustments have been made for material divergence, is remarkably like the West? So strong and powerful is the founding premise of difference that the ongoing invention and reinvention of African rhythm, far from buttressing epistemological claims, presents the writer with a mirror image of the dictates of this very ideology of difference.

The Politics of Notating African Rhythm

Consider an apparently purely technical issue such as transcription. Motivated, I believe, by the belief that African music is fundamentally different from Western music, earlier researchers such as Hewitt Pantaleoni and James Koetting decided that Western staff notation was simply not suitable for conveying the reality of African rhythm in its uniqueness and individuality.[38] They then proceeded to invent new and improved notations for the job at hand, notations that have fortunately fallen by the wayside in the subsequent practice of representing African rhythm. I say fortunately because the problems that Koetting and Pantaleoni wished to address, such as the importance of indicating timbre or method of playing, or of neutralizing the downbeat emphasis supposedly normative in Western music, are by no means unique to African music. In other words, Western music, too, suffers from being notated in the way that it has been notated so far; if a new notation should be developed, it should be developed for *both* African and Western music. The problem of notation is in this sense a universal one. To present it as a problem for African music alone is to deprive its specifically African manifestation of any claims to universality, any standing among influential discourses.

Even where it is designed to be descriptive, notation remains prescriptive because it involves the translation of actions, reading of codes, deciphering of signs, and ultimately, subjectivising of meaning. Notation relies importantly on the role of a *supplement*, a further set of signs set in motion by the process of interpretation. This supplementary knowledge, often carried orally or informally, is in the possession of many carriers of traditions. To load notation with more signs, or to introduce a new sign system altogether in the interests of descriptive precision or exhaustiveness, is, in effect, to attempt to reduce the size of the supplement, perhaps to deny the role of the supplement, and, with that, the creative role of the performer or interpreter. Descriptive notation, whether used by Pantaleoni, Koetting, or anyone else, embodies a resistance to the supplement; and it is this impossible attempt to eliminate the supplement that spells the doom of advocates of new notations.

One such alternative system of signs is the Time Unit Box System (TUBS) developed by Philip Harland in 1962 and applied most rigorously by Koetting in the analysis of West African drum ensemble music. TUBS uses dots enclosed in boxes to represent drum strokes, supplementing these with other signs that indicate manner of playing and that therefore convey a sense of sonority. Koetting says that TUBS "gives a clearer picture of sequential temporal relations within and among patterns than do the notes and rests of varying precise duration used in Western notation."[39] He is particularly anxious to avoid time signatures and bar lines—metrical measures with their "inherent stress structure." Unfortunately, Koetting's assumptions about African ensemble drumming are debatable. Meter, for example, is not so readily dismissed, and the gross beats which are conveyed by dancers' feet are as metrical as anything in European (Baroque) music.

In making his argument for the greater appropriateness of TUBS for notating African music, Koetting is forced to oversimplify and therefore distort the accentual implications of notated Western music. While granting that TUBS "is no more rhythmically accurate than Western notation," Koetting nevertheless emphasizes the importance of sonority and rhythm in African drum ensemble music. To do this, however, he must of necessity undercomplicate "Western rhythm patterns":

> Sonority and rhythm are generally equal in importance, rhythm being somewhat more significant in some patterns and sonority somewhat more in others, particularly those derived from speech patterns. For that reason, the drum ensemble patterns should be studied as rhythm/sonority patterns and must not be too much equated with Western rhythm patterns, which we often think of without pitch and tone quality as significant elements.[40]

Do we really think of "Western rhythm patterns" without including pitch as a significant element? Doubtless some people do, but even passing acquaintance with some of the more sophisticated theories of rhythm of

European tonal music will reveal that it is well-nigh impossible to exclude pitch from any account of accents or rhythm.[41]

Furthermore, if Stravinsky did not need a new notation for *The Rite of Spring*, if the persistent across-the-bar-line figures in Brahms's symphonies can be accommodated within the conventional representation, and if the highly embellished vocal styles in Romanian, Hungarian, and North African folk songs have been represented (by Bartók, among others) so as to communicate something of their essence, then it is not clear why African music must be held to a uniquely constricting representational mode.

This position may seem extraordinarily conservative, possibly reactionary. Why would anyone reject a new notation that promises greater representational accuracy? Must we all go through the same needle's eye, inhabit the same notational space, speak the same critical language? My position is partly pragmatic. Notations are read by communities of readers, so in order to consolidate African practices that can eventually gain some institutional power, it makes sense to use the existing notation, however imperfect. A very significant number of percussion students in the United States and Canada are, thanks to David Locke's transcriptions into standard notation (with a few modifications, of course) of the Southern Ewe dance, *Gahu*, able to perform this repertoire. And in the early 1960s, the publication of Jones's *Studies in African Music* brought some excitement to communities of European composers who could now study traditional African compositions. Had Locke and Jones not spoken a metropolitan language, such immediate reception would not have been possible.

This does not mean that every last African scholar should ignore TUBS or the tablature notation advocated by Moses Serwadda and Hewitt Pantaleoni,[42] or the circular representation made famous by David Rycroft,[43] or Doris Green's newly devised notation,[44] for there is surely room for such fringe activities within the pluralistic profile of African musicology. It only means that, as a communal practice, we should train our efforts toward the superior and extensive use of staff notation so as to make African music unavoidable in scholarly circles. Empowerment through scholarship comes in a variety of forms, and one way is to speak a language of which Westerners cannot feign misunderstanding. Is there not, in any case, something suspicious about Westerners telling Africans to use new notations for their music? Beware when the Greeks bring you gifts. . . .

The use of standard notation for pragmatic reasons does not eliminate difficulties at the level of representation, for much depends on an individual scholar's agenda. In the theories of A. M. Jones, for example, a premise of difference may have led him to make certain questionable decisions about transcribing African music. A cursory glance at the second volume of *Studies in African Music* confirms the complexity of African rhythmic systems. A sometimes rapid succession of meters, staggered bar lines tracing crooked paths from the top to the bottom of the texture, and unusual groupings of notes together with other features make it difficult to find the conductor's beat that would unlock the secrets of African drum ensemble playing. Jones, in fact, believed in noncoincident main beats. The graphic severity and unwieldiness of his transcriptions would seem to confirm the essential difference, the otherness, perhaps even the exoticism of African music. Yet, since Jones was transcribing a dance repertoire, it should have occurred to him that (even African) dancers need a regular, recurring beat to guide their negotiation of movements. By shunning regularity and isochrony, Jones encourages fantastic views about Africans dancing with their whole bodies, each body part performing a different rhythm in a different meter.[45]

Two specific flaws in Jones's work exemplify further the impulse to distance the Southern Ewe from the Europeans. The first, purely technical, concerns the use of staggered bar lines to represent perceived changes in accentual pattern. This aspect of Jones's work has been properly and extensively corrected in the work of David Locke, who, like Simha Arom, understands ensemble textures as isochronous rather than polychronous and based on a recurring cycle of beats.[46] A second, related flaw, apparent in Jones's transcription of play and fishing songs at the beginning of his book, stems from his equation of word accent with metrical accent, thus overlooking all the other types of phenomenal accent that emerge in a performance of Ewe song. One applauds Jones's effort to recognize the pertinence of Ewe speech accents in song, a feature to which subsequent transcribers have paid little attention. A pity that the technical means were not adequate to the task.[47]

The point of entering into these minutiae of transcription is not to quibble over minor details but to remind us that politics and ideology can exert a strong influence on something as apparently technical as the making of transcriptions. To his credit, Jones continued to use 'Western' staff notation, bar lines, time signatures, clefs, and phrase marks to render comprehensible Southern Ewe music, thus bringing the music into a sphere of discourse that is enabled by a distinguished intellectual history and undeniable institutional power. For power is what it is all about, warts, distortions, contradictions, imperfections, and all. A postcolonial transcription, then, is not one that imprisons itself in an ostensibly 'African' field of discourse but one that insists on playing in the premier league, on the master's ground, and in the North. From this point of view, an ideology of difference must be replaced by an ideology of sameness so that—and this is somewhat paradoxical—we can gain a better view of difference. In other words, only if we proceed from a premise of sameness and grant difference in the unique expression of that sameness are we likely to get at the true similarities and differences between musics.

"African Rhythm" as Invented by Africans: Ethical Theory or Epistemic Violence?

A third method by which "African rhythm" has been invented, a method that has been gaining in influence in the last two decades, is one by which the invention is attributed either directly or indirectly to African subjects themselves. The researcher ostensibly presents *their* viewpoint, a native or insider viewpoint, as opposed to an outsider one. For example, in an article on "Rhythmic Design in the Support Drums of Agbadza," Jeff Pressing states that "In *Agbadza Kpoka* an unvarying rhythmic background is provided by *gankogui, axatse,* and *kagan,* which is most correctly (in Ewe terms) conceptualized in 12/8 time."[48] These are the same Ewe who do not have terms in their language for "rhythm," "meter," or "time signature." How did they articulate the concepts attributed to them by Pressing? Clearly several acts of translation and inference have taken place in the construction of Pressing's ethnography, yet these acts are underreported in the article. It is not that one cannot guess what Pressing might mean; it is rather that the legitimizing phrase, "(in Ewe terms)"—framed, incidentally, by all-powerful parentheses—needs to be unpacked if its claims are to have force.

The foregrounding of native voices provides an attractive escape route for the resolution of certain moral and ethical dilemmas arising from working with Others. In contrast to researchers who ignore what their subjects say, we can claim that we are engaged in dialogue; our texts are layered and polyphonic, featuring a variety of voices in different registers. Indeed, when earlier I criticized A. M. Jones for failing to ask his informants what the Ewe word for *rhythm* was, I seemed to imply that Jones's error could simply be corrected by finding the appropriate Ewe word and incorporating it into what is unavoidably a prefabricated theoretical framework belonging to the researcher's field of discourse. In this way, consumers of the theory are lulled into believing that all due rights and privileges have been granted to the owners of native thought and expression. The theorist is heroically absolved from possible guilt stemming from the failure to acknowledge "the native's point of view."

But the nature of native discourses, their conceptual and logical frameworks, and especially the manner in which they pass from folk philosophy to a full-fledged ethnotheory: these issues are far too complex to be addressed merely by asking native informants for African language equivalents of English, French, or Portuguese words and phrases used in discussions of music and performance. Searching for such equivalents (or nonequivalents) without taking into account the complex histories of individual terms, and ignoring the important role that colonial and missionary discourses have played in granting these terms conventional status: these moves are likely to seriously undermine the explanatory value accorded the terms. Moreover, who orchestrates the dialogue, who owns or signs the text, and who gets paid for it are troubling questions that may not be facilely consigned to the margins of our theorizing, especially when such theorizing results in confident claims about our knowledge of other (living) human beings.

One could of course confine the discussion of dialogism or polyphonism to the strictly discursive level, a level that celebrates the internalism and even autonomy of critical texts. 'Dialogic editing,' rather than embracing an intricate series of transactions between historically situated researchers and researched, takes refuge in an all-consuming textuality, part of whose effect is a denial of certain social inequalities.[49] Unless it results in concrete political action, the dialogic impulse must be seen for what it is, namely, an attempt to continue to validate what is essentially a monologue by incorporating an image of 'native discourse' into the monologuer's theory and on his or her own terms. Not only do researchers exonerate themselves from the standard—and often ineffectually symbolic—charges of imperialism, neocolonialism, or anachronism, but they are able to lay claims also to an authentic African voice speaking a different (nonWestern) native language. Although this way of reporting field research may seem merely inefficient, naive, or unsubtle, it actually substitutes a particularly virulent from of political violence for 'mere' epistemic violence.

Is there a solution to the problems addressed in this chapter? Is there a correct way of representing African music? Obviously, there is no single solution, nor is there anything like a correct method of representation. Nor is the idea of "invention" avoidable. Indeed, if we cast a glance forward, we may speculate that future intellectual historians may well characterize the last quarter of the twentieth century as a time when the notion of invention was itself invented in the interventions of postmodernists and postcolonialists. But although one would be ill-advised to speak of a single solution, there are more or less ethical ways of representation, more or less precise ways of storing information, and more or less imaginative ways of constructing explanatory theories. These orders are not just logical or epistemological but political, practical, pragmatic, and ideological. And although there is a danger of overpoliticizing scholarly procedures, the greater danger lies in denying that politics plays a role in the construction of knowledge about African music. There is one possible solution to some of the problems addressed in this chapter, a way of countering the unfortunate effects of invention: eschew the "soft" strategies of dialogism and the solicitation of insider viewpoints and work towards the direct empowerment of postcolonial African subjects so that they can eventually represent themselves. And the guarantee that they will get it right? None, of course. But they will at least have the privilege of doing something that the West has always taken for granted, namely, to indulge their own representational fantasies—including and especially, self-representation at Others' expense—partly as an expression of power, but partly for sheer pleasure.

4
Polymeter, Additive Rhythm, and Other Enduring Myths

Persistent thematization of "African rhythm"—as remarked in chapter 3— has so far not produced a common analytical practice or metalanguage. In theories of African rhythm advanced during the twentieth century, from Hornbostel and Ward to Arom and Kubik, basic questions remain as to where the beat is, what constitutes a pattern, whether meter exists, how many meters are in operation within a given composition, how to notate rhythm, and so on. There is, in short, surprisingly little agreement about the basic organizing principles.[1]

If such divergence of perspectives arose simply from the fact of individual scholars working with different repertoires, if, in other words, theories were so data-driven that, taken together, they reflected the acknowledged and irreducible diversity of African music, we would not speak of confusion but rather of a rich pluralism. Unfortunately this is not quite the case. For one thing, there has been little institutionally prominent positive confrontation between theories, few attempts to falsify existing theories and replace them with new ones. Not only have Africanists not reaped the benefits of cumulative knowledge production but there has been a tendency to reinvent the wheel. Moreover, even within relatively canonical repertoires, such as that of the Southern Ewe (drumming, not singing), analytical research has not proceeded communally. The theories of A. M. Jones, Seth Cudjoe, David Locke, John Chernoff, Hewitt Pantaleoni, Nissio Fiagbedzi, and Jeff Pressing have not always derived from a direct and productive engagement with the work of others to produce a consensus about the core organizing principles. This absence of centralized efforts is also characteristic of research into musics of the Central African Republic, Nigeria, the Democratic Republic of Congo, and elsewhere.

For those suspicious of hegemony in any form, the absence of a common practice is welcome insofar as it undermines the possibility that a single, ostensibly "correct" way of understanding African rhythm can ever emerge. Others, however, will lament the practical circumstances that have allowed scholars to overlook or deliberately ignore the work of their predecessors so that they can rediscover Africa freshly, sleep with a virgin Africa, so to speak, own their bit of territory. The retreat from developing a general theory has in turn facilitated the propagation of certain myths, including notions such as polymeter, additive rhythm, and cross rhythm, among several others. In this chapter, which may be regarded as a kind of technical supplement to chapter 3, I argue that these concepts are untenable as a modeling of practice in the specific repertoires to which they have been applied. Such myths persist in both the popular imagination and scholarly writing, however, partly because of the absence of a regulating common practice and partly because of the incorrigible urge to represent Africa as always already different.

The absence of a common practice is signaled most obviously by the plethora of terms used to describe rhythm and related phenomena. Some of the terms that have appeared in the literature include:

additive rhythm	inherent pattern	polymeter
commetric accents	interlocking rhythm	polyrhythm
contrametric accents	isorhythm	resultant pattern
counter meter	linear rhythm	silent beats
cross rhythm	main beat	speech rhythm
density referent	megarhythm	strict rhythm
divisive rhythm	melorhythm	subjective beat
downbeat	metronome sense	subjective meter
free rhythm	multilinear rhythm	subjective pattern
gross pulse	nonsymmetric rhythm	suppressed downbeat
hemiola	off-beat rhythm	syncopation
hot rhythm	on-beat	time line
implied beat	phrasing referent	

Each of these terms has a history, a logical place within an economy of technical terms, and a range of intertextual resonances. Some are descriptively transparent (Kolinski's "contrametric accent"), some are locked in an active binary ("free rhythm" versus "strict rhythm"), while some speak of American imposition ("hot rhythm"). Although a full understanding requires much attention to context, origins, and influence, it is probably fair to say that no other dimension of African music has elicited more eagerness to name and rename.

Rhythmic *Topoi,* or Time Lines

Let us begin at the beginning by describing an aspect of everyday rhythm. As is well known, many West and Central African dances feature a prominently articulated, recurring rhythmic pattern that serves as an identifying feature or signature of the particular dance/drumming. These patterns are known by different names: time line, bell pattern, phrasing referent, and so on.[2] I prefer to call them *topoi*, commonplaces rich in associative meaning for cultural insiders. A *topos* is a short, distinct, and often memorable rhythmic figure of modest duration (about a metric length or a single cycle), usually played by the bell or high-pitched instrument in the ensemble, and serves as a point of temporal reference. It is held as an ostinato throughout the dance-composition. Although *topoi* originated in specific communities as parts of specific dances, they have by now moved from their communities of origin into a centralized, multiethnic, or detribalized space. The main catalyst for this migration is interethnic contact through boarding schools, government bureaucracy, trade, rural-to-urban migration, church, cultural troupes, and radio. The connotations of some *topoi* have thus been abandoned or transformed, even while their structural autonomy has been consolidated.

The key to understanding the structure of a given *topos* is the dance or choreography upon which it is based. According to William Echezona, "it is not easy for one to talk about rhythm without referring to (Nigerian) dance" (my parenthesis).[3] No one hears a *topos* without also hearing—in actuality or imaginatively—the movement of feet. And the movement of feet in turn registers directly or indirectly the metrical structure of the dance. Conceptually, then, the music and dance of a given *topos* exist at the same level; the music is not prior to the dance, nor is the dance prior to the music.

For cultural insiders, identifying the gross pulse or the "pieds de danse" ("dance feet") occurs instinctively and spontaneously.[4] Those not familiar with the choreographic supplement, however, sometimes have trouble locating the main beats and expressing them in movement. Hearing African music on recordings alone without prior grounding in its dance-based rhythms will not necessarily convey the choreographic supplement. Not surprisingly, many misinterpretations of African rhythm and meter stem from a failure to observe the dance. To say that in the beginning dance and music were together, like left and right, man and wife, or front and back, is not to exaggerate.

Recent research suggests that *topoi* constitute a most fruitful site for the exploration of African rhythmic practices. Kubik, in whose research time lines feature significantly, notes their distribution "along the west African coast, in western central Africa and in a broad belt along the Zambezi valley into Moçambique" and attributes to them great historical depth. He analyzes their "asymmetric inner structure" and reports on his discovery of a 24-pulse pattern said to be "the longest time-line pattern . . . among the pygmies of the Upper Sangha River in the Central African Republic."[5] Kubik has also searched the musical cultures of the African diaspora for asymmetric time line patterns and located them in Cuba, Haiti, Dominican Republic, Puerto Rico, Trinidad, and Brazil.[6] Jeff Pressing, taking a comparative perspective, has examined "cognitive isomorphisms" between rhythm/duration and pitch in various world musical cultures.[7] Jay Rahn, in an important article on ostinatos in African music, explores the numerical properties of 8-, 9-, 12-, 16-, and 24-beat cycles and offers a critique of Pressing's cognitive isomorphisms.[8] And Bertram Lehmann, in an unpublished paper, developed a "timeline database" of over 100 distinct items from various African and Caribbean repertoires.[9] It is beyond the scope of this chapter to review this specialized and deeply suggestive work. Rather, I should direct attention to the confluence of pattern and main beat in order to emphasize their origins in dance, and emphasize that dance feet are usually regular rather than irregular (Africans have only two feet!). "Polymeter" and "additive rhythm" overcomplicate African rhythm in unproductive ways.

Example 4-1 presents eight popular time lines (labelled A to H) to illustrate some structural features. (Although chosen in this instance from various Ghanaian repertoires, a number of them are found elsewhere.[10]) Each representation gives the main beats followed by the note pattern constituting the time line; notational variants are given where appropriate. A is the so-called standard pattern associated with southern Ewe music and typically heard as a bell pattern in dances like Agbadza, Agbekor, and Adzida (line 2). It has four main beats shown as dotted quarters in 12/8 meter or cycle (line 1). Out of its seven attack points, only two (attack points 1 and 6) coincide with main beats (1 and 4). The pattern has a latent off-beat feel and an extensive anacrusis that confers on it a strong, forward-pointing dynamic. Also shown at A are alternative ways of notating the standard pattern (lines 3 and 4). Line 5 gives a closely related *topos* found among the Yoruba; in fact, lines 4 and 5 are so close that they may be regarded as variants of one another. Their difference lies in the "exchange" of durational values of the last two attack points, 6 and 7. The Ewe and Yoruba patterns conclude with long-short and short-long successions respectively.

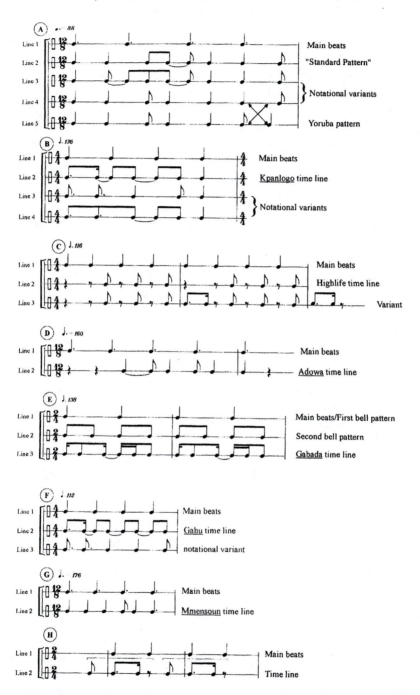

Example 4-1 Eight common time lines

Topos B is associated with a popular Ga dance, Kpanlogo (line 2), but has a very wide provenance. Like *A*, it has four main beats (given as quarter notes in line 1) and only two moments of coincidence between main beats and the pattern itself. *B* has a total of five attack points. Two notational variants betraying an additive conception are shown in lines 3 and 4. *Topos C* displays two cycles of the highlife time line (line 2). This popular pattern is notable for its extensive offbeat or anacrusic pattern that discharges into a silence or assumed beat on each successive downbeat. Here, none of the three attack points coincides with a main beat making for a very mobile, forward-pointing, and uplifting feel. There are, however, variants of the highlife *topos*, such as that shown in line 3 of *C*, which includes at least one point of common articulation (the downbeat) between main beat and time line. Note that if the highlife pattern is reckoned from its first sound then it is properly understood as originating on the third eighth-note of each 4/4 bar and terminating in the comparable place in the next bar. Thus, unlike patterns *A* and *B*, which are isomorphic with the metrical cycle, *C* features a surface displacement.

Something of this displacement is evident in *D*, the *topos* of the Akan Adowa dance. In the version written here, the Adowa *topos* has five attack points of which two (points 3 and 5) coincide with a main beat. Like *A* and, especially, *C*, pattern *D* is overshadowed by a long anacrusis that discharges not into a silence (as in *C*) but into a strongly articulated downbeat. Line 3 of *E* shows two cycles of the *topos* of Gabada, a popular northern Ewe dance. It, too, has five attack points. Like *B*, its cycle may be accommodated within the confines of a single measure. And of the four eighth-note main beats, the first and last coincide with articulations in the pattern. (Also shown in *E* are two other bell patterns that are heard with the *topos*. Line 1 marks the main beats while line 2 subdivides them into eighth notes. Lines 1 and 2 thus reinforce the basic pulse. Which is why line 3, with its distinct shape, is designated the time line.)

F is the *topos* for *Gahu*, another popular Southern Ewe dance, in the version studied by David Locke.[11] Like *B*, *D*, and *E*, *F* has five attack points, but it is most like *D* in achieving coincidence with a main beat once, this time, however, at the *beginning* of the pattern. Like *A*, *B*, and *E*, its pattern is coterminous with the metrical cycle.

The *topos* shown at *G* identifies the music of elephant horn ensembles of the Akan known as Mmensoun. Like *A* and *D*, it is written in 12/8 to accommodate four main dotted-quarter beats. Its first two beats are "crossed' with the main beats to produce a familiar cross rhythm, the two-against-three feel said to be characteristic of African music as a whole, while its third and fourth main beats are reinforced by the articulation of the *topos* pattern, the only difference being the subarticulation of the third main beat (attack points 4 and 5 of the *topos*). This *topos*, too, has the same boundaries as the 12/8 measure, and it is an indication of its relative rhythmic consonance that it has six attack points. Finally, the *topos* given at *H* is listed by Nketia simply as a time line.[12] Like *E*, its two halves are identical. Each half has three attack points only one of which—the second—coincides with a main beat articulation. And like *D*, it originates from an offbeat.

Another way of conceptualizing patterns *C*, *D*, and *H* is as a nonalignment between metrical structure and grouping structure. David Temperley, drawing on Lerdahl and Jackendoff's *Generative Theory of Tonal Music* (1983), clarifies this basic aspect of African rhythm.[13] Where meter functions as a constant but dynamic framework, grouping structure arises from specific forms of articulation determined by motivic structure, rests, and cadences. It is important to note, however, that oftentimes silences are an important part of groups in African music, that a silence is not an absence of sound but an intentional placement of silence as a substitute for sound. Thus the alternative version of the highlife *topos* 3, for example, includes sound on the downbeat, while the main version shown does not.

The morphology of a *topos* should never be divorced from its main beats and the referential cycle. Taking such a holistic view allows one to appreciate the degree of embeddedness of the time line function in a drum ensemble. Indeed, in ensembles that do not feature a clear timbral distinction between time line and other instrumental functions, the *topos* may remain implicit in what is played rather than made explicit. But it is no less important or functional for being an emergent or resultant pattern. It is, in short, the combination of the sounded and unsounded that gives a time line its meaning. If you ignore the role of the unsounded, you may miss the orientation provided by the choreographic rhythm. You might then be led to think that the first sound you hear marks the beginning of a metrical cycle, that relatively longer durations indicate downbeats, or that downbeats must be "filled" with sound rather than silence.

Example 4-2 hypothesizes a generative process for the highlife *topos* (*C* in Example 4-1) to show its conceptual origins in the dance feet that mark main beats. We start with the four main beats (1), suppress the downbeat (2), subdivide the remaining beats (3), and finally suppress the on-beats, leaving three off-beats (4). The reason for beginning with the main beats is to ensure that interpretation is grounded in the choreographic supplement, here a straightforward foot movement, perhaps alternating left and right, and coinciding with the four main beats. And the thought behind the suppression of beats is to introduce an element of play. The idea of knowing where the beat is but articulating it as a silence is part of an aesthetic of play found in numerous African communities. The generative process shown in Example 4-2 is thus consonant with indigenous habits of

Step 1: Establish 4/4 metrical cycle

Step 2: Suppress the downbeat

Step 3: Subdivide remaining beats

Step 4: Suppress the on-beats

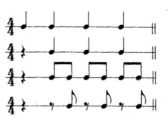

Example 4-2 Generating the highlife time (pattern C, line 2 of Ex. 4-1)

rhythmic organization, even if it is never framed as such. Other *topoi* may be similarly generated. Generating *topoi* in this fashion is of course a speculative exercise, but it has the advantage of inciting the analyst to modest acts of composition and thereby reinforcing the dialectical stance that facilitates understanding of African rhythm.

The basis for correct interpretation, then, is the background against which a different, more complex pattern is sounded. By background I mean an enabling structure, a simpler, regulating pattern that makes possible the accentual and durational patterns that constitute a particular *topos*. The background provides the condition of possibility for the time line. It is tempting to describe this feature as an at-least-two view, echoing a remark by A. M. Jones that Chernoff and others have repeated frequently, that "in African music there is practically always a clash of rhythms: this is a cardinal principle."[14] "Clash and conflict" are antithetical to African traditional philosophy, which is more likely to be communal and cooperative.[15] African musicians play with competing accents in order to enhance pleasure, delight the ear, and stimulate spiritual renewal. Such flights are possible only as temporary, imagined, or simulated departures from solid ground.

It should be obvious that the phenomenon we are discussing—of a foreground at variance with its enabling background, or, in Temperley's terms, a non-alignment between grouping and metrical structure—is characteristic of a great deal of European music, even if the gap between levels is smaller than that in some African compositions. Yet, we do not normally identify a "clash and conflict of rhythms" in the gavottes from J. S. Bach's keyboard suites, or in the opening theme of Mozart's 40th Symphony, or in the scherzo movement of Beethoven's early String Quartet, opus 18 no. 6. Nor do we invent a new vocabulary to account for the opening bars of Mozart's D minor Concerto, K. 466, where, in order to render the *alla zoppa* or limping style topic, the performer needs to have recourse to a pattern of regular pulsation: a background or choreographic supplement, in our terms. Although this particular background is sounded by the timpani, it need not be; it can be inferred from the confluence of rhythms. Nor do we take the nonalignment between grouping and meter in Brahms as a sign of metric change on a deep level. In this sense, African music shares with European music (and indeed much other music) a conceptual space describable in terms of a hidden background and a manifest foreground. It is somewhat amusing, then, to find commentators hailing Richard Waterman's notion of "metronome sense" as a breakthrough in the quest for understanding African rhythm.[16] Could African musicians have been relying upon anything else all these centuries? Why is the idea of a regular pulsation, the sine qua non of much of the world's music, not taken for granted when it comes to Africa?

Polymeter

Polymeter is the simultaneous use of more than one meter in an ensemble composition. Each functional component of the texture, be it an instrument or a group, is said to expose a distinct rhythmic pattern within its own metrical frame, apparently without any obvious regard for a larger coordinating mechanism. Constituent meters do not collapse into each other or into a larger meter, but persist into the background, creating a kind of metric dissonance or metric polyphony. Philosophically, polymeter indexes coexistence, not (necessarily) cooperation.[17]

Example 4-3 is a typical polymetric texture taken from the "apostle of African polymeter," A. M. Jones.[18] The eight layers represent different instruments as indicated. Layers 1 and 2 feature the bell and rattle in 12/8, the usual meter for Anlo-Ewe dances such as *Nyayito, Agbadza, Atsiagbekor, Kpegisu*, and others. Layer 3, hand claps, is also transcribed in 12/8, but notice that it begins its cycle on the third dotted quarter of the previous layers' pattern. Layer 4, the song, is not given a time signature, but on the basis of Jones's bar lines, we can assign a succession of shifting meters: 7/8, 4/8 (or 2/4), 6/8, 4/8 (or 2/4) again, 3/8, and finally two bars of 6/8 or 3/4. Layer 5, the so-called master drum, begins with two bars of 5/8 before going elsewhere, while the support drums in layers 6 and 7 are in 6/8. Finally, the last of the support drums is given a 3/8 time signature. When the entire ensemble is together in the last bar of the transcription (Jones's bar 6), you have at least four meters unfolding simultaneously: 12/8, 6/8, 5/8, and 3/8. We are asked, in other words, to imagine a master drummer playing in 5/8 while the guy next to him plays in 6/8, and the one next to them in 3/8. Meanwhile the singer is in 6/8 or 3/4 while the bell and rattle are in 12/8 or 6/8.

Polyrhythm versus polymeter

It is important to distinguish between polyrhythm and polymeter. Polyrhythm is generally understood as the simultaneous use of two or

Example 4-3 Excerpt from Southern Ewe funeral dance *Nyayito* as transcribed by
A. M. Jones (1959:ii/12)

more contrasting rhythms in a musical texture. Polyrhythmic usage in
African music is well documented by Arom, Jones, Ballantine, and Locke,
among others, and although the term itself remains questionable (as
Nzewi suggests[19]), the phenomenon it describes is easily grasped.

Example 4-4 reproduces a portion of David Locke's score of the Southern Ewe dance, *Gahu,* to illustrate polyrhythm.[20] Six layers representing
different instruments (1=bell, 2=rattle, 3, 4, 5=drums, 6=lead drum) expose six distinct patterns. All patterns are coordinated by a single grand
tactus or regulative beat in 4/4 meter. The drummers are not off doing
their own thing. You would not, for example, shift the bar line in the *kaganu* part (third layer) in order to eliminate the silence on the beat (as
shown to the right of layer 3 in the example). The *kaganu* pattern is consis-
tently, persistently, and permanently off the beat. Although the beat itself is
felt elsewhere in the ensemble, the *kaganu* player is not merely casually
aware of it but depends crucially on it. Nor would we rewrite layers 5 and 6
as shown in the example in order to align grouping and metrical structure.
How odd, then, to find John Chernoff insisting that African music "cannot

Example 4-4 Excerpt from the polyrhythmic texture of *Gahu,* a Southern Ewe dance, as transcribed by David Locke (1987:78)

be notated without assigning different meters to the different instruments of [the] ensemble."[21] And how uncharacteristically uncomprehending of Harold Powers, in an important reference article on rhythm, to rewrite David Locke's canonically correct transcription of another Southern Ewe dance, *Agbadza,*[22] so as to eliminate *kaganu*'s inaugural silence, to stagger the bar lines, and thus to enhance the interlocking nature of the rhythmic interplay.[23] The whimpish dotted vertical lines in Powers's version, found also in other transcriptions of African music, are misleading, because they collapse grouping structure into metrical structure. For the southern Ewe repertoire, at least, a single regulative beat exists for *all* members of the ensemble, not just one or two.

Polyrhythm is not, of course, unheard of in European music. The so-called *Ars subtilior* style of the fourteenth century, various passages in Haydn, Beethoven, and Brahms, and most obviously, twentieth-century repertoires from jazz through Stravinsky to Elliot Carter provide enough material for an account of European polyrhythm. What perhaps distinguishes the African usages is the degree of repetition of the constituent patterns, the foregrounding of repetition as a modus operandi. If this counts as a difference, it is one of degree, not of kind.

Inventing polymeter: Reading Merriam reading Ward

One source of the idea that African music is polymetric is the inflected transmission of ideas. We cannot review all of this scholarship here, so a single example will have to suffice. Alan P. Merriam, never guilty of shunning previous scholarship, provided the following statement about polymeter or "multiple meter":

> [a]lmost all students agree upon the fundamental importance of rhythm in African music as well as upon the fact that this rhythmic basis is frequently expressed by *the simultaneous use of two or more meters.* The organizing principles upon which multiple meter is based, however, are not agreed upon. Ward notes one drum playing a basically unvarying beat; Hornbostel sees the organization in terms of motor behavior which is the opposite of the Western concept; Waterman postulates the concept of the metronome sense; and Jones makes the point of lack of coincidence of the main beats. While these specific details remain to be worked out, *the consensus about the use of multiple meter is so strong as to remain unquestioned as the basis for African rhythm.*[24] (emphasis added)

This is a remarkably strong endorsement of a principle whose "specific details remain to be worked out." I would have thought that the normal procedure would be to specify at least the basic "specific details" before announcing that the principle "remain[s] unquestioned as the basis for African rhythm." Are different standards at work here? Imagine making a claim like that for European music!

Merriam, it should be said, did valuable service by periodically summarizing the results of other people's research, but he was not always a vigilant or disinterested reader. Look, for example, at the way he uses Ward to invent "polymeter" for West African music. "Broadly speaking," Ward wrote, "the difference between African and European rhythms is that whereas any piece of European music has at any one moment one rhythm in common, a piece of African music has always two or three, sometimes as many as four."[25] Ward the musician had sensed correctly that the music he heard in the Gold Coast during the 1920s was polyrhythmic. But observe the way Merriam the anthropologist glosses this quote:

> This principle [as described by Ward] is not to be confused with a simple elaboration of a single basic meter; different meters are used in combination so that while one drum is playing four beats, a second is playing three, a third, five and so forth, over the same span of time.[26]

This is a far cry from what Ward wrote. Ward spoke of different *rhythms* in combination, not different meters. Nor did Ward claim that four, three, and five beats were played "over the same span of time." He wrote, rather, that two, three, or "as many as four" rhythms may unfold simultaneously in a piece of African music. The extension of Ward's maximum hypothetical number from an even four to an odd number five may be a harmless slip in the interest of rhetorical emphasis. But the introduction of the notion of time span as a quantitative measure takes us into a different realm altogether. Indeed, Merriam elsewhere was so determined to establish an African difference on the topic of time that he failed to see that the simple distinction between the West's linear time and Africa's circular time represented a gross distortion of both realities.[27]

On the matter of the metrical background, Ward had correctly sensed that ensemble rhythms depend on something simpler, a duple rhythm:

> This [duple] deep booming regular beat is the fundamental beat of the piece, and sets the time for all the other rhythms and instruments. The other rhythms may have no possible similarity to it and no connection whatever, but on the first beat of the big drum all must coincide.[28]

Could one have been more explicit about the regulative and integral role of the so-called big drum? Doesn't Ward's statement suggest polyrhythm rather than polymeter? And, in any case, is there not something contradictory between Ward's claim, on the one hand, that he sees no similarity or connection between other rhythms and that of the big drum, and, on the other, that the other rhythms must coincide or connect with the big drum "on the first beat"? Perhaps Ward himself was not clear on this point. The right thing would have been for Merriam to convey some of that confusion.

Merriam then reproduces Ward's carefully worked out musical example in which the beats are correctly aligned with no hint of polymeter. Commenting on it, he sneaks in two words that Ward never wrote, enclosing them in parenthesis: "The following example illustrates both the diversity of rhythm (and meters) and the organizing beat of the big drum."[29] The parenthesis enclosing "and meters" says it all. Against all the evidence and Ward's careful if not always accurate description, Merriam seemed determined to infer polymeter from the earlier writer's study. So he invented it.

Slippage and cognitive failures of this kind might be overlooked—indeed, you might accuse me of making too much of an innocent parenthesis—were it not for the fact that polymeter and associated concepts are found repeatedly in reference articles, some of which may have mistaken Merriam's fantasies for an accurate report. To mention just two: Klaus

Wachsmann and Peter Cooke, in the article on "Africa" for the *New Grove Dictionary*, quote Merriam's statement that the use of multiple meter "remain[s] unquestioned as the basis of African rhythm," describing it as "an excellent short-cut to comparing various views about African rhythm."[30] A short-cut it certainly is, but excellent it is not, because, as I have suggested, the transmission of Ward alone is fraught with problems. Similarly, Helen Myers, relying heavily on Jones for an article on African music for the *New Oxford Companion to Music*, reproduces every one of the contentious concepts—the myths—with which this chapter is concerned.[31]

Contesting polymeter

Of the many reasons why the notion of polymeter must be rejected, I will mention three. First, if polymeter were a genuine feature of African music, we would expect to find some indication of its pertinence in the discourses and pedagogical schemes of African musicians, carriers of the tradition. As far as I know, no such data is available. There is, in other words, no ethnotheoretical discourse to ground or at least support the notion of polymeter. Some native discourses recognize ideas of measure by noting where dancers put their feet, but there is no hint of simultaneous use of different meters, for this would require dancers to respond at a fundamental level to different patterns within the ensemble instead of being guided by an emergent gross pulse, indeed one that may not be sounded by an individual instrument. All of which suggests that polymeter is probably an invention, an imposition on African music.[32]

Second, because practically all the ensemble music in which polymeter is said to be operative is dance music, and given the grounding demanded by choreography, it is more likely that these musics unfold within polyrhythmic matrices in single meters rather than in what Richard Waterman called "mixed" meters.[33] As with time lines, the choreographic supplement is an irreducible component of the rhythm, not an optional or decorative part of it. Strictly speaking, there is only one "rhythm" of the dance, all be it a compound "rhythm" expressed in a variety of internal articulations.

Third, decisions about how to represent drum ensemble music founder on the assumption, made most dramatically by Jones, that accents are metrical rather than phenomenal, to borrow Lerdahl and Jackendoff's terms.[34] I have suggested elsewhere that phenomenal accents play a more important role in African music than metrical accents. Because meter and grouping are distinct, postulating a single meter in accordance with the dance allows phenomenal or contrametric accents to emerge against a steady background. Polymeter fails to convey the true accentual structure of

African music insofar as it erases the essential tension between a firm and stable background and a fluid foreground.[35]

I am not, of course, the first to raise questions about polymeter. Kolinski, Arom, Anku, and Nzewi, among others, have either cast doubt upon it, or rejected it outright. In a 1973 article describing rhythmic procedure in European and African music, Kolinski records that he "came to realize that a performer or listener is not capable of a truly polymetric perception." Arom endorses Kolinski's terms "commetric" and "contrametric" while similarly rejecting the analytical relevance of polymeter:

> [T]he term "polymetric" is only applicable to a very special kind of phenomenon. If we take "metre" in its primary sense of *metrum* (the metre being the temporal reference unit), "polymetric" would describe the simultaneous unfolding of several parts in a single work at different tempos *so as not to be reducible to a single metrum.* This happens in some modern music, such as some of Charles Ives's works, Elliott Carter's *Symphony*, B. A. Zimmermann's opera *Die Soldaten*, and Pierre Boulez's *Rituel*. Being polymetric in the strict sense, these works can only be performed with several simultaneous conductors (author's emphasis).[36]

It is a sobering thought that Arom, who has devoted decades to the study of Central African music, and whose book *African Polyphony and Polyrhythm* is not only the most theoretically explicit study of African music but also includes a largely unprecedented number of transcriptions in extenso of compositions from the Central African Republic, should reject without equivocation any insinuation that the music is polymetric.

Willie Anku states near the beginning of a recent article that "polymeter . . . is now almost a thing of the past,"[37] while Meki Nzewi writes with characteristic forthrightness in a 1997 book:

> we remain bothered by such romance terms as polymetricity and polyrhythmicity. They are aberrations of African musical thoughts and practices, despite the artificial analytical sophistries and structural gymnastics employed to justify the illusions. Polymetricity and polyrhythmicity do not conform with the feeling, motion and organizational principles implicit in African ensemble music relationships and structuring.[38]

If Kolinski, Arom, Anku, and Nzewi are right, why are they not the dominant voices on the subject? Probably because the reception of theories of African rhythm has little to do with their epistemological cogency, internal consistency, historical or cultural grounding, empirical basis, or sensitivity to "musical" features. Rather, the reception of theories has everything to do with their narrative potential. By inciting certain acts of telling, by providing the conditions of possibility for exploitative fantasy, theories sanction consumer behavior that is only apparently enabled by the particular theory. And those behaviors are, in turn, determined by certain preconceptions, presuppositions, and prejudices. On the subject of polymeter and African rhythm in general, European investment in an ideology of difference so powerfully constrains what is ordinarily believed that, no matter what and how powerful the evidence is—and there is plenty of it in Arom, Locke, Anku, and others—an exotic notion like polymeter, rich in narrative potential, is not about to be relinquished without at least a fight.[39] Interrogating our love for certain ways of theorizing may be a step in the right direction; indeed, it may be the only option for those committed to an ethical scholarship.[40] But the extent to which students of African music are motivated by ethics is a complex and dicey issue that is perhaps best left alone for now.

Additive Rhythm

Additive rhythm, as opposed to divisive rhythm, describes a pattern of organization in which nonidentical or irregular durational groups follow one another. Additive rhythm operates at two levels: within the bar and between bars or groups of bars. For example, a single 12/8 bar may be divided additively into 5+7 or 3+2+2+5 but *not* into 3+3+3+3. Thus, the so-called standard pattern or time line in Anlo-Ewe music (*A* in Example 4-1) is sometimes counted (in eighth notes) additively as 2+2+1+2+2+2+1, while *Gahu*'s time line (*E* in Example 4-1) may be rendered with a sixteenth-note referent as 3+3+4+4+2. Similarly, at a larger level, an entire passage may display the metrical succession, 5/8+3/8+2/4+3/4. At both levels, the groups are irregular.

Example 4-5 quotes two competing transcriptions of a Mangbetu song by Rose Brandel to distinguish divisive from additive. In 1, the song is in 3/4 reflecting a divisive conception of rhythm. Phenomenal accents occur as shown, but the underlying feel of 3 beats per bar continues. In 2, Brandel uses bar lines to mark irregular groupings. Part of what motivates her here is a desire to place accented notes at the beginning of the bar, a fatal decision that also plagued Jones and others. So we have 3/8 followed by 5/16 then 6/16 then 7/16 and finally 3/8 again. Brandel actually prefers version 2, the additive conception, which she says is "truer to the Mangbetu conception," a claim that she herself was hardly in a position to substantiate.[41]

We owe the distinction between additive and divisive rhythms to Curt Sachs, author of *Rhythm and Tempo: A Study in Music History* (1953).

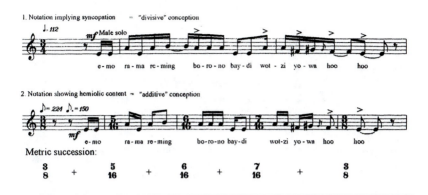

Example 4-5 Rose Brandel's demonstration of "two ways of notating the same [Mangbetu song]" (1961:74)

Sachs understood divisive rhythms as rhythms of the body, designed specifically for the dance. Such rhythms came to dominate European music from the seventeenth century onward. Additive rhythms, on the other hand, are rhythms of speech. They originate in language and are subject to the asymmetrical periodicities of speech. Sachs's terms were given prominence in the discourse of Africanist ethnomusicology, by his student Rose Brandel, from whose major study, *The Music of Central Africa*, Example 4-5 is taken. They appear in numerous writings. Jones claims that "the African approach to rhythm is largely additive, and so one is confronted with a series of rhythmic motifs of ever-changing time length which can only be intelligibly set down in a series of bars of continually changing value."[42] The equivocation implicit in Jones's phrase, "largely additive," disappears altogether in Nketia's formulation in *The Music of Africa*, where we read that "the use of additive rhythms in duple, triple, and hemiola patterns is *the hallmark of rhythmic organization in African music* (my emphasis).[43] Pantaleoni, Locke, Kauffman, Wiggins, Kubik, Walker, Rycroft, Pressing, and many others have also used the term "additive."[44]

The 3 + 3 + 2 pattern and counting words

Example 4-6 dramatizes two competing explanations for one of the commonest African rhythm patterns. (See also time line *B* in Example 4-1, whose first half is identical to this pattern.) The additive types write it as shown in line 2, using the sixteenth-note as density referent to produce a 3+3+2 pattern.[45] The divisive folks render it as a syncopated figure with a tie (line 1). In additive thinking the pattern is understood as an accretion

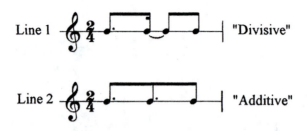

Example 4-6 Two different notations of a common rhythmic figure

of smaller values; its well-formedness as minimal unit arises purely contextually. From a divisive point of view, however, the pattern subtends a parallel quarter-note articulation that marks the main beats. The pattern is normally heard and felt with this background in mind, never without it. Its perceived well-formedness is owing to the presence of a palpable background.

Although the difference between the two ways of notating this rhythm may seem small, they stem from fundamentally different conceptions. Those who wish to convey a sense of the pattern's background, and who understand the surface morphology in relation to a regular subsurface articulation, will prefer the divisive format. Those who imagine the addition of three, then three, then two sixteenth notes will treat the well-formedness of 3+3+2 as fortuitous, a product of grouping rather than of metrical structure. They will be tempted to deny that African music has a bona fide metrical structure because of its frequent departures from a normative grouping structure.

One reason to be wary of the notion of additive rhythm is that African musicians do not normally conceive of the patterns they play additively. For the theorist, this absence is advisory rather than determining, because it is possible that indigenous structural conceptions—if one is patient enough to get at them—are entirely compatible with the quantitative orientation of European discourse. Still, one must wonder about the adequacy of durationally oriented descriptions like 3+2+4+1+2, 5+7, or 3+4+5 of patterns whose material mode of articulation on bells, rattles, and drums cannot possibly lay great store by sustained notes. More important, the syllabic structure of counting words in numerous indigenous African languages does not facilitate the kind of beat counting that would support 3+3+2 as a basic pedagogical mode. In the Ghanaian languages Ewe, Twi (Akwapim dialect), and Siwu, for instance, one, two, three, four, five, and six are two-syllable words, not one-syllable words as in English; eleven and twelve are three- or four-syllable words:

Ewe	Twi	Siwu	English
ɖeka	baako	iwẽ	one
eve	abien	inyɔ	two
etɔ̃	abiesã	itɛ	three
ene	anan	ina	four
atɔ̃	anum	iru	five
ade	asiã	ikuɔ	six
adre	asɔŋ	ikɔdzɛ	seven
enyi	awɔtwe	frãfana	eight
asieke	akron	kɔwẽ	nine
ewo	ɖu	iweo	ten
wuiɖekɛ	ɖubaako	iweoiwẽ	eleven
wuieve	ɖumien	iweoinyɔ	twelve

In teaching the 3+3+2 pattern, an English speaker would repeat: *one-two-three-one-two-three-one*-two several times. But try saying the Ewe equivalent: ɖeka-eve-etɔ-ɖeka-eve-etɔ-ɖeka-eve, and you will see that it works less well. The excess of syllables in the Ewe version produces an awkwardness that undermines its likelihood as a reflection of indigenous pedagogy. And it is for reasons like this that the entire durational-quantitative approach to African rhythm needs to be rethought.

The absence of a counting culture is not, of course, a strong enough reason to reject additive rhythm altogether. Theory involves negotiation, it may or may not take its cues from indigenous conceptions, and it appeals to different orders of authority, among them the divine or mystical, the logical, empirical, or rhetorical. So if some people find helpful the distinction between additive and divisive rhythm, we must not, in principle, deprive them of such a hermeneutic window. Only the outcome will provide justification for the course taken. While such a counter argument is plausible, it must nevertheless give us pause if a method that is supposedly "*the* hallmark of rhythmic organization in African music" (my emphasis) not only finds absolutely no practical corroboration in, but in some respects runs contrary to, the ways in which composer-performers and active listeners understand and interpret the resultant patterns.

Brandel and Nketia on additive rhythm

In her 1961 book, *Music of Central Africa*, Rose Brandel explains rhythmic structure in terms of hemiolas and additive processes. As Example 4-5 showed, and as the following quotation will further attest, Brandel explicitly rejects the notion of syncopation within regular time spans:

> African hemiola rhythms could be misinterpreted as being syncopated. Should a notation within a symmetric context showing a basic undercurrent of regular beats be utilized, the stressed offbeat

would make its appearance. . . . The subsuming of an independent, asymmetric line under a "counter" line of regularity, however, would be a falsification of the rhythmic intent of the music.

Brandel was surely right to broach the matter of "the rhythmic intent of the music" but she seems to have overlooked the choreographic component entirely. Transcribing mainly from published LP records, she did not always have the benefit of seeing the music and hearing the dance. And although she was alert to the preponderance of so-called hemiolas (or successive and simultaneous cross rhythms), her decision to represent Central African rhythmic patterns not within the constraints of a recurring metrical cycle but by placing a bar line before any perceived accent produced some unfortunate results. Brandel's Stravinsky-style scores confer an enviable complexity on ordinary African dance music, but they do not reflect the way African musicians conceive of their music. A Mangbetu woman dancing to the music of Example 4-5 is unlikely to think in terms of 3/8 followed by 5/16 followed by 6/16, then 7/16 then 3/8.

Unlike Brandel, Nketia confines his demonstration of additive rhythms to patterns within a 12/8 measure, not to successive metrical groups. The implication is that additive rhythm is operative at this local level of structure, not at a larger level. But there are two problems with Nketia's demonstration. First is the abstract rather than concrete nature of the discussion; second is the absence of culturally pertinent criteria for segmenting a given rhythmic pattern.

Example 4-7 reproduces Nketia's analysis of the so-called standard pattern. Heard within a 12/8 meter, the pattern shown at 1, consisting entirely of quarter notes, produces cross rhythms. In line 2 the pattern is also

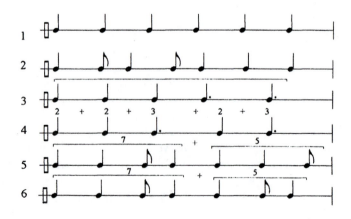

Example 4-7 Nketia's demonstration of additive patterns in "triple rhythm" (1974:132)

crossed with the main beats, but only in its second half, not the first. And line 3 reverses the pattern in 2 but suppresses the previous subdivided dotted-quarters. Patterns 4, 5, and 6 are versions of the standard pattern. Although it is not grouped as such, 4 may be represented as 2+2+3+2+3. Lines 5 and 6 at this level would be 2+2+1+2+2+2+1 and 2+2+1+ 2+2+1+2, respectively. On a higher hierarchic level, Nketia indicates a 7+5 grouping for 5 and 6.

Why is the pattern at 5 grouped as 7+5? As a matter of principle, no competent hearing of this pattern ever ignores the main beats, which are four dotted quarters in 12/8. The standard pattern makes sense therefore as a figure against a ground. But nothing about the ground sanctions a 7+5 segmentation, because once you take the main beats into account, you are more likely to interpret the pattern as syncopated, as heard against a regular accentuation. There is, then, something mechanical about Nketia's 7+5. His segmentation arises from treating the pattern in isolation, focusing on the morphology of the pattern without the ecology that sustains it. But if you accept the theoretical legitimacy of such treatment, then the door is open to other segmentations. Why not 5+7, 2+10, 4+1+6+1, 2+3+4+3, 2+7+3, each of them equally valid? In order to justify an additive conception, one must be explicit about one's criteria for segmentation. And those criteria should be culturally pertinent. Neither Nketia nor Brandel dwells on criteria for segmentation that originate from within the culture. Perhaps it is not possible to be forthcoming when the procedure itself is so questionable in the first place.

Cross Rhythm

Consider another basic device in the organization of African rhythm, so-called cross rhythm. Typically, two differentiated rhythmic patterns (Example 4-8, lines 1 and 2) unfold within the same time span but articulate

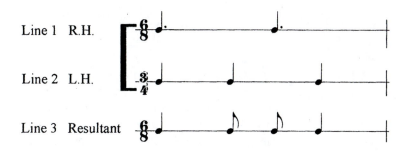

Example 4-8 "Cross Rhythm"

that space differently, at cross purposes, perhaps. According to the standard explanation, the African musician beats two equal beats in one hand (line 1) and three equal beats in the other (line 2) *within the same time span*, as Merriam would say. This would imply a low-level bi-metric organization: left hand in 6/8 and right hand in 3/4.

This extraordinary explanation is so much a part of the lore on African rhythm that it would seem almost perverse to question it. Yet one must ask whether African musicians really think of a span of time that they divide up by 2s or 3s and fill simultaneously. This seems unlikely. Because the two rhythms unfold together, articulation of one pattern presupposes the other. Therefore the resultant rhythm (line 3 of Example 4-8) holds the key to understanding. The resultant is in fact a straightforward 6/8 pattern. So when people say that they are performing this particular cross rhythm, they mean that they are performing in 6/8, not in 6/8 and 3/4 simultaneously! It is true that the resultant is articulated with timbral distinction between left and right hands, and that looking at what the hands play separately may encourage thinking in terms of independent articulations. But there is no independence here, because 2 and 3 belong to a single Gestalt.

As before, we ought to acknowledge the thoughts of other African musicians on the idea of cross rhythm. Meki Nzewi takes a philosophical approach that admits dependence as well as independence within the pattern as analogous to larger social transactions:

[The term "cross rhythm"] is antithetical to African social and, therefore, ensemble philosophy. A community/family/team does not work together at cross purposes. This musical structure [three quarters against two dotted quarters], which has depth essence, derives from the African philosophy of interdependence in human relationships. Personal/group identity and strength develop through structures of physical and emotional tension and catharsis. Motive as well as emotive suspense is generated when two moving entities which are at the point of colliding with each other unexpectedly veer off. A bounce-off affect is generated [Nzewi supplies a diagram]. The entities in missed-collision retain their individuality as well as motive or emotive energies/directions. When anticipations that develop in a motive or emotive relationship are not resolved or neutralised by actual contact, there is energy tension, a suspension. But a merger, subsumption or submersion of independence is avoided. In some African societies the bride price is never settled in full; in love relationships there is more emotional intensity when resolution is not attained through marriage or physical consummation. Thus the different characters, energies and qualities of the mutually relating entities are preserved.[46]

Drummer, dancer, and theorist C. K. Ladzekpo, who speaks of "the myth of cross rhythm" in his foundation course on African drumming, explains the technique with respect to "composite rhythm":

> A cross rhythm consists of a main beat scheme (a purpose in life) and a secondary beat scheme (a perceived obstacle). Each beat scheme has a significance and function in making up the distinct cross rhythmic texture. In performance, a cross rhythm becomes a composite unit by combining the contrasting beat schemes into a one line resultant rhythm or motif that recurs throughout the measure schemes as a unifying element. By the very nature of the desired resultant, the main beat scheme cannot be separated from the secondary beat scheme. It is the interplay of the two elements that produces the cross rhythmic texture.[47]

Thus Nzewi conveys the internal dynamism of the interacting parts while Ladzekpo insists on a hierarchic explanation. Both authors imply that the threat to a correct explanation comes from rampant atomisation of what is in effect a holistic practice.

Additive Rhythm in Vocal Music

If additive rhythm is problematic when applied to instrumental music, might it fare better in the analysis of vocal music? After all, given the consistent and natural asymmetries of speech rhythm, the accumulation of minimal units determined by syllabic accretion, and the placement of meaningful breath marks, it is not hard to imagine additive groupings. Indeed, in Sachs's distinction between additive and divisive, additive points to rhythms based in language and emanating from speech while divisive points to rhythms of the body expressed in dance.

A wide range of temporalities is domesticated in African song, but one enduring distinction, indeed one that is well-nigh universal, is that between unmeasured and measured song, between free and strict rhythm, or for certain readers, between something like secco recitative and aria. My interest here is in the measured or strict type. In general, the prosody of African songs of this type (syllabic count, speech tone contour, accentual scheme, and occasional rhyming effects) tends to be absorbed by the patterns implicit in hand claps, drumming, and dance. To say that the metrical structure of a song is most decisively articulated in such "extra-song" components may seem to devalue the internal structure of the sung elements, the song proper. But we must be careful not to impose an inappropriate ontological scheme on African song. Because there is no song proper without a sense of associated movement, deferring to extra-song components is entirely appropriate.

A. M. Jones was confronted with this issue, and he worked out a solution that reflects compromise. Having understood from his informant Desmond Tay that the hand claps and feet movement that accompanied play songs, for example, proceeded in a regular pattern—what Brandel calls "a basic undercurrent of regular beats"—Jones sought to reconcile the obviously shifting accents of sung words with the nonshifting choreographic accents. Transcribing the Southern Ewe song "Ta avɔ na legba" ("Clothe the idol"), Jones put the dance and feet movement (the extrasong components) in a straightforward 6/8 meter, thus signaling a divisive interpretation.[48] For the sung part, however, he opted for an additive conception whereby the singer begins with four bars of 6/8 followed by 3 of 3/4, one each of 6/8, 3/4, and 6/8 again, and finally two bars of silence referable presumably to the last active meter, which was 6/8. Jones, unlike some other transcribers, was sensitive to the placement of word accents, but he erred in using the bar line to mark such accents. His transcription reflects an understandable compromise between extrasong elements in divisive rhythm and song elements in additive rhythm. But this sort of compromise is weak, because it betrays a refusal to choose. Additive and divisive are not equal forces engaged in battle. The background is controlled by the divisive structure; additive, you might say, makes a lot of noise on the foreground.

We may compare Jones's transcription to two others. One by Hans-Heinrich Wängler shows a spoken as well as sung version of the Ewe text.[49] The sung version is grouped additively as three bars of 3/4, one of 4/4, and one last of 3/4. Since "Ta avɔ na legba" usually accompanies or is accompanied by dance-drumming, it is not clear what Wängler means to communicate by suppressing the extrasong components. Like Jones, Wängler's framework for the sung part is additive, but unlike Jones, he seemed to have been guided neither by the sequence of word accents nor by the silent choreography.

A third transcription appears in Nketia's *The Music of Africa* and is written in a single 6/8 meter throughout, the thought being that such a grid provides the ground against which word accentuation may emerge, not only structurally but within individual performances. Here, rhythm is understood as resolutely divisive, not additive.[50]

Additive rhythm, in short, is a highly problematic concept for African music. Like polymeter and cross rhythm, it is not in sync with indigenous conceptions of musical structure. It arises as a kind of default grouping mechanism for those transcribers who either disregard the choreography or fail to accord it foundational status. As a quantitative or durationally oriented concept, it finds no corroboration in other ordering procedures in African music. It is, in short, a myth.

Conclusion

If polymeter, additive rhythm, and cross rhythm are as problematic as I claim they are, why have they persisted in the literature? These modes of representing African rhythm are not isolated cases but part of a broader set of imaginings and constructions of Africa. They marked by the epistemological or perhaps cognitive constant that Edward Said has described as a discourse of "orientalism."[51] One could therefore postulate a parallel discourse of "Africanism" were it not for the fact that the word "Africanism" is already spoken for in writings by Herskovits and others as indicator of those nuggets of African cultural identity that survive in the New World.[52] Alternatively, we could describe polymeter and additive rhythm as inventions or myths, that is, power-based constructions of knowledge motivated in part by a search for self through imagined differences. Such constructions often betray the inventor's conscious or—more likely—subconscious desire for the people represented.[53]

There is, though, something a little facile, not to say merely fashionable, about invoking constructs like "orientalism" and "invention." You could argue that these sorts of error arise not from a peculiar cognitive disposition but simply from inadequate research: insufficient ethnographic data, wrong inferences, disregard for indigenous conceptions, hasty conclusions, and so on. And you might remind us that these same errors occur in other areas of musicological research: in Renaissance historiography, in music analysis, or in nineteenth-century studies. So, you would conclude, there is nothing unique about the African situation as presented here.

But therein lies the root of the problem: *the denial of nonuniqueness to Africa.* To imply that no portrayal of Africa is legitimate, complete, or of interest if it does not establish an ultimate African difference is to saddle Africa with an enormous critical burden. And yet this seems to be the premise (not always acknowledged and therefore rarely elaborated) with which many ethnomusicologists work. Unlike European music, which is ostensibly unmarked, belonging on a sort of zero level of conceptualization, African music is marked, different, Other.

A fuller exploration of difference will be found in chapter 8, and, although my own position boils down to a profound mistrust of difference, the issue is not productively framed as pro or contra. It rather lies in the interstices between difference and sameness, in the effort to mediate between ineradicable difference enshrined in the very act of representation and constructions of difference enabled by a particular ideology.

And so it is with African rhythm. The eagerness to construct African rhythmic patterning as essentially different from that of the West has produced certain myths and misunderstandings a number of which should now be jettisoned. To do this, one has to understand the motivations for such constructions, because the issue has less to do with a persuasive logical demonstration than with one's fantasy or desire for African reality. The fact that a number of African scholars have adopted—uncritically, let it be said—a Western problematic points only to the colonizing of our consciousness. It may be a while before these myths are replaced by others.

5
African Music as Text

As complex messages based on specific cultural codes, the varieties of African music known to us today may be designated as text. A text (from Latin *texere* meaning "to weave" and *textum* meaning "a web, texture"[1]) is something woven by performer-composers who conceive and produce the music-dance, by listener-viewers who consume it, and by critics who constitute it as text for the purposes of analysis and interpretation. "Text" as used here goes beyond the words of a song or the written trace of a composition. Performances of any sort can be conceived as texts: concert party entertainment, traditional drumming, or the pouring of libation. Festivals, rituals, outdooring ceremonies, the acts of medicine peddlers in public buses and at street corners, magical displays, and all-night crusades mounted by famous evangelists—these and many more count as text. Texts are thus primary data, basic resources, objects of analysis. Texts are not given but made; the conferral of textual status is a critical act. "Where there is no text," writes Mikhail Bakhtin, "there is neither object of inquiry nor thought."[2]

Designating African music as text has the advantage of liberating it from the yoke of ostensibly contextual explanations advocated by ethnographers and ethnomusicologists. This is not to say that we must gleefully ignore all matters of context and origin. But because context implies more text, and given that we can never be outside text, the work of interpretation is most fruitful when it proceeds in full awareness of this foundational impossibility. Registering the textuality of African music is in effect a way of foregrounding its essence as a performed art. It is a way of restoring a composition's fluid ontology by acknowledging its continuing life in reinterpretation. It is a way of "disprivileging" origins and first performances and coming to terms with the necessary acts of creative violation that must attend each new performance. For too long, the development of strong interpretations of the products of African musical genius has been hampered by overemphasis on the ethnomusicologists' classificatory schemes. We read of musical types, repertoires, and genres—always in the plural, as if the individual products were unworthy of analytical attention. Yet the aesthetic experiences of many Africans are shaped most memorably by a certain dirge, a certain song, a certain poetic text, a certain singer, a certain drummer, a certain occasion—in short, by specific performers, works, or performance situations. We recall specific moments of intensity, not necessarily complete configurations. It is appropriate, therefore, to fashion a critical approach that is more concerned with moments than wholes, and that draws strength from the wider range of possibilities made available in the pursuit of the textual status of African music. Such an approach is bound to lead into speculative realms, but that can only enhance our appreciation of African music.

Functional versus contemplative

As a preliminary, we need to explode a myth that has discouraged introspection about African music: the distinction between functional and contemplative music. In the process, we will restate the case for close listening.

Traditional African music is not normally described as contemplative art; it is thought rather to be functional. Functional music drawn from ritual, work, or play is externally motivated; it has a direct purpose. Thus funeral dirges sung by mourners, boat-rowing songs sung by fishermen, lullabies performed by mothers, and songs of insult traded by feuding clans are utilitarian musics that are said to be incompletely understood whenever analysis ignores the social or "extramusical" context. This music is then contrasted with élite or art music, whose affinities with European classical music are for the most part unmediated. Such contemplative or autonomous music is not tied to an external function; it is functionless. Although it is in principle consumed in a social setting, it demands nothing of its hearers save contemplation, meditation, an active self-forgetting. According to this distinction, then, analysis of traditional music, which is sometimes generalized to encompass all African music, must always take into account the particular activity to which the music is attached, whereas analysis of European music, unburdened of attachment to external function, can concentrate on the music itself, its inner workings, the life of its tones.

It does not require a great deal of imagination to see that the distinction between functional and contemplative is deeply problematic. It is especially so in failing to recognize the myriad opportunities for contemplation

Figure 5-1 Ga Lullaby

presented to makers of many so-called functional musics. I am not speaking merely of the existence of a genre of "songs for reflection" among the Gbaya,[3] or of the wordless chant *Gogodze* sung by the Ewe of Ve, Volta Region, Ghana. Rather, I am speaking of more familiar and ordinary genres of music. Consider a few speculative readings.

Example 5-1 quotes a Ga lullaby in Nketia's transcription.[4]

> Kaafo, kaafo, kaafo ni moko kwɛ oɖaŋ
> Don't cry, don't cry, don't cry for someone to look in your mouth

> Sika kɛ kpɔ yɛ oɖan
> A gold nugget is in your mouth

> Kaafo ni moko kwɛ oɖaŋ
> Don't cry for someone to look in your mouth

Mother speaks to child, trying to dissuade him from crying. There is a gold nugget in your mouth; if you cry, people will see it and want to possess it because it is precious. So hide it by closing your mouth, by not crying. The words themselves, delivered in a way that retains strong affinities with spoken Ga, already provide food for contemplation for both mother and child. Then there is the word oɖaŋ (your mouth), rendered twice in glissando style (bars 4 and 8), drawing the song away from relatively fixed pitches to the less determinate music of speech. And what about the long-range relationship between the endings of phrases (bars 3–4 and 7–8)? The latter phrase is transpositionally equivalent to the first at a distance of a perfect fourth. The latter lies lower in the singer's range. How does range signify? Does this particular transposition create tension or resolution? Is it a sign of closure, perhaps? And yet nothing in the melody's course prepares us for the lastness of the last phrase. We accept its finality only in retrospect, not in prospect.

Observe, too, the unfolding of the lullaby's message. The singer says to the child, *Kaafo* ("Don't cry"). Though modest from the point of view of syntax, the injunction is nevertheless semantically rich. It bears repeating. Then she adds to it, Kaafo ni moko kwɛ oɖaŋ ("Don't cry for someone to look in your mouth"). Thoughtwise, there is something incremental about the song's procedures. And timing is, of course, essential when trying to calm a child down in song. Notice how much expressive mileage our singer-composer manages to wring out of two pitches, G and A. Can it really be that only two pitches have been sung so far (bars 1–4)? Meanwhile, we are firmly anchored in duple meter.

Then, with the phrase Sika kɛ kpɔ yɛ oɖaŋ ("A gold nugget is inside your mouth"), new material is added, the music moves beyond its muted opening, signaling some sort of transition. Where might we be in transit to? That gold nugget phrase (bars 5–6), it turns out, fuses the functions of transition and contrast. Our singer-composer has declined to venture far afield (in structural terms). So she "returns" to the opening, to the third little phrase, Kaafo ni moko kwɛ oɖaŋ ("Don't cry for someone to look in your mouth"). She now dispenses with the two preliminary *kaafo*'s (bars 1–2). Perhaps this is the ending; perhaps it is enough to give us some but not all of what we heard before. And now the glissando at the end (bar 8) takes on a different meaning; it signifies transition from the world of heard song into the world of remembered song. What follows is not silence but the quiet echoes of what transpired before. Perhaps, then, the contradictory nature of the ending is motivated by the song's social function. Lullabies are meant to be sung over and over until their work is done, until the child goes to sleep, or until mother is exhausted. The social thus motivates the musical. When the work of the social is done, the musical relationships remain. Indeed, the only reason to sing at all is to depart from one temporal realm.

Here is another lullaby, this time from the Ewe-speaking people (transcribed in Example 5-2):

Nye ŋutɔ ʄe dzedzevi ye lo, toboli
S/he is my own dear child, toboli

Nye ŋutɔ ʄe dzedzevi ye lo, toboli
S/he is my own dear child, toboli

Mega fa 'vi le zãme nam o
Do not cry during the night for me

Nane/Sakabo na hɔ gbe l'asiwo nam
Something/Sakabo will take your voice away from me

Evinye lo, toboli
My own dear child, toboli

Figure 5-2 Popular Ewe lullaby

Lively, sprightly rhythms, musical phrases that close at first, remain open in the middle, then close toward the end, and the message of devotion and love: surely, these provide hermeneutic windows for mother, child, and implied audience. Important, too, is the song word *toboli*, which opens up a dimension of inner speech or inner singing that facilitates the accretion of various forms of content. There is some flexibility in textual construction. In place of *nane* ("something") in the penultimate line, you could sing *Sakabo* ("evil one," "childless one," "prostitute"). Our composer thus creates a sense not of re-beginning but of never-ending. Here, as in the previous lullaby, the social and the musical are thoroughly intertwined. Paradoxically, however, the work of the social appears to foreground certain musical details for the contemplating mind.

Consider another Ewe example, this one a funeral dirge (Example 5-3):

Alele, alele.
Alele, alele

Dzenɔ ɖeke me le du ke me o zã,
Is there not a singer in this town

ne va hɔ ha nam dzro?
to come and "receive" ("answer" or "respond to") my song for me?

Alele, alele, alele, alele, alele alele Tsalele, alele, alele
Alele, alele . . .

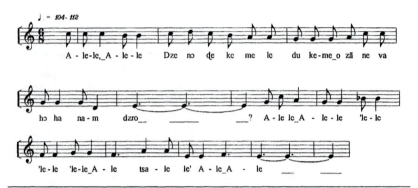

Figure 5-3 Ewe Funeral Dirge

When something tragic happens, it is the dirge singer who sings about it. Here, the dirge singer, presumably impersonating someone less gifted, someone with a less-cooked tongue, as the Ewe say, wonders where all the dirge singers have gone, and why there is no one to receive—or answer—her song. Perhaps, also, the tragedy has occurred to the dirge singer herself: Who will receive her song? Who will mourn with her? Textual ambiguity of this sort is common in Northern Ewe songs. Its purpose is to put performers and audiences in mind of certain deep or metaphysical questions, remind them of their own vulnerability and limitations, and thus confer on the occasion of performance a spiritual aura.

The invitation to contemplative behavior is achieved by repetition of the exclamation, *alele*. Beloved of singer-composers, the word *alele* has no fixed semantic referent; it merely conveys a sense of considerable magnitude. Repetition works literally to underwrite the process of enlargement even as it defamiliarizes the word and opens up empty spaces for reflection on the events that inspired the singing of the dirge. But the emptiness is only apparent, because the singer presses on, using the characteristic fourths of Northern Ewe melody to delineate an overall descending path to closure. Because we have all known sorrow, we are invited to contemplate it directly in those spaces of the song in which semantic information is frozen so that the underlying musical processes can be savored for themselves. The musical processes act as a stimulus to contemplation, and many singers either contemplate the death or tragedy directly, or, more often, retrieve from memory tragic events affecting them more personally. No one would deny that this dirge is functional, that it has an ascribed purpose, namely, to serve as a vehicle for the channeling of emotion in response to a specific death or to death in general. But it requires extraordinary deafness as well as a belittling of the dirge composer's art to deny the intrinsic interest of its elements and procedures, its invitations to contemplative behavior.

Consider yet another example, this time a children's play song recorded by Lester Monts from among the Vai people of Liberia.[5] The pitch content may be laid out in six phrases as follows:

323132
311332
332112
1121211
3233323212
11112(6)121

Distributing the reality of this dirge into numbers shows immediately the economical use of pitch: three in all, excepting the momentary incorporation of 6 toward the end. But closer inspection of patterns of movement reveals that the composer, probably some seven-year-old boy, has explored all the permutational possibilities of dyadic movement among the three principal notes of the song, 1-2-3. In other words, discounting repetitions and the brief appearance of 6 in the approach to the final cadence, the song consists entirely of adjacent motions 1-2, 1-3, and 2-3, and their retrogrades. Play songs are of course functional music, but because their function is to enable play, they are particularly rich in intellectual manipulation. And in order to admire the work of the composerly intellect, we have to inspect it, contemplate it. Should these "intellectual" processes be given short shrift just because the metalanguage I have used does not originate from the Vai themselves? Why should this sample of what is probably a largely unsung school of composition deep in Vai country be excluded from broader discussions of musical poetics?[6]

Consider, finally, another children's game, this one featuring verbal play and originating from the Northern Ewe people:

Kòkròkó lè còcôa tí mè lè kòkôm kákáká bé yeá dù koklô kúkú kòkòkò.

Kòkròkó is in the cocoa tree laughing hard and saying that he wants to eat a dead chicken by all means.

The play here is in the succession of speech tones, a kind of music that is inherent in words. The absurdity of the words suggests that the composer is more concerned with sound than meaning. According to this view, what matters, and what makes this play memorable, is the "music" resulting from this particular concatenation of speech tones. Of course the so-called absurdity of the text can never be erased entirely, so it could be argued that the semantic dissonance—the jarring effect conveyed by the sight of a man climbing a tree that is not usually climbed and insisting on something that is done but not said to be done—contrasts with a phonological consonance. (Strictly speaking, we all eat dead chickens, so Kòkròkó's desire is normal; however, the sight of dead chickens [from disease or accidents, and perhaps more than a day old] being picked up by the "Northerners" who lived among Ewes and did menial work on their cocoa farms may well play into their interpretation of the tone phrase.) The listener is then made to doubt that what she heard is what was intended by the composer. And this makes the "poem" memorable, inviting us to contemplate a play on sound and meaning.[7]

My point is obvious and probably overstated by now: the idea that African music is functional in contrast to a contemplative European music is a myth. Like others discussed in this book, this particular construct arose in connection with earlier ethnographies written for a Western audience and aiming to convey what might be different about African music. Difference betrays a subconscious desire to cast African music into an-Other sphere where it can complete Europe's lack.

This particular difference is fragile, however. For one thing, there is plenty of functional music in the Western tradition, but rarely is it said that it cannot be listened to for its own sake. Religious musics like masses, oratorios, and cantatas do not have to work hard to be accorded the status of "music alone."[8] Beyond the broad levels of genre, functionality is further evident within compositions. In opera, for example, music for a specific dramatic purpose may be provided by the composer to advance the action, but it never ceases to be music for contemplation. Think of the music that accompanies the duel between Don Giovanni and the commendatore early in Act 1 of Mozart's opera. Think also of the moment toward the end of the second act of *Tosca,* where Scarpia agrees to grant Tosca and Cavaradossi safe departure in exchange for a carnal favor from Tosca. Puccini's dark, foreboding music never sinks below the contemplative; and yet it is enlisted for dramatic work, for the passing of physical time as Scarpia writes, and for unveiling while at the same time obscuring, Tosca's intentions. This same F-sharp minor music will take on the role of a funeral dirge after the stabbing of Scarpia. In opera, there is no functional music that lacks a contemplative dimension. The opposition is artificial.

Think also of Haydn's "Farewell" Symphony, at the end of which orchestra members depart the concert platform one by one, ostensibly protesting their conditions of service at the Esterhaza. In one sense this "protest music" is functional, motivated by an extramusical—specifically dramatic—purpose. But the Farewell is also a form of wordless discourse, music to be contemplated. And think, finally, of those moments in Bartók's *Improvisations for Piano,* op. 20, where a figure is repeated in order to satisfy some aspect of compositional design, such as conformity to the proportions prescribed by the Fibonacci series. The repetitions are in that sense functional, but the *Improvisations,* based on folk songs, never cease to be contemplative music.

The point that African music can be legitimately listened to, that it never relinquishes a contemplative dimension—not even in theory—apparently still needs to be made in view of long-standing views linking music to dance. In his 1928 article, "African Negro Music," Hornbostel, claiming that "African music is not conceivable without dancing," identified "an essential contrast between our rhythmic conception and the Africans'; we proceed from hearing, they from motion."[9] An attempt by John Blacking to test the applicability of Hornbostel's absurd theory yielded no conclusive results.[10] More recently, John Baily, summarizing the researches of Hornbostel, Blacking, and especially Kubik, seeks to establish that "music is the sonic product of action," and that—quoting Kubik who was in turn quoting "an old view"—"African music is not sound alone." Baily later gives prominence to Kubik's view that "One can define African music in one of its fundamental structural aspects as a system of movement patterns."[11] And Kubik himself, in his seminal book, *Theory of African Music,* "designed to serve as a reader in African musicology for students, scholars and people with a wide interdisciplinary range of interests," devotes an entire section to "African music/dance as a motional system."[12] The implication is that physical negotiation of various musical patterns is as important as—if not more important than—the sonic trace itself.

Does European music lack a motional system? This seems unlikely. When you play five-finger exercises on a differently tuned (or out-of-tune) piano, do you not maintain the integrity of the fingering you learned? Would one then suggest that the movement of fingers is more important than the sonic trace? Given the margin of tolerance imposed by the technology with which many African instruments are made, and given the precariousness and contingency of our sound ideals, motional patterns ensure that compositions are anchored in a certain identity. Motional patterns do not take precedence over the resultant sound; rather, performers work with relative notions of sound.

The motional system of European music is equally evident wherever individuals make music. Turn off the sound on your TV while an orchestra is playing and observe the movement of string bows. The uniformity should assure you that European music could be said to constitute a motional system, no different from African music. More interesting is the discrepancy between the rhythm of bow movement and the rhythm of the sounds produced. Reconciling the physical constraints imposed on length and tightness of bow with the articulation demanded by the music/composer makes for a complex rhythmic polyphony even in relatively simple music. A researcher eager to construct European music as based on a motional system would find plenty of support in symphony orchestras. He or she could begin to develop theories to account for a lack of fit between motion and sonic trace. So, while it is true that certain performing individuals move more obviously than others, the distinction is not or should not be imposed as a set of gross categories distinguishing African from European music; its operation within traditions should be acknowledged as well.

In his "Music Structure and Human Movement," Baily concludes the section on Africa with remarks that may come as a surprise. Africa was singled out as a site at which "overt body movement is a prominent feature in the performance of many kinds of music."[13] Ethnomusicologists had drawn many valuable insights about "the relationship between sonic patterns of music and human movement" from research in Africa. But after reviewing this literature, Baily backtracks. He now concedes that "the importance of motional patterns in the performance of music is not unique to African music." Movement orientation only "seems" more pronounced in Africa than elsewhere. Indeed, "it seems probable that all musics can be usefully studied in . . . terms [of motional patterns]."[14] The equivocation is telling and strange, given its placement after the earlier incisive discussion. Once again, the urge to see Africa as intrinsically different may have influenced the theories of Hornbostel, Blacking, and Kubik.

The emphasis on motion, with its stress on context, easily leads to a denial that listening to African music without extramusical props can be a rewarding or even legitimate activity. In explaining why "it is a mistake 'to listen' to African music," John Chernoff draws attention to a number of supplementary texts that prop up the music sound.[15] Putting aside the one-sidedness of the argument (isn't European music similarly rooted in the extramusical?), we might point out that at no point is traditional music turned over to the deaf; at no point do its critics abandon aural engagement.

The functional attribute, then, is restrictive, and it is part of my purpose here to recommend its elimination. I want to dwell on the contemplative side and to exemplify some of the interpretive advantages it offers for engaging certain African repertoires. Now, to insist on the centrality not just of hearing but of listening is, paradoxically perhaps, to hint at an approach to African music that takes the partnership with language seriously. Music alone will not do it, because finally there is nothing like music alone. To be properly understood, African music must be approached at two intertwined levels: first, the level of musical language domesticated in various "compositions" and/or performances; second, the level constituted by a supplementary but necessary critical language.

Language and Music

If, as is generally believed, language dominates our conceptual apparatus, then there should be nothing surprising about invoking natural language as a point of reference in talk about music. According to Edward Sapir, language is "the communicative system par excellence in every known society."[16] Jakobson calls language a "purely semiotic system," functioning simultaneously as primary means of communication and as master discourse, as language and metalanguage. Music, too, as organized sound, may be construed as language but not—and this is of crucial importance—as metalanguage. As Émile Benveniste puts it, "language is the interpreting system of all other systems, linguistic and nonlinguistic."[17]

From a musician's point of view, the elevation of language above other systems of communication may appear odd at first. Performers are able to reach their audiences directly and can even carry out internal dialogues among themselves without investing heavily in spoken language. The linguistic and metalinguistic dimensions of an African composition are so thoroughly intertwined that their separation, even in theory, would seem difficult if not impossible. This is partly because of the thoroughly musical nature of African tone languages. To the extent that speech rhythm and speech tone serve as defining properties of natural language, we might think of African languages as forms of music. To reverse the equation and think of African musics as forms of language would work less well, for there is finally an asymmetry in the relationship. In one sense, then, it is musicians who should be adept at constructing and deploying the master discourse, not linguists or literary theorists. The argument that music constitutes not just *a* primary modeling system but *the* primary modeling system is not easily discarded in reference to Africa.[18]

I do not mean to start a territorial war with that last remark, only to underline the pertinence of African languages for the understanding of African music. According to Klaus Wachsmann, "there is hardly any music in Africa that is not in some way rooted in speech."[19] Chernoff says that "African music is derived from language,"[20] and Kubik writes that African music is "closely connected with language" and that "it is important . . . to link African music studies to the language map of Africa."[21] The close connection between language and music also explains the centrality of song in African modes of expression. "Vocal music," writes Francis Bebey, "is truly the essence of African musical art."[22] David Locke agrees: "Song is the heart of African music performance."[23] And Nissio Fiagbedzi confirms that view: "Although to the outside observer drumming and dancing might be regarded as central to Anlo music-making, to the traditional musician songs constitute the primary focus of musical activity."[24] These quotations—and they could easily be multiplied—may lead one to believe that the point of departure for any serious study of African music ought to be its linguistic dimension, "linguistic" conceived in the broadest possible sense to embrace textuality.[25]

There is, however, a difference between programmatic assertion and concrete action. Scholarly appropriations of Africa have still not made language study a priority. Nor is it common to find researchers who possess the appropriate reverential attitude to African languages. Consider a relatively trivial example like the routine mispronunciation of African names. Might this not be explained as a resistance to the music in language? Invoking music as pedagogical aid in the learning of African speech patterns sensitizes students to the tonal and accentual dimensions of language, dimensions that also exist fundamentally in song. At the acoustic and phonological levels, language study and music study can share many mutually valuable lessons.

So far, then, I have entered a few interpretive comments on a handful of songs, attempted to explode the functional-contemplative myth, restated the case for close listening to African music, and stressed the bonds between music and language. All of this has been undertaken with the aim of opening up windows for interpretation. A fuller discussion of analysis will be found in chapter 8. Here, I simply want to indicate the sorts of insights that come from treating African music as contemplative art while taking the partnership with language seriously. Rather than providing a comprehensive introduction to poetics, what follow are specific intuitions into certain aspects of the thought and practice of African music that may prove suggestive to other students. My examples are drawn from the traditions of two Ghanaian groups, the Northern Ewe and the Akpafu, and I have organized my remarks around four small topics: the uses of error; violence against natural language; singing in the throat; and signifying in instrumental music. (Ideally, these ideas would be presented with music examples sung, spoken, played, or listened to on recording. I beg the reader's indulgence in this less-than-ideal format.)

The uses of error

Errors made during rehearsal or performance—the distinction is not always firm—and the ways in which they are immediately corrected constitute rich sites for the study of aesthetic norms, conventions of grammar and syntax, and constraints on performance. In July 1986, I recorded a group of older women singing songs associated with puberty rites. This was in the village of Akpafu-Todzi, Volta Region, Ghana, where, according to the women, the practice had been outlawed by Christian missionaries since the 1950s. The women were thus performing a dead tradition, one that is resuscitated occasionally for the curious ethnographer. (None of this inauthenticity was lost on the performers on that occasion; indeed, their keen awareness that something called "culture" was being preserved points to a dimension of historical and critical awareness that ethnographers frequently miss when they read such texts on face value.)

First, a lead singer sang the entire song, ending with a signal for the others to join in:

Lele lele, mmɛ mma wu rã
Lele lele, me I have my husband

Things did not go well; the ensemble did not come together. These were not "participatory discrepancies" that arise normally in group performance.[26] No attempt was being made by the Akpafu women to create echo effects. Staggered entries, heterophony, or hocket technique were not part of the compositional or aesthetic intention. The sloppy entries of chorus members represented nothing but mistakes, pure and simple.

At this point, Mr. Danquah, my resource person who had organized the recording session, intervened using words that point in the direction of an indigenous metalanguage:

Kuka gɔgbe b'ɔmre ne mi ledzai ka kukakɔ si
This song is sweet, so sing it again well so that

mi silɔ oɖuɖuu ku mi kanya si ka kote.
all of your voices and your mouths agree (are in synchrony)

Mawẽ ɔtregu kuka kɛkɛi.
Some people ran away with the song (or, Some people took the song and ran).

To the Akpafu, the song's sweetness would invoke the sweetness of berries or sugar. It could also mean "delicious," as one might say of palm soup or bean stew. Mr. Danquah's phrase kuka gɔgbe b'ɔmre could thus be rendered as "the song is delicious." The idea of letting voices and mouths "agree" recognizes voice and mouth as separate entities, as functionally complementary but distinct at the levels of intention and execution. In a correct performance these two entities are synchronized as performers realize their intentions. Finally, the remark about running away with the song suggests that singing with others is like running with them, but not so as to win, not so as to be the first to cross the finishing line, because that would spoil the song. As in other spheres of African life, the ethos is communal rather than competitive.

After Mr. Danquah's remark, the singers tried again. This time, too, someone ran away with the song. At this point, the singers themselves became critics of their own performance. One said, "Lɔ kã atwe," which means "Be listening" or literally "Be propping up your ears." Another said, "Pɔkɔsɔɔ," which means "slowly" or "patiently." Then a third intervened with the most substantive corrective so far:

Nyo, wũi kpɛ ni, wũi ka ɔro
Look, she has not fetched it, she has not finished singing it

ɔ̃ka ɔsɔŋ ɖai ne kri boa moe ne
She will sing it and go and cut it, then we will catch it.

Again, the expression is telling. The song is fetched as one fetches water. It is also sung, as one sings a hymn. Then it is cut by the lead singer. In other contexts, a singer will first take a song to the "throwing-away place" (Kawrikɔ̃). Only then does she "cut it" thereby signaling to the Chorus to "catch it." To refer to the alternation between lead and chorus here by the catch-all term "Call and Response" would not be wrong, but it would miss the complex negotiation in which attitudes of fetching, cutting, throwing away, and catching are put in circulation in order to attain effective performance.

I imagine that many of us have encountered such performance errors among the musicians with whom we work. What I am suggesting here is simply that errors like these, recognized and corrected by the performers themselves—in other words, by performers turned critics in the moment of performance/rehearsal—can be extremely valuable sources of insight into musical aesthetics broadly conceived. The emergence of a metalanguage is an important by-product of this situation of error.[27]

Violence against natural language

Errors are errors only when recognized as such by the practitioners themselves. But there are other kinds of violation that have, in the course of time, hardened into metalanguage. Consider the following example from among the Northern Ewe. A typical performance combining dance, drumming, and singing often unfolds a dynamic trajectory. If you wait long enough, you will likely experience a moment of great intensity, a climax, a high point.[28] Different musical processes combine to convey a sense of climax: an accumulation of decorative patterns espoused by the lead drummer, the cleverness or topicality of the lead singer's improvisations, or the grace and elegance of a dancer's movements.

One expression that some Northern Ewe use to acknowledge moments of intensity (moments that, incidentally, are not necessarily brief) is èvùɔ́ sɔ́. The word vù denotes drum but it also denotes the occasion of drumming, which includes singing and dancing. There is no ordinary word like sɔ́ with a high tone, although there is sɔ̀ with a low tone, which means "agree," as when we say that àkayɛ mé sɔ̀ ò ("the gourds do not agree"). Sɔ́ with a high tone is probably a transformation of sɔ̀, so the expression èvùɔ́ sɔ́ could be rendered as "the drumming or dancing has reached a high level of agreement." (Another expression that conveys a similar meaning is "Éde éme nám ló," which means "It has really gone inside for me.")

We may speculate on the process by which the word sɔ́ entered the Ewe lexicon as a musicalizing of spoken language. In other words, the transformation of low tone to high tone is a transformation away from language and in the direction of music, away from the normal register of speech to a marked, higher one. The expression èvùɔ́ sɔ́ thus features a tonemic transgression, a form of violence against language, an implicit critique of language's ability to convey information about music. Only by relinquishing its ordinary referential sense, only by approaching the condition of music, it would seem, is language finally able adequately to represent one of music's deepest effects.

Singing in the Throat

African musics and languages may be understood as originating from the same background, because if a unit of language is marked essentially by tone and rhythm, then it might be described as a minimal unit of music, too. Identical origins, however, tell us little about subsequent use and the accretion of other identities in the course of time. It is for this reason that the coming together of music and language is of special interest.

Words and music are brought into alliance in song. One interesting, though perhaps uncommon, aspect of this alliance concerns situations in which words and music appear to go their separate ways, situations in which music escapes from language, as happens, for example, when a song is hummed rather than sung. In August 1986, I recorded a performance of the funeral dirge "Wo ɖo taa Agɔɖome" ("They are headed for Agɔɖome") in which sung and hummed versions followed one another. The performers described the humming as hadzidzi le veme ("singing in the throat").

Singing in the throat is used whenever the depth of sorrow experienced by the dirge singers is more than they can bear, forcing them to change registers. This stretch of "pure" music thus embodies a moment of excess, a moment of transcendence, perhaps, a moment in which words, once again, reach their limits, so to speak, unable to convey further meaning, and so defer to the more articulate music. While transcending language, however, music nevertheless remains dependent on it; it remains a supplement to language just as language remains a supplement to music. What was hummed was previously sung, so that, while singing in the throat with a kind of percussive articulation (that is, a kind of articulation native to speech), singers have the opportunity to reflect on the very words that they have abandoned or tried (usually unsuccessfully) to abandon, and to construct appropriate (new) meanings.

This clash or antagonism between word and tone, this forced cooperation between language and music, lies at the heart of the well-known question of how speech tones relate to melodic contour. The conventional view, advanced, it should be said, with more than a little ambivalence, is this: In song, words must be sung the way they are spoken in order for them to retain their meaning. This view is demonstrably false, however, because words can be sung any old way without losing their meaning. "Wrong" melodic contours do not necessarily give rise to alternative meanings; rather, they may undermine, without ultimately eliminating, the correct meaning.[29]

Although false, the conventional view is not lacking in implication. When a Northern Ewe singer sings a recreational song, for example, she is guided, on one hand, by an intonational contour, that is, a projection into pitch and rhythm space of an emergent linguistic shape, and, on the other, by the deep structure of the melody, a purely musical residue that embodies an intentional (i. e. nonarbitrary) aesthetic choice. These two constraints, then, are engaged in an active tussle: the melody pulls one way, the spoken language pulls another way. The resulting "drama" may or may not leave acoustic traces, but its psychological function and regulative influence cannot be denied. It is not, therefore, simply a case of music winning over language, as if the binary framework that enabled such an assessment was not fundamentally flawed, but of a rather more complex psychoacoustic profile in which music constantly resists the pull of language. To allow Ewe song this unsettled, dissociative, and agonic existence (to borrow Lawrence Kramer's characterization[30]) is not at all to compromise the challenge of defining song, but rather to recognize the conflicting impulses with which its ontology is composed.

Signifying in Instrumental Music

From the birth of metalanguages in performance errors through the pressing of language toward the condition of music to the active contestation of words and music in song, we have charted a path toward greater abstraction. I now come to the last of my categories, instrumental music. How does instrumental music or untexted music signify? Or—in order not to deny agency—how is instrumental music made to signify? Let us look at the predominant form of traditional instrumental music: drum music.

In his well-known study of Akan drumming, Nketia identifies three discrete modes of drumming: the speech mode, the signal mode, and the dance mode.[31] A drummer playing in the speech mode simply reproduces the tonal and rhythmic patterns of speech on the drums. In semiotic terms, this is an iconic mode of transfer. Second is a signal mode of drumming, in which a spoken phrase, recognized iconically but understood symbolically, is repeated several times to convey a message. Third is the dance mode, where apparently purely musical dance rhythms, domesticated within a specific cycle of beats or meter (12/8, 4/4, or 2/4), provide a continuous or near-continuous texture for movement, singing, and dancing. The speech mode is isomorphic with ordinary language, the signal mode with poetic language, and the dance mode with a heightened form of poetic language that at the same time points beyond itself.[32]

It is obvious that the lines dividing these modes of drumming are by no means firm. Nor are the modes as discrete as Nketia's taxonomy would imply. In the speech mode, for example, the apparently direct transfer of speech texts to a different medium is not as direct as has been thought, because to play a verbal phrase on a pair of drums, without the benefit of vowel or consonant articulation, is to engage in an act of translation constrained by performance. Because the active vocabulary used by talking drummers is relatively small (500 words in Akan surrogate languages, for example, excluding proper names and strong names, according to Nketia[33]), the performer is forced to cultivate the conventional or symbolic element extensively. It is therefore somewhat misleading to say that the speech mode of drumming is simply isomorphic with speech. No matter how versatile, a drummer cannot "talk" in the way that a native speaker can generate a potentially infinite number of sentences on a given subject. The transformation of spoken speech into drummed speech entails a deletion of parts of the linguistic universe. Anecdotes about talking drummers saying, "Go and bring two bottles of strong beer for this white man and me," or, "Find me a woman for the night," in the speech mode must be interpreted carefully.[34] Such messages *can* be communicated, of course, but only through generalized and conventional signals expressing thirst or carnal desire that are then interpreted by addressees of the message according to the coordinates of a local context. Both iconic and symbolic modes of signification are at work in the speech mode.

I should note, by way of parenthesis, that the speech mode of drumming is frequently appropriated by popular musicians, who mime the morphology of speech without necessarily saying anything, without necessarily speaking words. This kind of appropriation suggests that in some parts of the post-colony, the practice of talking drumming has passed into history, has become a relic of an older, more functional practice, now simply remembered as something our people used to do. When thus enacted, the speech mode betrays the self-consciousness of an invented tradition. The error in certain popular representations of talking drumming is that they overlook or deny this invention.

The speech mode of drumming thus collapses into a signal mode more readily than has hitherto been granted, even though an essential difference between speech and signal modes is the higher degree of repetition found in the signal mode. The signal mode, in other words, gives rise to a further contraction of the linguistic universe. Drummers deliver proverbs, praise names, and summons ("burden texts," Nketia calls them), whose rhythmic and tonal patterns have been previously internalized by members of a given community. Through regular use, some of these phrases have been defamiliarized, allowing a certain degree of interpretation on the part of the receiver of the message; consequently, if the speech mode enables performed speech, the signal mode enables stylized speech. Again, it is the ascendancy of the symbolic element over the iconic that separates signal from speech.

One would predict that in the dance mode, the increasing functionality of the symbolic element, that is, the process by which the speech mode is deprived of its semantic element, is carried to its logical extreme. This prediction would not be entirely accurate, however. The crucial marker of the dance mode is the introduction of metric articulation into most—but by no means all—parts of the dance. The dance mode does not abandon speaking and signaling; rather, it becomes a repository for all three modes of drumming.

Conclusion

I have been meditating on the relationship between music and language in Africa, using the metaphor of text as a point of entry. Because the discussion has gone in several directions, it would be inappropriate to attempt to impose a unity on its diverse strands. My main concern has been to encourage direct engagement with African music, and surreptitiously to challenge the privilege accorded professional (ethnomusicological) discourses, especially those that bar individuals who lack certain forms of contextual knowledge from participating in the processes of meaning formation. So rich and diverse are African compositions and performances that no interpretation can finally be said to be anachronistic. If this impossibility holds, it should prove inspiring; it should empower African-language speaking critics to speculate freely upon the meanings, associations, connotations, and values subtended by African music. It should recognize the value of insights produced by critics who prefer a hermeneutics of moments to one of wholes or genres or classes of song. It should allow a more fluid mode of constructing metalanguages so that the constructions of specialists are treated as one among several competing discourses. And it should dispense with the facile distribution of insights into ostensibly Western or African categories, for these only serve a certain divisive institutional mind, one that fails to appreciate the advantages of redrawing boundaries in the process of identity formation. It is through the accumulation of such discourses, the accretion of views born of individual contemplation, that we can display the expressive range and structural magnificence of African music.

6
Popular Music Defended against Its Devotees

Have we underestimated the potency of popular music? In his widely read *The Music of Africa*, Kwabena Nketia rigorously excludes sustained discussion of African popular music, basing his study largely on traditional music, an understanding of which is regarded as necessary for a secure interpretation of newer forms. Although he acknowledges the "legacy of Europe" and "horizons expanding," and although he elsewhere reviews recreational music, adequate recognition or attention is not given to popular forms like jùjú, fújì, afro-beat, afro-rock, highlife, makossa, taarab, and several dozen others.[1] Similarly, Francis Bebey, in a colorful primer on African music, explores—not without a certain amount of mystification—the traditional heritage, conceived as the backbone of African musical expression.[2]

Nketia's book appeared in 1974, Bebey's five years earlier. These were not only the first but remain the most influential African-authored surveys by musician-scholars. Although neither author could have been unaware of the vital role played by popular music in culture (Bebey, in fact, composes and performs in a popular medium, as well), academic protocol and a long-standing fascination with ethnographies of old music had rendered popular music avoidable for anyone attempting a survey at the time. Things have changed since the mid-1970s, however. Ideas that were once lodged in the margins of texts by Kubik, Ward, Hornbostel, Jones, Sprigge, and others have migrated to the center of newer work. In 1980, *The New Grove Dictionary* gave token coverage to African popular music, while in the recently published revised version (2001), coverage is extended to other genres as well as to individual performers like Salif Keita, I. K. Dairo,

117

Baaba Maal, Youssou N'Dour, Koo Nimo, Ashter Aweke, Alpha Blondy, "King" Sunny Ade, and numerous others. Similarly, the Africa volume of *The Garland Encyclopedia of World Music* includes a number of essays on African popular music.[3] Real ethnographic and theoretical advance have come, however, not in officially sponsored surveys but in the research of individual scholars such as David Coplan, Christopher Waterman, Kazadi wa Mukuna, John Collins, Ronnie Graham, Atta Annan Mensah, Christopher Ballantine, Veit Erlmann, John Chernoff, Louise Meintjes, Wolfgang Bender, Tejunmola Olaniyan, and Michael Veal, among many others.[4] While it would be excessively optimistic to think that the study of popular music will soon catch up with or indeed outstrip the study of traditional music (nor is the desirability of such a change beyond dispute), the collective work of these scholars has helped to counter some of the prejudice against popular music and to generate excitement about its interpretive possibilities.

Resisting Popular Music

Why is the most widely heard music on the continent not also the most written about, the most taught in our institutions, the most valued? The reasons for our reticence reside in the very circumstances in which knowledge is produced in Africa, in the models of scholarship inherited from European musicology, in the relative lack of participation by emancipated African actors, and in the absence of methodologies suited to music that apparently falls between stools. Rehearsing these factors necessarily entails pointing accusing fingers at certain individuals and institutions, but because this personalizes the debate in ways that may not always be productive, I will confine comment here to two factors: first, the paradoxical role played by ethnomusicologists in (under)valuing popular music; and second, the prejudices against our own cultures instilled by colonial education.

Although redress has come from among their ranks, ethnomusicologists are in part to blame for the relative neglect of popular music. According to Ronnie Graham, author of one of the most valuable surveys of African popular music, "ethnomusicologists are in the main much more comfortable with tradition than with innovation and are often biased against music with any overt Western influence."[5] Similarly, Karin Barber, introducing a collection of articles on African popular culture, writes:

> Popular music, the most protean, adaptable, transferable of arts, and the only one to make a noticeable impact on popular audiences outside Africa, was one of the first popular African arts to be seriously studied; but even that was quite a recent development, after many decades in which ethnomusicologists deplored the contami-

nation of authentic indigenous traditional sounds by the infusion of Western rhythms, melodies and technologies.[6]

It is possible to counter Graham's claim by pointing to ethnomusicological works that deal with musical change and innovation, and by noting a growing interest in Western-influenced non-Western music, including the products of so-called urban ethnomusicology. And it is possible to wonder how extensive is the offending literature that Barber refers to. Nevertheless, their core claim retains a kernel of truth for the 1980s and before: Insofar as ethnomusicology inherited an anthropological ethos built on a search for difference, a number of its earlier, classical contributions were less concerned with conveying a first-level (naive, ordinary) African reality than with a reality produced in a discourse that necessarily conveyed the sense of Africa's distance from, rather than proximity to, Europe. In such a climate, a male, guitar-playing African musician, wearing a pair of imported jeans and dark glasses, or a church musician steeped in tonic solfa who wore jacket and tie on Sundays and composed hymnlike anthems for his congregation were of considerably less interest than the fierce-looking bush African sporting a grass skirt, teeth finely chiseled, bare breasted, beating on a drum, and invoking ancestral spirits without irony! Only after Euro-Americans experienced their own crises of representation in the 1960s did it become not only legitimate but also desirable to begin to theorize the fascinating contradictions and ironies of modern African living exemplified in popular music.

The paradox in ethnomusicology's contribution arises because, although the difference-producing machine dominated ethnographies of the early days (the 1950s), it would not be long before the discipline's profoundly ethical avoidance of a priori valuations of music imposed itself on fieldworkers. Whether expressed as the study of all music, music in culture, non-Western music, nonurban music, or nonart music, ethnomusicology in principle valued all musics equally. Thus popular music, with its undisguised appropriation of European and American idioms, was as valid as funeral dirges, ritual music, or the praise-singing of griots. Ethnomusicology's flexible methods made it a more suitable place to undertake research into music that was not written, dealt directly with everyday matters, did not always last, and was made by poor and rich alike.

It should perhaps be mentioned—especially because African patterns of scholarship often mimic those of the metropolis—that the undervaluation of popular music is characteristic of European musicology, too. Centered on a narrow definition of texts the majority of which have little to do with the musical experience as such, musicology has only recently begun to study popular music seriously. As far back as 1941, Adorno published an article "On Popular Music" which includes a criticism not of the scholarship but of the very phenomenon. In Adorno's view, popular music breeds standardization and pseudo-individualization. The glamour required for its effective presentation sometimes produces "baby talk." Recognition as opposed to adventure or exploration marks the extent of some listeners' experience. The existence of leisure time is a factor in the sustenance of the industry. And popular music functions as a kind of "social cement," engendering ambivalent feelings in its consumers.[7]

Adorno's concerns were probably widely shared, even if few had the courage to say so. Musicology silently endorsed this negative valuation, and it was not until the work of scholars like William Austin and Charles Hamm that the scales started to fall off our eyes.[8] It is possible, then, to see metropolitan prejudice reflected in former colonies. For if musicology as an academic discipline in well-endowed Euro-American institutions had still not fully embraced the study of popular music, then what chance did a fledgling African musicology have of giving it proper attention? The emancipatory potential in studying African popular music stood little chance of being pursued.

A second and related aspect of the popular-music tragedy concerns Africans themselves. As is well known, part of the legacy of colonialism is a persistent and resolute denigration by schooled—but not necessarily educated—Africans of certain cultural forms. We have probably all heard anecdotes about the speaking of indigenous languages once prohibited in certain schools, about parents preferring modern Christian names to indigenous ones (the latter packed in too much history, too much significance), about imported (canned) foods being given a higher premium over fresh, local varieties, and so on. In the case of music, some schooled Africans "lucky" enough to be exposed to Handel, Bach, Mozart, or Beethoven stuck with them; very few listened with interest to contemporary African art music. And while popular music such as highlife served an important social function as dance music, its incorporation into the curriculum was slow to emerge.

An anecdote may be helpful here. As recently as the early 1990s, the Department of Music in the School of Performing Arts at the University of Ghana at Legon still lacked staff trained to teach the varieties of African popular music. When the intention to appoint a lecturer in that area was announced, a number of people vehemently opposed the idea, arguing that an expert in popular music belonged not in a music department but in the department of sociology or African studies—in short, some place other than the music department. The music department was reserved for those who could talk of crotchets and quavers, sonata and rondo forms, diatonic and chromatic harmony. Fortunately, and thanks to the vision of the acting director of the school, the dissenting voices were put in their place, and the appointment was made. Today, courses in popular music attract more enrollments than any others; and the degree of student engagement with these repertoires—both practically and theoretically—is unmatched by any other.

Similar anecdotes circulate about the teaching of African literature, African philosophy, or African art. They speak to a form of self-hatred that in turn testifies to the success of the colonial project. Listening to Mozart, playing hymns at the harmonium, singing a chorus or two from *Messiah*, being able to orchestrate a piano piece for instruments you have neither seen (except in pictures) nor heard, being able to harmonize a chromatic melody are thought to chart a better, more civilized path into modernity than studying or performing the music of hooligans who stay up all night, play instruments with unfortunate associations (like guitars), sing lewd and funny songs in the vernacular or broken English, drink beer or akpeteshie, and have sex before they marry.

It is a pity that only a handful of our intellectual leaders have been troubled by the mediocre level of European music instruction in our institutions of higher learning, even where programs are dubbed "bi-musical." Students trained in these places often leave with a flawed, incomplete, and jaundiced view of the European canon, overvaluing its procedures—such as counterpoint—while underappreciating its cultural embeddedness. A little reflection might have led to the consideration of alternatives, including the implications of the largely untapped competence in popular music possessed by many students. Beginning in the 1950s, and intensified by the 1960s, popular music has been made sonically unavoidable for most urban dwellers. Even in rural Ghana, radio boxes mounted after independence to enhance citizens' allegiance to a precarious nation-state ensured its wide dissemination. Reflection would have revealed that students possess a large repertoire in memory, that some have internalized—naively, no doubt, but authentically—its enabling procedures, and that none would lack insight into the social meanings set in motion by the sound and especially words of the popular music they had grown up with. Reflection might have led to the discovery that students are able to speak popular music as a language, to modify a remark of Nietzsche's. They can complete utterances begun in it, recognize idioms, and evaluate not only the grammatical correctness but also poetic depth of other people's performances. Sadly, many students who had such competence simply had to kiss it goodbye as they were put through the grueling and wicked tasks of trying to resolve diminished-seventh chords (for reasons that could not be adequately explained by instructors), avoiding parallel fifths and octaves (when all the traditional music around them gloried in parallelism), scoring keyboard minuets for small orchestra (when only a small number of them had any inkling of the sound ideal that they were ostensibly emulating), and memorizing dry facts about Verdi's middle-period operas (when there was no chance in their life times of ever seeing one). It is hard not to conclude from this that the educational ethos bequeathed by British colonialism was not centrally concerned to instruct, edify, enable, and thus ultimately empower, but to trip up, punish, and subject to difficult tasks in order to guarantee failure on the part of some, if not many. Indeed, the fact that some instructors themselves barely made it through these oppressive regimes as students explains why they have become their strongest advocates and implementors today.

Readers of Adorno will recognize my lifting of the title of his 1951 essay, "Bach gegen seine Liebhaber verteidigt," translated by Samuel and Shierry Weber as "Bach Defended against His Devotees."[9] Adorno's concern was to rescue Bach from those who had turned him into a theological figure, those who sought his significance not in the purely musical procedures he cultivated, complete with internal contradictions between Baroque and Classical impulses, between a thoroughly modern and an archaic melodic element, and between constructions of objectivity and subjectivity. Adorno sought to reinforce the pertinence of the musical essence of Bach, because without this emphasis, Bach was reduced to texts for social decoding, an exercise that left untouched the true and deep significance of his work. By the same token, and to the extent that it is possible to argue the position without resorting to technicalities, I want to suggest here that there is a deep musical stratum in popular music that constitutes its essence. Imbricated as it is in other texts and discursive systems, popular music nevertheless evinces a "specific musical content." To say this is not to suggest that the musical and the social are easily distinguished; on the contrary, as Adorno showed, they are thoroughly intertwined, and analysis must embrace this fundamental duality, a duality that, in any case, is not peculiar to, but merely finds its most engaging and immediate dramatization in, popular music.

Defining Popular Music

What exactly is popular music? It is first and foremost a repertoire, but the diversity of its forms and the absence of widely accepted names for its genres have delayed the emergence of reliable taxonomies. While terms like highlife, jùjú, afrobeat, makossa, taarab, and rumba have acquired some currency in the literature, none has so far formed the basis of a broad and sustained critical discourse. Indeed, one only has to look at the provenance of a term like "highlife" to see the range of heterogenous elements that it absorbs. Perhaps we should stop dreaming of an adequate taxonomy and speak simply of *varieties* of African popular music.

All acts of naming, whether of musical forms, genres, or musical instruments retain a degree of arbitrariness. Some names are assigned not with the needs of a pedantic archivist or curator in mind, but under the influence of specific ambitions for ownership, power, and a desired identity. Two dances may share roughly the same compositional structure but be assigned different names depending on who is doing the naming, when, and for what purpose. Names may originate in the very act of resisting naming, some may reflect an ironic response to a dominant power, whereas some have purely euphonious value. In some cases, genres with near-identical compositional structure may nevertheless be called different things depending on the social function for which the particular music has been coopted.

A corresponding multiplicity of meaning attaches to the tripartite grid traditional-popular-art/élite that many a commentator has invoked to distribute the reality of African arts. "Traditional," defined by its deep associations with the core institutions of precolonial society, has had to be reinvented in modern times in order to ensure its survival in the face of contemporary influences, erasures, and new creations. And so, without doubting the palpable presence of expressive forms that retain a strong connection with the precolonial past, one must also consider the accretions to this base, accretions whose morphological sameness makes them often indistinguishable from the models that they seek to emulate. The term "neotraditional" is sometimes used, not in the manner of disguised or invented traditions, but to symbolize a self-conscious renewal of tradition. Thus certain recreational dances use core elements from the tradition but incorporate foreign or outside influences as well. Urban Bareis and Kubik, for example, use the term "neotraditional" to characterize the popular Ewe dance Bɔbɔbɔ and the repertoire of the Kachamba brothers of Malawi, respectively.[10] In some cases, ostensibly traditional genres attain such a degree of popularity across ethnic boundaries that they are best thought of as irreducibly hybrid, "traditional-popular" forms.

At the other end of the pole lies art music, which seems easier to define because of its association with elite culture, its relatively few adherents, and its normative insistence on fully notated scores, including notations that evacuate their signifying function by handing improvisatory license over to the performer. Yet the folk operas claimed by art-music composers, in combining music with drama, occupy a place in the stylistic register that has none of the alienation of the more abstract symphony, concerto, or sonata. Similarly, the choral anthems beloved of church, school, and community choirs, although written down in tonic solfa or staff notation, are taught within the routines of an oral tradition associated with traditional music. Some anthems are well known, frequently heard, and may thus claim a degree of popularity. By contrast, the avant-garde experiments of our more daring composers have more of an audience outside Africa than within it.

If the terms "traditional" and "elite" are thus polysemic, "popular" is even more so. In a magisterial survey of the popular arts in Africa, including music, visual art, literature, and theater, as well as one-off genres involving portrait photography, coffins, and decorated beads, Karin Barber dwells at length on the strengths and especially limitations of the triadic scheme. While she finds some use for it as a tool for managing heterogeneity, she is also keenly aware of the fluid nature of its internal boundaries:

> Traditional, popular, and elite must not be taken as empirical classes of products; they represent expressive fields with their own centers of gravity, characteristic tendencies, pulls of influence, and modes of orientation. They are concentrations of certain styles of expression at different locations in the social map, rather than hard-and-fast categories. Treated in this manner the distinctions are valuable, indeed crucial, if we are to understand what is happening in African culture today and what the practitioners of the arts themselves conceive themselves to be doing.[11]

Nevertheless, heterogeneity is more marked in the middle term "popular" than in the other two. There is an excess here. "Popular," Barber says, is a "fugitive category," migrating up or down conceptually depending on the context. And so one way to define popular is negatively, in terms of what it is not, rather than what it is.

The difficulty with the negative approach is that it takes the other two categories with rather too much confidence. As indicated earlier, traditional and elite are not stable categories where popular is unstable. Barber is of course fully aware of this, although dwelling on the fluidity of the two outside categories would have taken her too far afield in an article devoted to the popular arts in Africa. She does, however, insist, following the Russian formalists, that analysis is most meaningful if it respects the peculiar materiality of each art form rather than consign all arts to a single broad category. And given music's paradoxical property of being at once totally adaptable or complicit, and at the same time resistant to cooptation, it will be necessary to read the triadic scheme with music's peculiar features in mind.

There have been a number of attempts to theorize African popular music. Writings by Waterman, Coplan, Erlmann, and others have yielded many valuable insights into the juncture between the social and the musical, the (non-)issues of race and identity, the economics of transmission, globalization, hybridity, syncreticism, the internal dynamics of performance, the significance of song words or poetry, and a host of other concerns. The breadth of issues may be said to mirror the breadth of the phenomenon itself. One thing that is clear from these writings is that theory works best when it is data-driven. And so, rather than summarize and critique competing theories of popular music, I embark on something far more modest, namely, to engage in some speculation about modes of signification in the popular genre, highlife. I have chosen highlife because, thanks mainly to the research of John Collins, its history is well established while its recorded products are readily available. The analyst can thus take the background for granted and proceed with the self-indulgent task of listening into the interior of highlife.[12]

Reading Highlife

Highlife is rooted in song, an amalgam of words and tune. While tunes follow diverse structural models and elicit their own associations, words, freighted with semantic content, offer the critic numerous pegs on which to hang an interpretation. So we might as well begin with the words that highlife musicians sing not because they are fundamental but because they facilitate interpretation.[13]

To the extent that Ghanaian highlife evinces a dominant language, it is Twi, the language of E. K. Nyame, Nana Ampadu, Koo Nimo, Amakye Dede, Kojo Antwi, and Dasebre Gyamena. Asante Twi is most common, but Fante is used, too. Kwaa Mensah, an early exponent of palm-wine guitar highlife, sang in Fante, like the more recent mainstream artist, A. B. Crentsil. Ga is not unheard of either. Bands like Uhuru and the Black Beats feature songs in Ga. One of E. T. Mensah's hits from the 1950s, "Yei Ngbewoh" ("The women are killing us") was sung in Ga. Significant, too, is the 1970s band Wulomei, which offered an imaginative blend of highlife with traditional singing in Ga. Ewe is heard only occasionally, notably in the music of Togolese migrant Agboti Yao. Varieties of English are used by various highlife bands, as in E. T. Mensah and the Tempo's "All for You" or "School Girl." I refer to "varieties" in order to include pidgin or broken English as well as the many subtle ways in which sung English is inflected by the intonational contours of Twi, Ga, Hausa, Dagbani, Nzema, Anlo-Ewe, and so on. Such inflections, hard to describe in words but immediately recognizable by insiders, are an essential conduit of ethnic, class, and gendered meanings.

One consequence of the existence of a range of language options for highlife singers is the practice of polyglottism, the mixing of languages within a given text or utterance. Contemporary highlife star Dasebre Gyamena uses such mixture to great effect in songs like "Kɔ yɛ me ho adeɛ" and "Kɔkɔɔkɔ." In the former, a woman says to her lover in Twi that he should go and ask for her hand properly, in the traditional way—introduce himself to her family and offer the required libations. Otherwise, she continues, "You can't touch me." Crossing over into English to deliver this prohibition gives it added significance: a strategic invocation of tradition by a (presumably) educated woman. In another song, "Kɔkɔɔkɔ," the title of which is an onomatopoeic reproduction of the sound of knocking at someone's door, a lover says in Twi that he is standing behind his lover's door knocking "Kɔkɔɔkɔ," wanting to be invited in; he then intersperses in English the self-explanatory phrase "I can never live without you." (I believe that Gyamena means "live" rather than "leave," but his difficulty with the short /i/ in English brings another semantic vista into view.) Later, the singer supplements the English content with the phrase, "O dear, darling, I can never live without you." ("Darling," too, is rendered with a longish /i/ approaching /ee/.) There is, on one level, a seamless continuity in this use of English and Twi, because the two languages are conjoined, entered, and left without preparation, without self-consciousness, as if one were speaking just one language. On another level, however, the languages signify differently: Twi signifies the inside, the oral, the local, and the natural; English suggests the outside, the written, the foreign, the acquired. And when you factor in Dasebre Gyamena's intonation in the delivery of English, you're made aware of additional connotations.

What, then, is the significance of language for highlife? Singing in one's language is an invitation into an intimate space, home, the ancestral home, perhaps, a place unspoiled by linguistic boundaries or barriers. For people whose sonic environments are constantly being bombarded by various foreign musics and tongues, entry into this space brings much inner solace and assurance. In practice, however, home is a contested space, summoning varying degrees of commitment. For many postcolonial subjects, home is linguistically constituted as a set of fragments; home is the sum of (necessarily) partial competence in indigenous and colonial languages. Language thus occupies different functional and stylistic registers and elicits affiliation at fluctuating levels of intensity. The languages of highlife mirror this range of expression, making highlife an important milieu for understanding how we think and form our identities.

How crucial is it to understand what singers say? To the extent that enunciated words supply the listener with a set of images to aid the listening process, their meanings may be said to be important. And the fact that a key word or catchphrase or choral refrain is presentationally marked ensures that competent listeners will profit from its semantic residue. Yet, even when highlife is sung in languages that one understands, the words are not necessarily heard, recognized, or understood. Under pressure from melodic forces or performance imperatives, words may be articulated indistinctly or unfolded rapidly; idiomatic expressions may be culled from archaic or obscure sources. And so we hear but do not necessarily understand. Or we understand but only at a first level. While there are exceptions to this rule, it is possible to enter a generalization here: partial rather than full comprehension seems to be the intended mode of reception for song words. We hear but faintly, as if overhearing, as if trapped in the traffic of numerous conversations unfolding simultaneously. It is true, in any case, that meanings are normally never fully present to us. But there is a difference between intended and unintended partiality and the ambiguities that flow therefrom. Word meanings are never irrelevant to the aesthetics of popular song; it is the degree of relevance that remains variable.

Beneath the sonic exterior of highlife lies a world of great imagination and poetic depth. Highlife provides an insight into the imagined realities of modern living while also exemplifying with unparalleled lucidity African modes of play (joking, making fun of, jesting, entertaining, teasing, amusing, acting, dallying). No subject is taboo for the highlife singer as long as he observes the appropriate conventions of speaking. Topics can be sacred or secular. Songs may deal with witches and nightlife, accidents, death, religion, birth, and one's relatives. Poverty is a favorite, as are envy, jealousy, and retaliation. The relationship between men and women occupies an important place, but very rarely is it presented in exclusive, narcissistic terms. In highlife, love is expressed within a broader network of social relations. Few lovers can afford a mode of aloneness.

The expression in highlife can be direct and straightforward, or, more usually, indirect, allusive, or enigmatic. Because metaphor and indirect speech are favored in traditional society, highlife in part reproduces these modes of speaking while also making possible the cultivation of related communicative skills. How an elder talks to a young person, an *okyeame* ("linguist") speaks for the chief, house boys speak to their masters, peers express their membership of social groups, women lament loss, deception is unveiled—these and dozens more ways of world-making make highlife an important reservoir of rhetoric, philosophy, and pedagogy.

There is plenty of humor in highlife, but some of it is accessible only to cultural insiders. Humor may be dry and self-deprecating or it may be outwardly directed to underscore the ironies of modern (urban) living. Highlife, finally, is the repository of an emergent morality made up in part by the peculiar alchemy of New Testament, heaven- and hell-oriented Christianity and a more complex ethos based in communal, small-society living. Thus attempts to correct wayward or antisocial behavior, to lament loss or tragedy, or to remind us of the punishment that awaits evil doing are regularly enacted in highlife songs.

Rehearsing some of these themes should not lead to the supposition that highlife is about this or that. Highlife composers explore the interstices separating the real from the imagined. What they say may or may not have happened, may or may not refer to actual people, may or may not be historically accurate. Highlife text-making begins as an exercise of the imagination and goes on from there. This should make us wary of some of the things that have been claimed for highlife, including its predictive power. E. K. Nyame's song "Nsu bet a nframa di kan," ("before it rains, the wind blows,") has been credited with more power than it should. The idea that some actions follow others is obvious enough, but to politicians in office, the performance of this truism may acquire an uncanny sense, including the forecast that incompetence may lead imminently to a downfall. The expression is so general, so adaptable to many circumstances, that it may be invoked opportunistically and retrospectively—which is why some eager commentators once credited highlife musicians with predicting the fall of Nkrumah's government in 1966. One should never deprive such self-styled social commentators of opportunities to envision societal change. But because song predictions as a rule have never been subject to any kind of empirical test—no one has tallied the many predictions that did not come to pass—it would be more accurate to say that "Nsu bet a mframa di kan" took on particular significance in retrospect for certain people who sought such realist value for art. Popular song's fluid ontology makes possible its cooptation for social work.

Language, words, and themes: we have only scratched the surface of an endlessly fascinating subject. But there is a danger of overvaluing sung words. Words in song have a precarious existence. While this widespread phenomenon tends to be resisted by people who use words as an interpretive crutch, the tendency of music to "colonize," swallow up, or assimilate words is not easily dismissed. Reviewing Don Harrán's *In Defense of Music: The Case of Music as Argued by a Singer and Scholar of the Late Fifteenth Century* in 1990, Daniel Leech-Wilkinson cuts to the heart of the matter:

> Argument over the relative importance of music and text in song is as everlasting as it is pointless. From Plato through Renaissance Humanism, the Reformation, the birth of opera, through Gluck and Wagner, musicians have argued with themselves and with authors about the duty of music to mirror the stresses and quantities of spoken text. Music history, as a result, has woven a drunken path back and forth between enforced recitation and more natural melodic exuberance as writers and musicians have exchanged the upper hand. The endlessly repeating arguments, which will continue as long as there remain articulate people unresponsive to music, are so much wasted energy; for music always wins. As was well understood in the Middle Ages, music dominates whatever it accompanies, imposing its shape and character in a process which appears to be psychologically unavoidable. However it may be restrained by diktat, therefore, there follows inevitably a drift back to-

wards a style in which musical rules determine musical details: the two cannot be separated in a satisfying way. But attitudes are governed by ideology, not art.[14]

There are doubtless many exceptions to this rule, but in writings by Schoenberg, Nietzsche, Dahlhaus, and numerous others, the asymmetry of the relationship between words and music in European (mainly German) art song is demonstrated repeatedly.[15] Similarly—to mention a different tradition of music—in the analysis of Euro-American pop, Simon Frith has raised doubts about the importance of words to the reception of sung song.[16]

To reduce the significance of highlife words to their articulatory value—and this is especially important in non-Islamic African styles, where word setting is, as a general rule, syllabic, with only an occasional brief melisma—may seem perverse, an eager musician's attempt to restore some of music's autonomy or self-sufficiency. Were we to be in possession of hard data from reception history about what aspects of highlife are responsible for listeners' most intense responses, we might be in a better position to judge the influence of words. Lacking such data, however, we fall back on introspection and anecdotal evidence. While it appears that recalling a heard highlife song is often facilitated by some reference to its words, the nature and depth of experiences associated with such hearing may not have much to do with semantic meanings. Let us turn, then, to some of these musical elements.

The Compositional Structure of Highlife

The pleasure in highlife derives from the confluence of a danceable beat, fresh, inviting melody, unobtrusive harmony, modest, playful improvisation, and an overarching musicoverbal "message." The beat is expressed as quadruple (never triple) and is enlivened in the foreground by distinct rhythmic *topoi*, the commonest of which is the familiar offbeat pattern said to derive from the Akan dance Sikyi (Example 6-1).[17] The beat is

Example 6-1 Four cycles of highlife *topos*

danceable in the sense that it shares with other beats an irresistible invitation to dance, to move the body in response to a rhythmic pattern. Listeners respond differently to this invitation. In a dance hall, disco, or student assembly hall, boys and girls, men and women may dance overtly. In taxis or beer bars or at home, the dance may be realized silently and imaginatively without any loss of aesthetic pleasure. Sometimes both modes of response are operative.

There has obviously been an evolution in listener-response to highlife. In the beginning (1920s), highlife, as performed by a dance orchestra like the Excelsior, was live music played to live audiences. With the burgeoning of recording technology in the 1950s–1960s, however, highlife has gradually become a listener's repertoire. The so-called palm-wine guitar styles played by Kwaa Mensah and later Koo Nimo boast an intimacy that indexes mind before body. Today, imaginative dance has overtaken externalized dance.

Certain structural features of the highlife *topos* make it especially suited to the dance (Example 6-1). By articulating the off-beats only of beats 2, 3, and 4 in a 4/4 meter, the *topos* maximizes the energy in the margins and enshrines a potential for movement. As explained in chapter 4, listeners know where the main beats are and so coordinate foot movement with these unsounded parts of the *topos*. The dancer thus becomes an active interpreter, contributing to the implementation of the pattern. Of course, in the case of dance-band highlife, the unsounded parts of the *topos* may be sounded by other instruments or voice; the background is thus activated. Whether the background is assumed or externalized, it remains an indispensable dimension of the music.

Highlife melody takes different forms. At its most basic, it borrows the outline of a popular melody or hymn tune. This could be a complete tune with a clearly defined beginning, middle, and ending, or it could be a series of fragments of which one, sung as the response in a call-response mode, is projected in such a way that it imposes itself as the most memorable. These largely diatonic melodies serve as subjects for improvisation. Highlife's studied elegance speaks to an aesthetic of restraint; as such, it demands modesty in improvisation. American listeners accustomed to the improvisational manners of Louis Armstrong, Charlie Parker, Dizzy Gillespie, or Ornette Coleman may find highlife relatively tame. And this is because— brief, contrasting moments aside—virtuosity as such is alien to the spirit of the genre.

The best highlife tunes are those that manage to be economical rather than elaborate, concise and well-shaped rather than ornate and complex. This aesthetic bias does not necessarily hold for other African popular music forms. In Mali or Senegal, for example, the Islamic-influenced vocal styles of

Youssou Ndour or Salif Keita feature broad, descending melodic sweeps in which the voice as voice is an indispensable part of the aesthetic conception. Highlife singers are in this sense impersonators rather than actors.

Highlife melodies are not essentially text-bound; rather, they take their shape from certain melodic archetypes that are diatonic at the core and typically expressed as descending contours. Not unlike melody in neotraditional or recreational music, highlife melody is in a perpetual state of tension, seeking to balance the pull of an intonational, language-based pattern against that of an invariant, harmonically driven, precompositionally determined one. Part of the pleasure in listening to highlife comes from an awareness of this layering of not-quite-different melodies. One is reminded of the indistinct unisons (*unscharfe Unisono*) that Adorno heard in Mahler,[18] and that are magnificently illustrated in duets featuring one-stringed fiddle (goje) and voice.[19] The indistinctness in highlife melody is a cumulative profile based on singers "speaking" in different registers and intonations.

The repeated chord schemes on which popular music is based impart a cyclical, nondevelopmental quality to highlife. Highlife's tonal types juggle the pressures of a closed I-V-I progression with various open modal structures. What some listeners hear as a less than complete control of tonal cadencing is in fact a more complex outcome of the attempt to balance indigenous melodic and multipart tendencies against the goal-oriented, cadence-based harmony of Bach or Beethoven. Thus the singing in parallel thirds that one often hears in highlife may seem to derive directly from traditional Akan singing; yet, while traditional singers can use contrapuntal procedures like voice crossing to maintain the integrity of the texture of thirds, a I-V-I progression cannot be expressed in idiomatic voice leading without interrupting the succession of thirds. From a harmonic point of view, then, highlife maintains conflicting procedures at its most fundamental level.

One does not normally credit highlife music with subtle form. Rather, the extensive use of repetition confers a circular sense, a feeling of going over the same ground. This underlying strophic impulse is subject to different levels of projection and composing out. In some big-band highlife, songs are framed by tutti sections, whereas the middle portions feature several sung verses broken by one or two instrumental improvisations. There is an order and stylization to this way of doing things that suggests standardization. But there are other approaches to form. Through-composed forms arise from following the shape of the verbal text. Additive form may also result from such prioritization. In any case, the idea of return is never sacrificed to any other principle, not even in songs that end with a volume fade-out.

Form in African music is not often singled out for praise. Rhythm, dance, timbre, some multipart techniques, and certain melodic gestures are by common agreement the most distinctive aspects of African music. Yet, as work such as Willie Anku's on *Adowa* or Kongo Zabana's on form in African music has shown, long-term thinking and planning are not the exclusive preserve of metropolitan musicians.[20] In *Adowa*, the master drummer has at his disposal a set of themes that he orders in a particular way. Themes have different lengths and relate differently to the bell pattern. The master drummer, working within a modulus of 12, deploys sets, subsets, and supersets in full awareness of their temporal extent. What appears to the lay listener as an improvised succession of complex rhythmic patterns is in fact rigorously ordered. The resultant form is not predictable from the beginning, nor do we doubt its intuitive rightness at the close of the composition.

Nor is such thinking confined to traditional music. E. T. Mensah's "You call me Roko," for example, provides a tiny example of long-term melodic thinking that suggests that we may profit from exploring larger trajectories of musical thought. If you pay attention to verse endings, you will notice that while each one closes, the sense of an ending is not definitive. There is always more to come. Thus the introduction ends with the succession of scale degrees 5-5-5-4-3 (equivalent to the five syllables "You call me Roko"). The three verses sung by the singer end with 5-5-6-4-3, 5-5-5-4-3, and 3-4-4-2-1. Descent to 1 is thus reserved for the singer's parting shot; indeed, this is the only time in the song that the voice goes below 3, taking up the lower octave in the manner of an emptying out, a reaching for home, rest, and finality. The vocal ending is thus a long-delayed attainment of full closure, several times postponed. Although not especially dramatic, this example suggests that there may well be more to the longer-term intuitions of African musicians than has been granted by those who refuse to discipline African popular music in transcription in order to observe its inner workings.

The example of "You Call Me Roko" reminds us that only by analyzing specific compositions (or portions thereof) will we be in a position to make valid generalizations. While it is beyond the scope of this chapter to offer detailed, technical analyses, a few comments about three highlife songs may be in order.

E. T. Mensah's "205"

The capitalist machine continues to produce guides to cultural products. One of these, a CD dubbed *West African Music: The Rough Guide*, offers the following:

Few areas of the world can match the range of rhythms, melodies and musical textures of West Africa. From Senegal's dramatic mbalax to the lilting highlife guitar sounds of Ghana, from the soaring Manding music of Mali to the pounding percussion of Nigerian fuji and juju, the region steams with good sounds. Especially compiled by the World Music Network to accompany the Rough Guide To West Africa travel Guide, this mid-price compilation features many of the top artists from the region; Ali Farka Toure, E. T. Mensah, Toumani Diabate, Dimi Mint Abba, Sona Diabate, Oumou Sangare, Mansour Seck, Super Rail Band, Bajourou, Kante Manfila, Moussa Poussy and Orchestra Baoba. Essential![21]

Copyright constraints must have discouraged a more representative collection, for despite what the blurb announces, five of the twelve tracks are of music from Mali. Guinea and Senegal have two each, while Niger, Ghana, and Mauritania each have one. Nigeria is not included, nor are Sierra Leone, Cameroon, Togo, Benin, Burkina Faso, or The Gambia. Of course a truly representative guide is nearly impossible, so the issue here is not what was included or excluded. The interest for us lies simply in the inclusion of a single item from Ghana, E. T. Mensah's song "205." Whatever reservations one might have about the genre of Rough Guides, "205" is as good a guide to highlife as any other.

"205" unfolds in 7 sections. First is an introduction featuring the full band. Then follow six "verses': lines 1–4; lines 5–8; an instrumental rendition; lines 9–12; lines 13–16 (part sung [lines 13–15] and part played [line 16]; and a closing fade-out section, lines 17–20.

1 Ahɔɔfɛ bɛn na ɛba yi a?
   Who is that beauty approaching?

2 Na mo se yɛ frɛ no sɛn ni ee?
   And you say what is her name?

3 Na mose ɔfiri he?
   And so you say where does she come from?

4 Ayee, na ɛno na mo ka no sɛ yi e, Koforidua ababaawa oo,
   Ayee, is that what you are saying? A young lady from Koforidua

5 Ahɔɔfɛ bɛn na ɛba yi a?
   Who is that beauty approaching?

6 Abena Serwah ana?
   Is this Abena Serwah?

7 Ekua Bafo ana?
Is it Ekua Bafo?

8 Ayee, na ɛno na mo ka no sɛ yi e, Koforidua ababaawa oo,
Koforidua flowers ni o
Ayee, is that what you are saying? A young lady from
Koforidua, this is Koforidua flowers

Instrumental interlude

9 Ahoɔfɛ bɛn na ɛba yi a?
Who is this beauty approaching?

10 Abena Serwah anaa ah?
Is this Abena Serwah?

11 Ah, ɔkita neɛma paa
She has got a lot of things (i.e., she is well endowed)

12 Ayee, na eno na mo ka no sɛ yi e, Apedwa Yaa Amponsa nana
nono, Ayenkwa ɔnom Birem o
Ayee, is that what you are saying? Grandchild of Apedwa Yaa
Amponsa, who drinks from the river Birem

13 Ahoɔfɛ bɛn na ɛba yi a?
Who is this beauty approaching?

14 Owusu neɛma paa
She shakes a lot of things

15 Wo hu no a, wo bɛ fa no hye paa, Hye hye hye, Hye a yɛfrɛ no
hye, Wo bɛ fa paa, Ah ɔkita o,
You will be mesmerized by her presence, mesmerized,
mesmerized, mesmerized, you will like her a lot, Ah, she's got it

16 Instrumental completion

17 Ahoɔfɛ ben na ɛba yi a?
Who is that beauty approaching?

18 Ah, wo tua koraa a, won te koraa
Ah, even when you pay, you won't feel it

19 Biribiara a ɔbɛ ka biara, wo de bɛ ma no
Whatever she asks for, you'll give it to her

20 Okura, okura neɛma paa, neɛma nyinaa okura bi
She's got it, she's got a lot of things, she's got everything

Men, probably in a drinking bar, watch a woman walk by. Who is she? Where does she come from? What is her name? Is it Abena Serwah? Is it Ekua Bafo? She must be from the town of Koforidua. From the fourth verse on, her physical attributes are mentioned. She is said to have a lot of "things." That is another way of saying that she is well endowed: presumably with breasts and buttocks. And we know this because she is shaking them well. You will be so taken with her, so mesmerized by her presence, that you won't feel it when you pay. In fact, she has everything.

From one point of view, this text has all the ingredients of politically incorrect language: the lecherous gaze of men on a woman, their fantasies about sleeping with her, the presumption that money might buy some services. She is here reduced to a body, a body with sizable protrusions in back and front. And the men seem to be having fun. Political incorrectness, however, must be understood contextually. In 1950s urban West Africa, male-dominated highlife bands thematized whatever had the potential to amuse, titillate, or entertain an urban audience. And the objectification of women was one such theme.

The form and content of "205" suggest another, quite different interpretation, however. The Akan genre *mpre* features a listing of attributes of a Chosen one. "205" may well be modeled on *mpre*. She is a beauty, she comes from Koforidua. She is physically attractive. Her grandmother is Apedwa Yaa Amponsa, who herself drank from the river Birem. By naming her, the speaker ensures that she is valued fully as a member of the culture; she is not merely an object of desire. The act of naming is solemn, not trivial; it carries responsibility. There are, indeed, other Akan genres that feature similar acts of naming in the course of praising. An example that can be readily consulted by North American readers is the fourth track on *Rhythms of Life, Songs of Wisdom: Akan Music from Ghana, West Africa,* recorded by Roger Vetter, which includes a drum text played and spoken.[22] The text is in three sections. First is an introductory greeting to those present, then comes drum language glorifying the king of Denkyira (this is the longest and main section of the text), and third is a section of poetry honoring the river Tano. The language in which the king is glorified makes evident the affinities with "205": he is the devourer of the elephant; he is grandson of parrot whose winds sweep and devour even the stones; he is quicksand. It is he who flies and the skies become still like the cemetery. He is Amponsem's grandson, the first grandson of the Agona line. He always fulfills his promise. And so on.

Of course, the king of Denkyira has a different status from our beauty from Koforidua, and this is reflected in the way they are constructed. The king's mighty deeds are recounted, his historical standing reinforced; the girl from Koforidua's lineage is established, too, alongside the "things" she has that appeal to men. E. T. Mensah's "205" may thus be understood in terms of the competing interests between tradition and modernity, between a "traditional" mode of praise appellation and a casual topic of conversation common among drinking partners in an urban setting. This subtle interface between rhetorical modes provides a tiny example of the sort of "complexity" sometimes denied popular music.

There is, however, a carelessness in the way that the words are sometimes delivered, and this suggests that verbal communication may not hold the highest priority for the performer of this highlife song. In lines 4, 8, and 12, delivery of words is rushed rather than disguised. It is as if melody is calling the shots here, not words. But these rushed moments are the places in which the attributes of our beauty are enumerated. The singer rushes to dispense the words without any concern for elegance. And although there is plenty of melody in "205," the sung portions are not its best exemplar, because they seem more routine than poetic. It is the failure to capitalize on the musically "routine" to deliver a memorable verbal message that is significant.

A few musical details may be worth close observation. As shown in Example 6-2, "205" begins with a four-bar bass guitar introduction, itself divisible into two-bar phrases mapping a move from tonic to dominant and back. Then the trumpets enter with a catchy tune, essentially an elaboration of a simple perfect cadence. (Example 6-3 hypothesizes a model and two successive variants, the second of which brings us right to the surface of "205.") This two-bar cadence figure, which concludes melodically with a little fanfare in the trumpet (bar 8), is repeated twice more (bars 7–8 and 9–10). In bar 11, the melody reaches for its highest note (F) and begins a gradual descent spanning six bars (bars 11–16). The fanfare figure in bar 16 is an echo as well as a prefix to the repetition of the cadence figure. The voice enters for the first time in bar 18, where our sketch breaks off.

The musicality and memorability of the refrain are conveyed by longer notes and by stepwise descent. And these four bars (11–14), when heard in the context of the succeeding two, suggest a continuity in underlying structure, as shown in Example 6-4. Thus bars 15–16 supply the 4-3-2-1 portion of a larger 8-7-6-5-4-3-2-1 descent in the form 4-2-3-1. (Notice that the 3-2 order is reversed.) Many African melodies, both traditional and modern, rely on descents like this. An occasional gap may be introduced and the interval span may be less than an octave. Something like this deep, diatonic song may well lie in the memories of singers and their listeners. It holds their attention and stimulates their fantasy by promising something beyond, something ultimately unattainable. In the particular case of "205," the relatively disjunct melodic contour in bars 5–10 suggests a speech

Example 6-2 E. T. Mensah's "205," introduction. bars 1–18 (bass and treble only)

Example 6-3 Generating bars 5–6 of "205"

Example 6-4 Stepwise descent in bars 11–16 of "205"

mode of articulation. In bar 11, song mode takes over and interprets the earlier "speech" as "song."

One feature that conveys the complexity of tonal thinking in highlife is the relationship between treble and bass. Our bass guitarist begins with a Dagomba-style walking bass based on a tonic-dominant succession (including their functional as well as phenomenal equivalents). Between bars 5 and 6, the progression, predominant-dominant-tonic, is articulated a little more complexly: there is "internal" movement within the predominant chord (B-flat down to G) while the dominant note is represented by 7. In bars 7 and 8, the dominant note is restored on beat 3, followed by another chord tone, but now the result is a bass that is nearly identical to its partner melody (see Example 6-5). This is a species of parallelism akin to heterophony, whereby the bass player literally reproduces, in rhythmic alteration, the notes of the trumpet melody.

The elaboration of a few details in "205" should not take attention away from the coherence of the song's overall narrative. An introduction (Example 6-2) sets the pace, creates a lively atmosphere, invites us on to the dance floor, and familiarizes us with the song's musical essence. Verse 1 uses this music to announce the subject of the song, verse 2 restates it, and verse 3, a purely instrumental rendition, allows us not only to contemplate what has just been said but also to forecast an outcome. Verse 4 reinforces the cumulative message of verses 1, 2, and 3 and then begins to flesh out our beauty's attributes. Verse 5 highlights these attributes, but at the refrain phrase, instruments, not voices, complete the utterance. And verse 6 rapidly multi-

Example 6-5 Parallel movement between treble and bass in bars 9–10 of "205"

plies the list of traits even as the singer faces certain death: The story must end, closure is unavoidable, and so a mindless listing of the woman's physical features will not help. The singer is in fact cut off by the literal turning down of the volume dial.

Although I have referred to the song's narrative, there is a sense in which this narrative does not progress from one point to another linearly, but goes over the same ground in circular fashion. This is evident in the trumpet commentaries that support but also compete with the singer. These delightfully spontaneous commentaries lie at the heart of trumpeter E. T. Mensah's art, and they exemplify both the parasitic and communal nature of dance band highlife. E. T. first comments around line 2 with a laid back, deceptively casual phrase. Another comment is made around line 5, this time beginning on a marked high C, and signifying distance as well as something otherworldly. At line 9, E. T. comments again, but where before the mode of enunciation had been songlike, it is now speechlike, in patter mode. The commentary around line 13 makes use of a turn figure, an embellishment. Finally, commentary around line 16 is no longer E. T.'s affair only, but involves other supporting "voices." The harmony is richer and homophonic, serving to underline the sense of an ending. These charming, behind-the-scenes commentaries lack any sort of urgent profile. No one is in a hurry here; on the contrary, this highlife song sports a feeling of self-satisfaction.

E. T. Mensah's "You Call Me Roko"

Although "You Call Me Roko" (track 4 on *African Music: The Glory Years*, OMCDO11) is akin to "205" in spirit, its structure is more rigid and perhaps more formulaic. (Example 6-6 transcribes the main melodic material.) There are a total of eight verses. The first is the purely instrumental, full-band rendition of the song at the beginning (labelled 1 in the example and shown with its accompanying bass line). This sets one half of the song's frame, establishes the 12-bar period as reference point, and acquaints listeners and performers with the music that will regulate subsequent utterance. (The other half, labelled 8, will come at the end; notice that 8 is virtually identical to 1, the only difference being its modified ending.)

Verse 2, a sung version of verse 1, is in (standard) English:

My dear, you call me Roko
My dear, you call me Roko
In the daytime you call me Roko
In the nighttime you call me sweetheart
In the daytime you call me Roko
In the nighttime you call me sweetheart.

Example 6-6

This is all we need to infer the overarching verbal message. Our protagonist is a male of humble origins—a laborer, porter, or messenger. He is addressing his lover. When she sees him during the day, she joins others in using the conventional and derogatory designation, "Roko." "Roko" categorizes without naming, assigns an identity that is not. In the privacy of their bed at night, however, she's glad of his labors; she now calls him "sweetheart." The text's enabling binary oppositions are not hidden: lower versus upper class, public versus private naming codes, diurnal versus nocturnal interchange, and, of course, male versus female.

Example 6-6 (continued)

Verse 3 maintains the message of Verse 2 but substitutes "Alaru" for "Roko." "Alaru" is another popular designation for a day laborer and so intensifies the sentiment expressed previously. Verses 4, 5, and 6 (not shown in Example 6-6) feature improvised solos on the 12-bar tune. Trumpet, then alto saxophone, and finally tenor saxophone probe gently the secrets of the theme. As paraphrases of previously sung melody, these solos retain the core message of the song—whatever it is—but allow thoughtful listeners time and space to reflect on the ironies of the apparent mismatch. Is "You Call Me Roko" a lament by our lover, a complaint that he is not being given proper recognition? Or could there be a hidden message, a criticism of an upper-class woman who is forced to descend the social ladder in order to find love?

After the three improvised solos, the voice returns to finish off its business (verse 7). As explained earlier, this verse brings the sung portions to a resounding close with a strong 3-2-1 progression in the lower register marking what Schenker called "the definitive close of the composition."[23] In this verse, too, there is a substitution: The word "Kaya," another name for laborer, specifically a species of porter popular in market places, occurs in place of "Roko" (verse 1) and "Alaru" (verse 2). We now have three complementary images of our protagonist, and all three locate him among the working classes. Finally, the other half of the song's frame follows as verse 8. The symmetrical equivalent of verse 1, its rhetorical presentation is enhanced by a persistent bell/rattle sound that marks it differently and retroactively as a sign of closure.

"Cool" would not be an inappropriate word for "You Call Me Roko." E. T.'s band creates a distinctly relaxed ambience; and the verbal message, which in other highlife songs can inflect the temporal feel, is marked by a studied reticence; a rush to inform is simply not part of the song's burden. There is a sense that we are here to play, but the peculiar play of highlife music is not that of a game, not a win-or-lose situation. The song expresses the redundancy of a noncompetitive game, a casual exploration of our surroundings as a way of passing time. This refusal to act is implicit in the paradigmatic representation of the song's melodic content in Example 6-6. Here we see/hear the sung melody first as unsung song, then sung twice, then paraphrased three times by different instruments, before being concluded first by the singer and then, as if in echo, by the band. (The fact, by the way, that the chronological ending renders the "You call me Roko" phrase 5-5-5-5-5 indicates some ambivalence perhaps, some unfinished business.)

This analysis has been biased toward the compositional structure rather than toward a specific performance. Indeed, apart from the bandleader and trumpeter, we have reduced other performers to generic classes; we have referred to the singer, not to Kwadwo from Sunyani or Nii from Bukom; we have mentioned a saxophone solo but have not identified the saxophonist as a flesh and blood individual. And yet, in contemporary popular music criticism, such anonymity is no longer encouraged; rather, we are encouraged to restore agency, to name the specific historical/cultural actors involved in the little drama that we know as "You Call Me Roko."

Might there be a good reason to deny agency, however provisionally, in the analysis of highlife? I would argue that there is. In order to counter some of the prejudice against popular music, we need to present its compositional structure *strategically* as a viable structure independent of specific performances or performers. No one would claim that the impact of "You Call Me Roko" is fully accounted for by merely observing that the highlife time line is heard throughout, the melody is delivered in short fragments, the harmonic rhythm increases in the approach to cadences, or the definitive close occurs at the end of verse 7. At the same time, it would be perverse to deny that such structural elements play an important role in establishing the identity of the song. Listeners unable to verbalize their responses in technical language are not necessarily innocent of the work of structural techniques. So if our aim as devotees of popular music is to value it by ranging over its vast structural and expressive resources, then there can in principle be no inappropriate mode of analysis.

Uhuru's "Eyaa Duom"

If E. T. Mensah's "205" and "You Call Me Roko" represent the classic phase of highlife, Uhuru's "Eyaa Duom" (track 13 on *African Music: The Glory Years*, OMCD011) marks one of its experimental tributaries. This remarkable song is highlife in the sense that its main section features the highlife time line followed by an alternation among full tutti, instrumental solos, and singing. But "Eyaa Duom" neither begins nor ends as highlife. It begins in fact with the sound of thunder and rain, a kind of African *musique concrète*, allowing the singer to sing words heavy with prophesy:

Nsuo betɔ a
Before it rains

ɔdi nframa di kan
Wind precedes it

ɔno a ɔyɛ adeɛ yie
The one that makes everything right

Duom na mereba e
Take the lead, I am coming

To these the chorus responds:

Iyaa duom o
Take the lead

Ee barima duom
Ee, gentleman take the lead

Ee ɛyaa duom
Ee, take the lead

Osabarima duomo
The great warrior, take the lead

Owuo si aso o
Death deafens the ear.

All of this singing is in a declamatory or free style, not a dance or strict style, and is reminiscent of the declamatory portions of traditional dances, whose nominal function is to provide food for thought for performers. If there is any doubt that highlife incorporates an invitation to contemplative behavior, the beginning of "Eyaa duom" should settle the question.

Declamation is followed by a time line played on a bell, and insiders immediately recognize this as the elegant Akan dance *Adowa*. *Adowa* is associated with funerals nowadays, and although there is no one-to-one correspondence between the structure of funeral music and its social function, the dissolving function of death and mourning makes any and all music appropriate for a funeral. And this hermeneutic license allows us to merge funereal symbolism with the prophetic nature of the declamatory text.

The move from free to strict rhythm at the beginning of "Eyaa Duom" is balanced by a retention of melodic material across those two segments of the song. Declamation is thus turned into dance. Up to this point, we have been hearing not highlife but *Adowa* played by a highlife band. *Adowa* is thus defamiliarized, made to bear the weight of a modern setting. The resulting tension is part of the aesthetic conception. Tradition exists within modernity.

Perhaps the aesthetic disjunction achieved by placing *Adowa* in highlife's (orchestral) dress will have led some listeners to expect a proper emergence of highlife later in the song. And this is precisely what happens next. In a remarkable metric-tempo modulation, the time line of *Adowa* is replaced by the off-beat time line of highlife. The sung element retains its *Adowa* lineage so that this new *Adowa*-highlife eschews the predictable, hymnlike harmonies of, say, "You Call Me Roko," and substitutes a more intricate pattern in which the bass line is forced to incorporate melodic function as well. The highlife portion of this song will predominate, as we soon find out, for not only was the *Adowa* gesture curtailed but also the highlife gesture is expressed more generously through characteristic improvised solos. The predominance of highlife is a matter not of proportion but rather of generic weight. So, when the highlife portion is complete, and the *Adowa* material returns in its original form, complete with responsorial declamation and time line, we are fully prepared for the beginning of the end. Rain and thunder replay the realist melodrama of "Eyaa Duom"'s opening, and the last word is left to a talking drum, muttering something in speech and signal modes.

The ontology of "Eyaa Duom" supports the view that the expressive field of highlife is wide enough to accommodate diverse traditional influences. Indeed, one only has to cast a brief eye on the history of highlife to recognize a very wide variety of styles, some more folk in orientation, some more traditional, some more indebted to American swing bands, and some strikingly original in their refusal to be like anything else. In "Eyaa Duom," *Adowa* is not assimilated as such but is swallowed whole; *Adowa,* in other words, is not absorbed, for to absorb it would be to probe its compositional structure, select some of its features while discarding others, and then incorporate them into a new musical form thereby wiping out (part of) its ancestry. Yet, a listener who has just heard "Eyaa duom" cannot easily "unremember" *Adowa* because not only is it prominent as the song's framing music but also its inauthenticity lingers in the memory long after the last sounds have faded.

Perhaps, then, the enduring message of "Eyaa Duom," the prophecy that before it rains the wind blows, is salient because it is projected within an unorthodox form. But the unorthodoxy of "Eyaa Duom" is confined to the 1960s and 1970s. In more recent times, hyphenated forms have proliferated. Thus sikyi-highlife, gospel-highlife, reggae-highlife, cultural highlife, Dagomba-highlife, and even hip-life all testify to highlife's unyielding compatibility. Part of this compatibility rests in the simple quadruple or duple beat, which can be readily adapted as the creative mind desires. Highlife's fertility is likely to endure for some time to come.

The Significance of African Popular Music

These observations about structure and meaning in three highlife songs may help stimulate interest in those particular songs or in the analysis of other highlife compositions. I will argue more fully for analysis in chapter 8. In closing this chapter, however, I want to return the discussion to a broader level and comment on three characteristics of West African popular music: its use of repetition, allusive quality, and contemplative capacity.

The key musical procedure in popular music, as in much other African music, and indeed in much of the world's music, lies in repetition and attendant processes of variation. Repetition enables and stabilizes; it facilitates adventure while guaranteeing, not the outcome as such, but the meaningfulness of adventure. If repetition of a harmonic progression seventy-five times can keep listeners and dancers interested, then there is a power to repetition that suggests not mindlessness or a false sense of security (as some critics have proposed) but a fascination with grounded musical adventures. Repetition, in short, is the lifeblood of music.[24]

Variation, a form of repetition, offers a glimpse into the psychology of composition and performance. When E. T. Mensah plays a phrase and varies it the second time round, he does exactly what a fortepianist like Malcolm Bilson does when he embellishes the repeat of a sonata exposition. Both artists challenge listeners' memory while effectively soliciting their attention with the promise that the text will be altered with each repetition. As simple as this device is, it remains extremely effective. Although the degree of variation differs from genre to genre and according to the skills of the interpreter, the idea of freshly constituting a musical text can have a spellbinding effect on some listeners. If this example is valid, if different world repertoires can be meaningfully compared from the point of view of their investment in the repetition principle, then we might be wary of separating popular music from other music. Differences may be more meaningful not in the assignment of broad generic categories but in distinguishing one performance from another, even within the same stylistic category.

A second feature of popular music is its intensely allusive quality. Anyone seeking support for the frequent claim that African musical traditions are unusually diverse will find it in the promiscuity of African popular music. European harmony, melodic style, periodic organization, and instruments coexist with African rhythmic procedures, musical instruments, vocal and rhetorical styles, and performing sensibilities. Allusions may be quite precise, going beyond the broad Euro-American versus African gross categories. E. T. Mensah's improvisations may suggest Louis Armstrong. The formal arrangement of highlife songs may reproduce the protocol of big bands of the Swing Era. Harmonic progressions may come directly from the Methodist or Presbyterian hymnbook or from Jim Reeves, the Beatles, or the Temptations. Melodies may be based on dirges, play songs, recreational dance songs, or modeled on European pop hits while incorporating African-language words. Intertextuality extends to mutual citation. Nigerian highlife musicians like Victor Olaiya and Bobby Benson owe much to E. T. Mensah, while Fela's jazz-influenced saxophone improvisations have proven suggestive to Ghanaian bandsmen, even as Fela himself borrowed from Ghanaian drummer Guy Warren. Calypso, Cuban rhythms, and other idioms of New World music are found in highlife. And in more recent times, American rock, African-American gospel (complete with performing practice), and, perhaps most spectacularly, rap have made their way into African popular music. In light of such an astonishing diversity, notional oppositions between high and low styles, urban and rural musical spheres, local and foreign influences, and sacred and secular musical idioms are placed under considerable strain when deployed without qualification in analysis.

In listing these diverse influences that are layered in popular music, we may encourage listeners to adopt a mode of hearing that seeks the origins of the things they hear, that reads the concept of intertextuality rather too literally and transposes it from a poietic to an esthesic realm. This would be a mistake, however, for music's temporal tyranny discourages sideways listening. Listening that allows itself to be distracted by allusions and intertextual resonances runs the risk of missing the essence of the currently unfolding drama. This is not to deny that listeners are routinely "distracted" by such allusions but to suggest that a more self-conscious choreographing of the act of listening may curtail in-time interest in such allusions.

The point, then, of producing a list of influences is not to recommend a way of listening but simply to inform about what is there. It is to frame popular music as an accommodating and incorporating medium. But these deposits are not just left there, like rocks on a riverbed. Some of them move, as the Northern Ewe singer recognized when she sang in apparent disbelief:

> Etsi mekplɔɔ kpe o, tɔnye kplɔ kpe va yiɛ ɖee,
> The river does not normally sweep away stones; why is my river
> sweeping away its stones?

Just as the river's moving stones collide with others, form new enclaves elsewhere, and follow movement patterns that cannot be predicted, so various elements interact to create other expressive forms, forms that are not merely the summation of discrete elements. While some elements remain intact in their new environment, others acquire new identities.

The irreducibly allusive quality of popular music makes it something of a paradoxical art, an art in which certain apparent incongruities and downright opposing tendencies—from a logical point of view—are brought into mutual play without necessarily seeking to reconcile them. This is why notions of hybridity and syncreticism have emerged as appropriate terms in popular music analysis. It is well to remember, however, that popular music is not the only music that communicates by using (radically) contrasting primitives, be they procedures or materials. The music of Beethoven, too, lays great store by contrasting ingredients. French and Italian styles, Scottish folk song, Russian folk tunes, various *topoi* associated with everyday musics, and dance elements—these ingredients of Beethoven's language perform comparable functions as those found in popular music. That there is a significant popular element in Beethoven is well known.[25] Less often discussed, however, is the fact that Beethoven's language is akin to a kind of Creole. A late work like the A-minor String Quartet, op. 132, with its invocation of and allusions to numerous styles and techniques, cannot in any meaningful way be said to conform to a pure musical dialect.[26] Of course, there are differences between the tradition of composing to which Beethoven belonged and that of popular musicians, but these differences stem not from the nature of materials as such but from the conventions by which one displays competence, erudition, learnedness, and indeed genius. Again, recognizing the parallels between Beethoven and highlife musicians may prove liberating to aficionados of both Western Classical and African popular music.

Valuing influences, borrowings, or allusions depends on the interpreter's perspective. If you take a slice of African popular music and examine its constituent elements, you may find a number of ingredients of diverse provenance. Examining the slice synchronically, that is, as a self-sufficient system complete and adequate for its immediate purposes, will render the question of origins moot, while showing how the peculiar nature of the interaction among elements becomes a source of aesthetic pleasure. A diachronic view, on the other hand, forces us to acknowledge origins. The question for critics of African popular music then becomes: How long will we continue to talk about this or that feature as originating in this or that foreign culture? For example, what sense does it make, after a century and a half of regular, continuous, and imaginative use, to describe the guitar as a "foreign" instrument in Africa, or a church hymn as representing an alien musical language, or a perfect cadence as extrinsic?

Many aspects of culture are formed by contributions from different parts of the world. The history of food, for example, provides many spectacular examples of transplantation and cultural appropriation. We may, with time, suppress (aspects of) these histories or leave their production to academic historians. We may, in time, naturalize procedures depending on the meaning they have come to have for us. Otherwise, we would have to insist, every time we hear the Beethoven Violin Concerto, that the violin originated in the Middle East, that strictly speaking, it is not a European instrument, and therefore that all compositions for violin by Europeans are hybrid at the core, always already marked as "oriental." If the merest trace of a foreign element were allowed to inflect our interpretations of European cultural products—not to mention American ones—we would have our hands full for some time to come.

Thematizing or not thematizing origins thus represents an ideological choice, and it is my claim that too much adherence to origins wreaks havoc in the analysis of African popular music. Many listeners to highlife have so internalized its harmonic progressions, for example, that they associate them spontaneously with African practice, not an erstwhile European one. An aspect of functional harmony has thus become naturalized for them as a first-order language. Musicians speak it at a first level of articulation, not with an accent, so to speak. And similar arguments could be made for other elements and procedures. We should beware, then, of histories that value origins. We should be wary, also, of postmodern critical investments in paradox, incongruities, and intertextuality, some of which postulate uncomplicated origins in order to be able to characterize present practice as complicated. Perhaps, in time, we may hope for ideologically committed histories of African popular music that celebrate its viability within our cultures rather than look over shoulders to give credit to others: Portuguese, Brazilians, Jamaicans, North Americans, or Cubans.

Popular music, finally, is contemplative art—a surprising claim, perhaps, given its association with dance and its divergence from danceless art music. Yet a moment's reflection on the patterns of consumption of popular music will confirm that it appeals primarily to listeners, not dancers. The element of dance has not been eliminated; rather, it has been transformed into an imaginative one. As is well documented, recording, not live performance, has been the major catalyst in the dissemination of African popular music. When people listen to or hear highlife on their car radios, in taxis, at beer bars, in restaurants, or even in their living rooms, overt dancing is neither the immediate nor the most frequent response. They may nod their heads, stamp their feet, continue in conversation as the music plays, express delight at an aspect of performance, or sigh in agreement with the message. None of this is to deny that highlife is performed in dance halls by live bands, or played on records and CDs for people to dance in cafés, hotels, schools, community centers, village football parks, cinema theaters, on state occasions, and so on. However, not everyone can afford to go to dances; and not everyone of the largely and nominally Christian population approves of going to dances. Yet all at least hear, and in many cases listen to, highlife. Highlife is first and foremost contemplative; only secondarily is it functional art.

Popular music as a contemplative art? Devotees may balk. Some may hear in it an old-fashioned, German romantic, specifically Hanslickian prejudice, namely, the attempt to claim music as autonomous, as constituted in essence by "forms set in motion by sounding."[27] If this is in fact the view of devotees, then African popular music needs to be defended against them. For surely the point is not to deny popular music's many-sidedness but to contextualize it so that its fluid musical essence is not lost. Interpretations based in historical, sociological, philosophical, or literary methods, although necessary and enriching, remain incomplete, for popular music never renounces its ontological specificity as an art of tone.

If I end by saying that there is no more urgent task for African musicology than the comprehensive, musical study of our popular music, I do not mean to imply that this is in any way a new or unprecedented call, or that there aren't rich, pioneering studies (many of them in the metropolis, unfortunately) that might usefully orient future work. Writings by Sprigge, Richards, Collins, Coplan, Yankah, Geest, Owusu Brempong, Sackey, Mensah, and others have enriched our understanding of highlife.[28] Kubik, Waterman, and Erlmann and his team of contributors, have contributed much to our understanding of other African popular music.[29] And the work on Euro-American popular music by Tagg, Forte, Walser, Brackett, Middleton, Frith, Taylor, and—like it or not—Adorno is deeply suggestive of how we might approach these repertoires analytically.[30] The immense range of expressive strategies found in African popular music is yet further testimony to African musical genius. We begin to do it justice by engaging it at close range in order to reveal its depths and complexity.

7
Contesting Difference

Difference may well be *the* sign of our times. In the United States, for example, feminist theories seeking to negotiate the problematics of gender, to come to terms with various essentialisms, and to counter real-world discrimination have placed difference firmly on the critical agenda. Gay and lesbian studies, too, are centrally concerned with the validity of alternative epistemologies, and thus with resisting coarse constructions of difference that may prove sociopolitically disadvantageous to their communities. And, perhaps most notably, race as a category permeates a good deal of American humanistic discourse, providing innumerable opportunities for a wide range of reflection on difference. There are, as is to be expected, many points of divergence, but if we had to isolate an overriding concern, it may well be the attempt, in Gayatri Spivak's words, to undermine "the story of the straight, white, Judeo-Christian, heterosexual man of property as the ethical universal."[1]

Discussion of difference among music scholars is already under way, inspired in part by a number of interdisciplinary conversations, and in part by a widely shared feeling that only a few of music's many contexts have been given adequate scholarly attention. *Musicology and Difference* is the title of a pathbreaking collection published in 1993 featuring essays on "gender and sexuality in music scholarship."[2] Another important collection with a self-explanatory title, *Queering the Pitch: The New Gay and Lesbian Musicology,* appeared the very next year, edited by Philip Brett, Elizabeth Wood, and Gary C. Thomas.[3] And in 2001, a pioneering and wide-ranging collection devoted to race, *Music and the Racial Imagination,* was published by the University of Chicago Press, edited by Ronald Radano and Philip Bohlman.[4] There is evidence, too, in the kinds of papers read at music conferences, in journal articles, and in the sorts of topics being explored in doctoral dissertations nowadays that more and more people are interested in difference.[5]

It is perhaps a little surprising that such discussion is not more prominent in ethnomusicology, a field which regularly traffics in and exploits difference. According to Martin Stokes:

> [Ethnomusicology during the 1990s] was absorbed by the question of difference, particularly in relation to matters of ethnicity, nation, race, gender and sexuality. It has also reflexively generated concern with the ways in which the discipline of ethnomusicology itself constructs difference, and the consequences of this process.[6]

However, signs of this absorption and reflection are not prominent in the subfield of Africanist ethnomusicology. Reviewing competing approaches to African rhythm in a 1991 essay, Christopher Waterman cited "the portrayal of similarity and difference" as a subject "infrequently discussed" by Africanist ethnomusicology. This was not to deny that Africanist ethnomusicology had always drawn *implicitly* on notions of difference, distance, and alterity. Critical discussion, however, had been strangely muted. It continues to be. It might be timely, then, to revisit the subject.

The purpose of this chapter is to develop a more sustained critique of notions of difference than has been possible in previous chapters. My aims are fourfold: to observe the foundational status of difference in ethnomusicology; to recall a handful of thematizations of difference in Africanist ethnomusicology that reflect a particular representational bias; to inquire as to whether difference is "real"; and finally—and taking an explicitly political stance—to urge a resistance to difference. Although ethnomusicologists with other field experiences have written about difference, I will maintain a focus here on writings about African music in order to avoid the very real danger of dissolving a specific but by no means unique African problematic in some global formulation on account of its not being different from what has been reported of encounters between Euro-America and India, China or the Middle East.

Difference as Foundation

Ethnomusicology is founded on difference. Notions of unlikeness or dissimilarity lie at its core both in concept and, more spectacularly, in practice. From its antecedents in Enlightenment representations of world cultures through its concrete emergence as *die vergleichende Musikwissenschaft* or "comparative musicology" to its institutionalization as a formal fieldwork-based discipline in the 1950s, ethnomusicology has invested considerable stock in the production of cultural differences and notions of otherness. To say that ethnomusicological epistemology is an epistemology of difference is to utter a virtual truism.[7]

Mappings of the field by insiders tend not to dwell on difference as such but to recognize multiple agendas. Bruno Nettl, for example, proposes the following as core activities in ethnomusicology: study of music in oral traditions; study of folk music; study of music in/as culture; and comparative study of world music cultures.[8] Such a seemingly straightforward list acquires added meaning, however, the moment we ask who studies what, where, for how long, and why. As we restore the human actors who give face to a sometimes faceless ethnomusicology, and speculate on the motivations for scholarly study, notions of difference, otherness, and alterity come rapidly to the fore.

Klaus Wachsmann once wrote that ethnomusicology "is concerned with the music of other peoples,"[9] thus speaking directly to difference while conveniently suppressing reference to asymmetries of power. Pace Wachsmann—and choosing a hypothetical example—a Togolese scholar specializing in the music of Debussy is not normally considered an ethnomusicologist although such a scholar is "concerned with music of other peoples." A French scholar studying any of the diverse Togolese repertoires is, however, likely to be described as an ethnomusicologist (or ethnologist). In one sense, then, Wachsmann's definition works principally in one direction, namely, "for" the scholar of metropolitan origins, "against" one from the Third World.

Nor will such a definition win universal approval among today's professional ethnomusicologists. The emergence of urban ethnomusicology, the proliferation of studies of folk or traditional music of Europe and America, and the sporadic appearances of Asians and Africans described not as "scholars" but as "native scholars" are signs of an ongoing and more nuanced reconfiguring of the field that goes beyond Wachsmann's. Ethnomusicologists will probably not wish to dwell on the fact that their field, as Wachsmann implies, thrives on versions of the classical binary opposition between Self and Other, between the privileged and the underprivileged, between the haves and have-nots, between the powerful and the powerless, between the First and Third (or Fourth) worlds, and between whites and nonwhites. Is it not enough, some will ask, simply to acknowledge such asymmetrical binaries and get on with the task of knowledge production? Still others will argue that these binaries have been problematized in recent writing and folded into less bald and more ethically responsible constructs. Such protestation is understandable, for asymmetries of power, exploitation, and ethical violations are not comfortable topics of conversation. Ethnomusicologists' self-image as "the great egalitarians of musicology,"[10] however, sits rather uneasily beside their frequent unwillingness to dwell on the material nonegalitarianism that they (must) regularly encounter in their places of (field)work. When compelled to concede, in response to a familiar but easy charge, that they sometimes send copies of their videotapes to the "natives," we are right to suspect that a thorough interrogation of difference is not the first thing on their minds. Talk about videotapes while our subjects face war, disease, famine, and death?

Wachsmann further noted that ethnomusicology "operates essentially across cultural boundaries of one sort or another" and that, in general, "the observer does not share directly the musical tradition that he studies."[11] This characterization remains valid for Africanist ethnomusicology—a field, incidentally, to which Wachsmann himself contributed significantly. He does not go on to observe that cross-cultural boundaries operate within a politically and ideologically circumscribed world, a world of communities with individual histories, marked by conflicts and migrations. He does not say, in other words, "on whose terms" and "into whose culture" such hybridity is to be domesticated.[12] We are thus presented with a vision of "cross-culturalism" (or for that matter "multiculturalism") not as an even-handed dealing between cultural groups but as the age-old hierarchized transaction in which Euro-America retains its hegemonic status. Read in the context of Africanist ethnomusicology, Wachsmann's "across cultural boundaries" indexes a form of what Spivak calls "Eurocentric cross-culturalism."[13]

To be fair, ethnomusicology carries a burden that none of the musical subdisciplines quite share. At its moment of second birth in the 1950s (the first birth having coincided with the emergence of comparative musicology at the end of the nineteenth century), the need to define itself against a larger musicology had already committed ethnomusicology to a search for effective distancing strategies, a will-to-difference as a gesture of self-definition. As the hegemonic discipline in academic musical studies, musicology instituted itself as "the scholarly study of music wherever it may be found historically or geographically,"[14] a modern formulation that has proved defensible more as an exclamatory ideal than as a reflection of daily practice. In the United States at least, musicologists by and large concentrate on Western art music, smuggling in a dash of non-Western music under the aegis of "world music" in response to external demographic pressures and only in order to rejuvenate and diversify theory, not necessarily to embrace human ("world") subjects.[15] The burden that ethnomusicology placed on itself at its birth was thus considerable insofar as it deprived practitioners of the privilege of invoking difference as a naturally occurring, self-evident quality or truth. Ethnomusicology could not, in other words, take its difference for granted but needed to justify its very dissimilarity from the start. To say, therefore, that ethnomusicology is founded on difference is to point to these peculiar and complex conditions at the origin. Some musical disciplines, we might say, are born different (ethnomusicology) while others strive to achieve difference (the "New Musicology"). Ethnomusicology, alas, also has difference thrust upon it.[16]

Ethnomusicological knowledge may be defined as knowledge produced by scholars from the metropolis (Europe or America) about the musical practices of less-privileged others (in Africa, Asia, or Australia) often (but not always) on the basis of (brief) periods of so-called fieldwork. This is neither the customary definition nor a comprehensive one, but it has the virtue of compelling attention to the confluence of knowledge, difference, and power. Like anthropologists, producers/owners of ethnomusicological knowledge stand in a relation of power to those represented. The acts of naming, representing others in our language and notational systems, and laying down the terms for subsequent discourse betray ethnomusicology's collusion with colonialism. For colonialism sought justification in part from an imagined difference between Europe and geocultural spaces variously called the Orient, the non-West, Africa, and so on. Colonial domination served as an enabling condition for the cultivation of anthropology and later ethnomusicology.[17] Understanding ethnomusicology as a discipline nurtured by colonialism is not the same as branding every ethnomusicologist a colonialist. But acknowledging the link between a decisive set of historical events in Africa at the end of the nineteenth century and the emergence of the discourse of an academic discipline is a precondition for adequate historical analysis. Africanist ethnomusicologists have so far shown little interest in thematizing their colonial filiations and affiliations. Nor have they rushed to work toward the transformation of the very conditions of political society so as to liberalize, for example, the movement of global labor. Think how dramatically research into African musics might change if Nigerian or Malian fieldworkers, say, could enter the United States as readily as Americans visit Nigeria or Mali! This is not (necessarily) to recommend that every ethnomusicologist become a placard-bearing activist advocating the removal of travel restrictions. Rather, it is to remind us that the asymmetrical relation between the ethnomusicologist and his or her subjects is not fortuitous; it is, in fact, the very condition of possibility for the production of ethnomusicological knowledge.

Thematizing Difference

Difference is regularly invoked by ethnomusicologists in their ordinary discourse. Erich von Hornbostel, for example, opened his 1928 article on "African Negro Music" with a question that directs attention to the comparative method and thus to difference: "What is African music like as compared to our own?" Hornbostel's brief but subsequently worked out answer was: "African and (modern) European music are constructed on *entirely different principles*" (my emphasis).[18] Why Hornbostel chose to emphasize differences over similarities, instead of granting similarities alongside differences, probably had less to do with the comparative method as such than with an inherited tradition of European representations of others. Could it be, perhaps, that Hegel's ghost was hovering over Hornbostel's pages, reminding the comparative musicologist of words written a century earlier: "[The African character] is difficult to comprehend, because it is so totally different from our own culture, and so remote and alien in relation to our own mode of consciousness."?[19]

Nonetheless, it is interesting that Hornbostel, in the course of the article, concedes many points of similarity between the two musics. In fact, his phrase "entirely different principles" could easily be replaced by "similar principles" or, more daringly, by "the same general principles" without altering (the [in]coherence of) his argument. There is a danger of under-complicating the issue, however, because in the absence of explicit criteria for distinguishing between similarities and differences, a rigorous analysis cannot be undertaken. My interest here is not in proving the truth or falsity of Hornbostel's remark but in observing that his initially declared "difference" is a summary of his knowledge, not some fictional, unenlightened starting point to be proven untenable by a process of discovery. As such, it contradicts the other summary of his knowledge, the analytically achieved sameness that emerges from the article per se. This contradiction is fascinating: by constructing phenomena, objects, or people as "different," one stakes a claim to power over them.

A. M. Jones, too, opens his *Studies in African Music* of 1959 with a loud bang on the difference cymbal:

> Anyone who goes to Africa is bound to hear the music of the country and is equally certain to notice that it is not the same as our Western music. True, the people sing, in solo or chorus, as we do, and their instruments though lacking the precision of Western technology, will still recognizably belong to the familiar families of wind, string, or percussion. Yet the music produced is obviously not the same sort of music as that to which we in the West are accustomed. . . . The plain fact is that African music is a strange and novel object when encountered by a Western musician.[20]

Jones acknowledged similarities and differences but, like Hornbostel, he *chose* to give the edge to "strange[ness] and novel[ty]." Difference for him constituted premise as well as conclusion. As premise, difference served to enliven the process of discovery by allowing the Englishman to read "exoticism" (or difference) into various African objects and procedures. As conclusion, difference facilitated a symbolic affirmation of a prior, indeed, naturalized view of African music as phenomenologically unlike that of the West. Such acts of framing are not inevitable; they represent choices made within a broader economy of representational practices.

Hugh Tracey was equally forthright when, as honorary secretary of the African Music Society, he addressed the International Folk Music Council on July 14, 1953, on "The State of Folk Music in Bantu Africa":

> We Europeans are at a great disadvantage in talking about African music. Unlike most other members of this conference we do not represent or discuss our own music but that of *a people radically unlike ourselves* among whom we live. It is only because we have found that the African is pathetically incapable of defending his own culture and indeed is largely indifferent to its fate that we, who subscribe wholeheartedly to the ideals of our International Council, are attempting to tide over the period during which irreparable damage can be done and until Africans themselves will be capable of appearing at our conferences as well-informed representatives of their own peoples.[21] (My emphasis)

The ringing reference to Africans as "a people radically unlike ourselves" speaks to a persistent strategy of "differencing," one that remains as alive today as it was in the 1950s, though in less blatant forms. Although Tracey understood one consequence of the rise of global capital to be the subjugation of African voices, construed the European's role in Africa as historically temporary, and felt confident that Africans would eventually possess the wherewithal to represent themselves, his own project and that of other Africanist ethnomusicologists did not pursue a strategy of transferring power to "Africans themselves" with any urgency. Nor was such a strategy finally implementable because maintaining the imbalance of power is, as we have seen, logically necessary for ethnomusicological practice. To balance the distribution of power is to remove one of ethnomusicology's crucial enabling mechanisms.

As argued in chapter 4, one subject in particular has provided fertile grounds for the enactment of various fantasies in the name of difference: rhythm. The sheer number of terms invented or used by scholars to explain rhythmic organization in African music is noteworthy. While it is true that these terms are not applied exclusively to African music, and that a similar lack of convergence is evident in other areas of rhythm study, there is an excess here, a ludic abundance in the act of naming that bespeaks a strong predisposition to exploitative play and fantasy. While the plethora of terms may be understood as a sign of the richness of the phenomenon, it may also represent an inducement to mystify by cultivating difference. Why, for example, have scholars systematically neglected dance, when African music's metric structure is easily ascertained from the pattern produced by the *pieds de danse?* These patterns of thought undermine one's hope that intuited difference at the initial stage of research will be treated as no more than a sense impression to be critiqued subsequently in order to gauge its validity. The temptation to remain at the level of sense impressions can be especially strong in Africanist ethnomusicology.

Hornbostel, Jones, and Hugh Tracey belong to an earlier generation, and so it may be thought that the tendency I am criticizing no longer holds. Yet, in more recent writing, Hegelian ideas of difference continue to be promulgated, sometimes in a crude and aggressively essentialist mode. Consider the following anecdote.

Some time in 1998, I met an American professor who had been spending his sabbatical at the University of Ghana. Although he was there to teach mathematics, the vibrant atmosphere at the School of Music had caught his attention, and so he had decided to join the bamboo flute (known locally as *atenteben*) ensemble. I asked John West (not his real name) toward the end of his stay how he had enjoyed performing in that ensemble. His immediate and quite assured answer was, "Africans learn music very differently from Europeans." Hearing the word "different" made me curious. When African students were asked to read music from staff notation, things slowed down considerably, and they played with less confidence. But as soon as the notation was removed, and they were asked to improvise, African students came to life. This, West said, was in direct contrast to his own abilities. *He* (a white American) could read music but could not readily improvise; Africans could improvise naturally but had trouble reading music.

It is doubtless possible to support these positions, but not with the evidence culled by West. He had neglected to point out, for example, that, unlike the Ghanaian students, he had had several years of clarinet lessons as a young man. The students, on the other hand, had only recently begun to learn to read music. Their "inability," therefore, had little to do with feeling constrained by written music; it was simply a practical one stemming from their lack of practice. Nor did West bother to point out that the musical style in which students were expected to improvise was familiar to them from years of enculturation, whereas his own exposure to it had been brief.

But why was John West so eager to produce this particular difference? Probably because among the stories he planned to tell when he returned to the United States was a package of difference stories. These would justify his trip abroad, and make his interlocutors envious of the new experiences he'd acquired on the "dark continent." Better then to frame things in terms of nature rather than nurture, in terms of innate ability rather than training. Better to reproduce long-standing stereotypes about literacy being the exclusive preserve of people in the North than find out who these students were and what opportunity they might have had to develop comparable literacy. And better to ignore the many African musicians who read music as fluently as any European—some of them teaching in the very institution West was visiting—and cite a bunch of (not necessarily gifted) students as paradigmatic African music students.

But we musn't be too hard on a colleague who was, after all, a tourist, not a professional ethnographer. I relate this anecdote because of the spontaneous way in which it was told to me. West's construal of different ways of learning music is not that far removed from the way some ethnomusicologists construe the learning methods of the musicians they work with. To describe West's behavior as unethical may seem unduly harsh; perhaps he erred sincerely. But there may be some who will read in his facile construction of difference an eagerness to reinforce a certain power differential by abrogating the right to name accurately. West went searching for differences, and so he found them. He knew that in the metropolis difference stories sell better than sameness stories. And he was not against increasing his capital.

Or consider a recent essay on "hearing" in West African idioms, in which John Chernoff recalls an incident from his first visit to Ghana many years before.[22] He was taken to a restaurant in Accra for a Ghanaian meal. When the pot of soup was brought and uncovered, Chernoff's interlocutor asked, "Can you hear the scent?" Chernoff was a little surprised at this locution, for where he grew up, people did not normally hear scents. (He did not mention that European poets down the years have provided us with image after image of such crossing of domains.) Although he later admitted that his friend was not fluent in English, that he was probably translating literally from Twi into English, Chernoff did not dismiss "Can you hear the scent?" as a wrong translation, an epistemological gaffe. "In Ghana," he wrote, "when something smells, one doesn't smell it; one hears it."

Having established this ostensibly peculiar link between sense modalities, Chernoff proceeded to listen hard for usages of the verb "to hear." "Do you hear such-and-such a language?" some Ghanaians would ask, when what they meant was "Can you understand—do you speak—such and such a language?" Although it is unlikely that a competent translator would render understanding as hearing, Chernoff infers that "in the Ghanaian context, the notion of 'understanding' is the major attribute of hearing." Thus, to learn to perform—"hear" correctly—the rhythmically intricate ensemble music that is a favorite subject of ethnomusicological analysis, you have to "learn to keep the four-beat [pattern] with [your] foot while playing a triple-time apart." Movement and dance are thus important parts of the equation. "Movement," he says, "is the key to 'hearing' the music. If the music relinquishes its relation to movement, it abandons its participatory potential." Having thus urged us to regard this "broader connotation" whereby "hearing" implies "demonstrated comprehension as a companion to receptive perception," Chernoff is able to conclude that "'hearing' music, like 'hearing' a language or 'hearing' the truth or 'hearing' the scent of a soup, refers to perception as a form of recognition."

It should be noted that Chernoff always put the word "hearing" in quotation marks in the article, signaling some discomfort, some equivocation. But so intent is he on establishing a West African difference that he overlooks a number of factors that might argue against the view that Western conceptions of hearing simply refer to the registering of auditory phenomena whereas African conceptions suggest more than sound, incorporating understanding as well. For this argument to make sense, we need many more contexts of ethical translation. What about the references that Ghanaians routinely make to sound: the sound of an animal, the sound of drumming, the sound of a corn mill? Conversely, how is it possible for Westerners to hear sound without understanding? Isn't recognition as much a part of the processing of sound as sound in the West as it is in Africa? Don't people distinguish regularly between musical and nonmusical sounds?

What finally motivates this hunt for differences is not easily inferred from the article, but it is just possible that an invitation to a distinguished Africanist to contribute an article on hearing to a special issue of the journal *World of Music* prompted Chernoff's celebration of difference. It is also possible that he was merely continuing the project begun in *African Rhythm and African Sensibility*, in which a homogenized Western musical culture enabled the author to play up differences with Africa, itself represented principally by the Dagomba and Southern Ewe traditions of Ghana.[23] Giving free rein to the impulse to difference, Chernoff, in the 1997 article, retrieves Hornbostel's famous but dubious statement that "We proceed from hearing, they [i.e. the Africans] from motion" and suggests that it "makes a strange kind of sense." This is the same Hornbostel who announced at the start of his 1928 article on "African Negro Music" that African music and Western music are built on "entirely different principles."[24] Both authors, then, are tempted by essentialism, Hornbostel explicitly, Chernoff implicitly.

Finally, Peter Cooke, in an article subtitled "Listening to Instrumental Music in Africa South of the Sahara," sets out to prove that Africans "may well listen in a different way from the way Europeans do."[25] The difference lies in Africans' habitual association of instrumental music with verbal texts. Citing remarks by a number of musicians (harpists, xylophonists, horn players, and others), Cooke proposes that Africans do not hear instrumental music as pure or absolute. If they are not familiar with a given composition, some compose words to it silently.

Cooke's argument might have been more convincing if he could have shown that Europeans hearing their own "absolute music" do not associate it with verbal texts but hear it as absolute patterns of sound. No compelling data from the European side of the equation is reported, however. Indeed, Cooke is forced to embrace ambiguity at certain moments and to suggest that Africans use a "dual mode of listening"—part absolute, part word-based.

While it is not possible to review all of Cooke's "data" here, one brief illustration will convey their fragility. This concerns Ghanaian xylophonist Kakraba Lobi. Refusing to accept the merely metaphorical nature of some of the terms used by Africans to describe instrumental music, Cooke cites an article by Ghanaian musicologist Ben Aning on Kakraba to show "a basic difference between what Europeans and Africans south of the Sahara are listening for with regard to instrumental performance." About his composition "Sidigidi mengo o" [accurately: "Gidigidi menyo o," an Ewe phrase meaning "fighting is not good"], Kakraba is supposed to have said:

> It is like no other Lobi music. . . . It does not speak. It has no words.
> It is like European music. When you listen to "Sidigidi mengo o"
> [sic] it is played in a western style, the way they play loud and soft.
> So I can say It is a very interesting composition.

Does Kakraba have a suasive agenda? What are his referents for "European music" and "western style"? Cooke's intervention fails to address these possibly pertinent questions: "Kakraba is clearly distinguishing between his traditional repertory, which 'speaks,' and European instrumental music, which does not."

But what does Kakraba know about European music? Is he conversant with its language, can he understand what Bach, Mozart, or Wagner "speak"? Sensing the fragility of his argument, Cooke is forced to append a footnote: "During his performing tours to Europe, Kakraba had ample opportunity to attend classical concerts and to experience 'absolute' music. He became aware of a basic difference between such music and his own traditional music."

But Kakraba's biographer, Ben Aning, does not dwell on the classical concerts that Kakraba attended. He mentions only one orchestral concert in West Germany in 1966, which apparently inspired Kakraba to acts of imitation. But the imitation does not touch the heart of the musical language, because it is confined to tempo (fast-slow) and dynamics (loud-soft)—effects that Kakraba found intriguing. What about periodicity and harmony, form and rhythm? If it could be shown that Kakraba was more knowledgeable about European music, his comparative statements would carry greater weight, of course. Nor does Aning indicate what Kakraba heard at the various concerts he attended. But if Kakraba really did attend numerous "classical concerts," as Cooke implies, we need to know what he heard. Did he go to recitals of art song, for example, where the partnership between pianist and singer might have resonated with fiddle-accompanied praise singing of northern Ghana? Did he ever see an opera, where the spectacle and formality might have reminded him of festival dramas? Was he alert to the dance element in Mozart, for example, to the gestures of singing style, learned style, fanfare, Sturm und Drang that enliven Mozart's language, and that might have elicited a mode of verbalization akin to what he experienced in the song-based traditional music of his native tribe? Did Kakraba ever hear paraphrases of existing song, such as Liszt's paraphrases of Schubert, about which no knowledgeable listener would deny a verbal association?

I do not doubt that Kakraba found classical music different from his own, but I doubt that his understanding was deep enough for his words to be cited as evidence of a "basic difference" between European and African hearing. Even more puzzling—and basic—is the fact that all the instrumental repertoires cited by Cooke in his article openly acknowledge some basis in preexisting song with associated verbal text. But such repertoires are not confined to Africa. A listener who is familiar with the original song and declares that Art Tatum's improvisation on "Willow Weep for Me" reminds him or her of the song's words is not displaying any peculiar mode of response to absolute music. Nor would we consider it unusual if, listening to the finale of Berlioz's *Symphonie Fantastique*, I say that it makes me think of the day of judgment, for the invocation of the old chant "Dies Irae" is meant, in part, to impel such an association. So why should the listening habits of Africans be different? Again, the point is not that listeners hear uniformly but that differences may be more significant among individuals rather than at the gross level of "Africans" and "Europeans."

Cooke's argument, like many that seek differences between African and European music, undercomplicates European music. Difference is thus bought at a price. What happens when we look at the aesthetic discourses of the West, examine reported listening habits of Europeans? The word is never far off. Hearing someone say that a particular performance does not "speak to" him, or that the cello "sings passionately," or that a quartet begins in "singing style"—these sorts of locutions reinforce the embeddedness of musical metalanguage in word-based conceptual schemes. They do not index a unique European sensibility.

So if there is a "basic difference" between the way Africans and Europeans listen to instrumental music, it is certainly not demonstrated by

Cooke. But there is more: to undercomplicate European practice in order to show Africa's uniqueness is to deprive Africa of full participation in global critical acts; it is to confer a sham uniqueness on Africa. This patronizing and pernicious form of conceptual violence is designed to keep Africa away from center stage. Africa deserves full recognition of whatever unique attributes it possesses, but it does not need fake attributions.

One could go on to cite many more instances of the "differencing" of Africa by ethnomusicologists, but I hope that what has been said provides a fair sample of this way of treating our continent. I will return to the matter of difference in the next chapter in connection with analysis, but I hope that the examples given so far will confirm that acts of "differencing" do not belong to a forgotten or remote past but are very much alive in our own time.

Is Difference Real?

At first sight, difference is a real, commonsensical phenomenon. When faced with a range of objects, I can distinguish them by number, size, color, texture, function, and so on. The system of language enables me to invoke basic, meaning-producing oppositions. Thus, notes played on an instrument may be high or low, short or long, soft or loud, dark or bright. Chords can be consonant or dissonant, mellow or harsh, open- or close-spaced, and so on. These and thousands of other such distinctions are employed routinely in (musicians') daily discourses. They are, for the most part, self-evident at this first level of articulation.

Meaning is difference. This fundamental insight has been worked over many times, with discussions extending into semiotic, linguistic, psychoanalytical, and other areas but without ever giving up the notion of a first-level differentiation. Without difference, the ethnomusicologists would say, after Saussure, there can be no meaning. And so, although the specific construction of meaning can accentuate one or another political or ideological motivation, the will to communicate is shared by all producers of texts about music. The enterprise of ethnomusicology is, in this sense—and contrary to the earlier assertion that the discipline is founded on difference—not different from other branches of learning that seek to communicate research results through publication.

A little reflection on the complex processes of meaning formation, however, undermines our confidence that differences are self-evident or natural. They are, in fact, propped up by other textual constructions and motivated in ways that are not (necessarily) immediately apparent. What, for example, does the term "black" mean when applied to a group of people in the United States? To some, it is a perfectly adequate descriptive category for one's racial makeup. "Race" in this understanding is distributed into two essential categories, "white" and "black." ("Yellow" is underused because it does not carry the force of the two polar opposites while various hybrids are generally consigned to the category "black," not "white"). But since very few people are literally "black" or "white"—"brown" and "pink" might be more accurate substitutes for the metaphorically challenged or those enamored of iconic signs—we need to translate signs from one realm of experience into another. (In Irish, I'm told, black people are called "blue" [gorm]!) But what about "black" as a social construction? Here, and depending on context, one might consciously or—more often—subconsciously tap into a series of historical or social texts that construe blackness in terms of slavery, sports, entertainment, preferential policies, urban violence, and so on. So, while at one level the terms "black" and "white" seem self-evident as descriptive categories, they are, if we are prepared to listen to what they subtend, burdened with meaning.[26]

There is, in any case, nothing natural about racial categories. Pointing out that race has no firm biological basis may come as something of a shock to those who accept certain constructions—usually in a monolingual world—as given or natural. In West Africa, for example, identities are constructed with minimal reference to race. Ethnicity or class are more crucial markers.[27] To approach West African cultures with hard and fast notions of "black" and "white," therefore, would be to impose dangerously inappropriate perceptual categories. To refer to West African music as "Black music" is to compel a set of associations with various diasporic communities. Nowadays, however, with the advent of colonialism, white and black as oppositional categories *do* register in some "native" discourses, where they may index meanings that sometimes alter their conceptual origins. The Akpafu refer to whites as *mafudzaa,* which translates literally as "those who are white," a color-based designation that the Akpafu never use for other human beings, not even Albinos. Their neighbors to the south, the Anlo-Ewe, however, refer to white people as *ayevu* or "cunning dog"! Things get more complicated as individuals cross linguistic barriers, suppress the origins of words, or enter into various forms of power-based transactions with others. That these processes take place all the time suggests a high level of fluidity in the process of difference construction.

Differences, then, are not simply there for the perceiving subject. We do not perceive in a vacuum. Categories of perception are made, not given. Every act of perception carries implicit baggage from a history of habits of constructing the world. It should not seem strange at all—to choose a final set of examples—that not all of us notice hair types as markers of distinction among people. Similarly, in societies where aging does not carry a stigma, reference to an ethnographer as "an old man" is not considered an insult. Nor does one balk at the equivalent of "fatso" as a description and evaluation of physical size in communities in which plumpness is regarded as a sign of well-being. (Those who are thin are those who have not had enough to eat.)

There is nothing self-evident about the categories, borne of difference, put forward to distinguish African musics from Western music: functional as opposed to contemplative; communal rather than individualistic; spontaneous rather than calculated; rhythmically complex rather than simple; melodically unsophisticated rather than ornate; improvised rather than precomposed; and based in oral rather than written practices. These binarisms range from the real to the irrational. Each subtends an asymmetrical relation in which one term is marked, the other unmarked. As ideology, these enduring characterizations speak to meaning as difference constructed by particular individuals for particular purposes.[28]

We are thus faced with a somewhat paradoxical situation in which difference is necessary but available only through a process of construction. To say with the structuralists that meaning is difference is, in a sense, to do no more than identify a condition of language use. To say with Fabian that the production of ethnomusicological knowledge depends crucially on a denial of coevalness—a posture designed to keep the Other in a different time frame—is also to identify a condition of knowledge construction. The challenge, therefore, is not whether but *how* to construct difference. It is here that we need to attend to factors of an ethical, political, and ideological nature.

Resisting Difference

There are signs that models of knowledge construction that privilege an all-powerful, all-knowing (white, male) ethnographer are receding in favor of models that incorporate overt dialogue and collaboration with the Other. The dialogic turn superficially signals a turn from difference but far from initiating a decisive reorientation of the field, such a turn has simply made possible a repackaging of an older set of practices and objects. Where previously Tracey or Jones referred to "the African," I might now specify Tiv, Kpelle, Shona, BaAka, or Ewe. But who is the "I" who spoke in the last sentence? Is she or he not the latest incarnation of the very "I" who authored "the African"? Again, it might be said that, unlike earlier scholars who failed to pay much attention to the actual words of native informants, we now routinely reproduce page upon page of transcribed conversations in our publications in order to underline the collaborative nature of our research. But collaboration depends on translation, and, since translation virtually guarantees that any and all things attributed to informants can be incorporated into an ethnotheory, it is not immediately clear that the more explicit presentation of native voices finally overcomes the shortcomings of the implicit procedures of previous scholars. There is, to be sure, an ontological radicality in quotation, even in translation, but whether the ethical imperative of Africanist ethnomusicology has changed as a result remains an open question.

Glossing the turn to dialogue as a turn from an "us-versus-them model" to a "we model" does not eliminate difference; it merely disguises it. And disguise, in some respects, manifests a more salient presence than "undisguise." Prominently displayed photographs of native informants on book covers; generous acknowledgment of insiders who placed their "extensive knowledge" at the ethnographer's disposal; and citations of what one or another semiliterate musician said in English or French: these and other strenuous efforts to assure the reader that one's data is authentic and that differencing has been minimized are framing tricks. The very framework of knowledge production has not been recast, nor has the balance of power shifted. Rather, by claiming even more of the cognitive geography of African musicians, the metropolitan scholar paradoxically acquires more territory, more power to celebrate difference.

A radical critique of Africanist ethnomusicology, one that openly confronts the problem of differencing, might adopt a model of knowledge production in which local scholars—many of whom are, after all, fluent "speakers" of various musical and verbal languages—are installed in place of ethnomusicologists. How about letting Others speak for themselves and on their own terms, instead of hearing their refracted voices through the ethnomusicolgist's texts? How about facing up to the possibility that ethnomusicologists' commitments are not to the givers of knowledge, not even to the producers of the raw materials used in knowledge production, but to their own careers in the Western academy? Is it not at best dubious to build careers on other peoples' backs even while styling yourself an "egalitarian" engaged in "dialogue" and "collaborative research"?

These are tough questions, and they are probably overstated; the positions they advocate are extreme. For beyond their short-term economic consequences, they advocate the eventual disappearance of the ethnomusicologist. No sane ethnomusicologist will voluntarily pursue a course of action that leads to self-annihilation, certainly not at a time when, in the U.S. academy at least, notions of diversity and multiculturalism have enabled ethnomusicologists to cash in on their knowledge of other musical cultures. Some will question the moral efficacy of substituting a new group of native differencemongerers for the earlier metropolitan one. Will it not be morally imperative to eliminate such natives eventually? Or should natives be given the privilege of "messing up" like their metropolitan colleagues?

And some will insist that the task of ethnomusicology is first and foremost the production of knowledge, not political or social action.

These counter assertions enjoin us to search for a less radical solution, one that achieves a compromise between the extremes of continuing with business as usual and abandoning the Africanist ethnomusicological project altogether. In what alternative terms might we cast a principled pursuit of difference? Charles Taylor has written about this issue in the context of a discussion of multiculturalism.[29] His task was to find ways of approaching the challenge of interpretation when dealing with degrees of difference and distance between cultures. Here is Taylor's Gadamer-inspired recommendation, one that has the added benefit for us of a musical analogy:

> [F]or a sufficiently different culture, the very understanding of what it is to be of worth will be strange and unfamiliar to us. To approach, say, a raga with the presumptions of value implicit in the well-tempered clavier would be forever to miss the point. What has to happen is what Gadamer has called a "fusion of horizons." We learn to move in a broader horizon, within which what we have formerly taken for granted as the background to valuation can be situated as one possibility alongside the different background of formerly unfamiliar culture. The "fusion of horizons" operates through our developing new vocabularies of comparison, by means of which we can articulate these contrasts.[30]

This sounds like a very reasonable course of action, one that, far from being new, has been more or less enacted by social anthropologists committed to participant observation. It is a strategy that is well known to ethnomusicologists whose ethnographies have been shaped, sometimes decisively, by fieldwork and the incorporation of "the native's point of view." Taylor's strategy for cross-cultural understanding promises to overcome certain ethical dilemmas raised by our dealing with Others. It provides a way of acknowledging, contextualizing, and eventually containing difference.

But Taylor's program (and numerous others that resonate with it) is essentially "Western" or "European." How does one decide, to start with, that a given culture is "sufficiently different"? If differences are constructed, then the judgment that one culture is "sufficiently different" from another presupposes a prior set of analytical acts. There is a danger of monopolizing the ability to name something as different, a danger of granting that ability to those in the metropolis, and denying it to those in the South. Second, whose are the resulting "broader horizons"—ours or theirs? Are they not essentially an expansion of Western horizons? Is it possible to achieve a genuine fusion of horizons between cultures located in radically different economic spheres? Is cross-cultural understanding ultimately possible?

These questions prompt us to consider an alternative strategy. Pace Taylor, one might approach a raga with "the presumptions of value" implicit in Bach's *Well-Tempered Clavier* in order to pursue to the limits our initial impression—for it is no more than that—that the two musics are "sufficiently different." If we probe the contexts of both musics with equal commitment and sensitivity, and if we recognize the translatability of the impulses that lie behind certain expressive gestures,[31] we may well find that operating at different levels of perception are differences as well as residual similarities. More crucially, it is to be hoped that the "presumptions of value" implicit in a raga will be brought to bear on an investigation of the *Well-Tempered Clavier* as well, thus allowing flow in both directions. For although Taylor, writing from "our" point of view, naturally assumes that we have the first option of checking out the other's horizon, it ought to be possible to imagine a reversal of this scheme.

Taylor's efforts here might suggest an attempt to relativize and decenter the West in order to draw other world cultures into a more egalitarian discussion space. ("Organized by whom?" we might remember to ask, in order not to forget that the construction of egalitarianism itself represents an exercise of power in the deployment of material resources.) Among the things we might expect from such a reorientation is a convergence at the level of background of ostensibly different cultural systems. For backgrounds or deep structures bear uncanny resemblances to one another, so that what Taylor calls our "background of valuation" could easily be a version of the Asian's, Australian's, or African's background of valuation. But as we approach this "fusion of horizons" from the discrete polarity separating "our horizon" from "their horizon," we might wonder where this third space is located. And, because space is usually owned, we might ask to whom it belongs. Taylor implies that the new space is ultimately an extension of the West's; it is *our* "vocabularies of comparison" that will be enriched in the process. So while bringing more of the Other into view, Taylor's program does not—indeed cannot—eliminate the foundational terms of Self or Other, terms locked in a violent hierarchy in which Self is subject, Other is object. More tragically, perhaps, Taylor does not make it possible for Others to other us, so to speak. So, once again, a version of "Eurocentric cross-culturalism" is what is likely to emerge from this course of action.[32]

Embracing Sameness?

If differencing has produced such distorted, ideologically one-sided, and politically disadvantageous representation, and if a reasonable proposition to fuse horizons fails to overcome its core difficulty, why not eliminate it altogether and substitute a carefully defined sameness? The proposition that we dispense with difference might sound reactionary at first, scandalous perhaps, or merely silly. To attempt to eliminate that which is not ultimately eliminable is to attempt a critique in the spirit of a deconstruction.[33] It is to gnaw at limits, resist the naturalized oppositions on which knowledge of African music has been based without being able to escape the regime of oppositions. It is to insist on the provisional nature of our musical ethnographies, to persist in reordering concepts positioned at the center or margin. Only through such a persistent critique can we hope to refine theories born of a will to difference; only through critique can we stem the tide that reduces the hugely complex edifice of African musical practices to a series of "characteristics."

There is no method for attending to sameness, only a presence of mind, an attitude, a way of seeing the world. For fieldworkers who presume sameness rather than difference, the challenge of constructing an ethnographic report would be construed as developing a theory of translation that aims to show how the materiality of culture constrains musical practice in specific ways. The idea would be to unearth the impulses that motivate acts of performance and to seek to interpret them in terms of broader, perhaps even generic cultural impulses. Such a project would ultimately look beyond the immediate material level, not by denying that Africans blow on elephant horns, cover drums with animal skin, or make flutes out of bamboo, but by emphasizing the contingency of their investment in certain material objects and practices. Objects function as means to an end, and it is the complex of actions elicited by such objects that betrays the translatable impulses behind performance. Focusing on such impulses promotes a cross-cultural vision without denying the arbitrary specificity of a local (African) practice.

Contesting difference through an embrace of sameness might also prompt a fresh critique of essentialism. Such a critique should facilitate a better understanding of the peculiar juxtapositions of cultural practices that define modern Africa. As argued in the introduction, it would explain how a Sierra Leonean, Nigerian, or Ghanaian can be equally moved by a hymn, a traditional dance, a local proverb, a quotation from Shakespeare, a piece of reggae, the Wedding march, and the latest highlife music. To eliminate the will to difference is to highlight the precarious grounds on which contemporary African reality stands, grounds shaped by religious, political, and ethical impositions that are layered at various levels of depth in various places. Sameness prepares an understanding of (modern) African culture as a form of improvised theater. African culture, in this view, is a makeshift culture whose actors respond to specific pressures on an ad hoc, ongoing basis. It is not a culture of frozen artifacts imbued with spiritual essences.

A premise of sameness might also reorient our studies of theoretical (including aesthetic) discourses by causing us to regard with suspicion some of what is reported to have been said by informants in their own languages. Languages evolve according to need, and needs are defined across a spectrum of human activities. Accidents occur just as frequently as intended actions. So the condition of any African language today is best considered in light of its genealogy and refracted histories, including real and hypothetical occurrences. The "fact," for example, that there are no terms corresponding directly with "music" in many African languages—a fact, incidentally, that has caused difference-seeking ethnotheorists to rejoice— is significant only in a restricted sense. Its significance is retrospective, not prospective. What matters is not what is known but what lies in the realm of imaginative possibility. The issue is not, "Do the Venda have a term for 'absolute music'?" but the more dynamic conception whereby changes in the material circumstances of the Venda breed changes in cultural practices that in turn make it possible for them, if they so desire, to articulate ideas about "absolute music." This future-oriented appraisal paves the way for empowerment in that it places the accent not on what an objectifying Western discourse deems significant but on the potential of African languages to support a self-sufficient and sophisticated practice of critical reflection.

The transformative, contingent, if-only, frankly political approach advocated in the last few pages has certain practical consequences. One of them concerns the production of ethnography. Awareness of the precarious nature of material investments should lead to an abandonment of ethnography and an embrace of fiction. It should lead to a rejection of all first-level, ostensibly objective descriptions, and a substitution of second- or third-level suppositions, some of them openly speculative, none of them realist. We would not presume a shared descriptive vocabulary, and would insist that if "nose flute" appears on our inventory, it be understood in terms of a series of texts speaking to music-making.

An aspect of this approach has already been adumbrated in the work of comparative musicologists who, by presuming a rhythmic or melodic content in African and Asian music, made it possible to observe readily the expressive investments that cultures make at certain historical junctures. The arbitrariness of their framing, however, is easily noted and corrected: one can imagine a rewrite of Schneider or Hornbostel using the parameters of Hausa or Karimojong musicking as point of reference. Sentimental and nostalgic attachments to certain cultural practices would be left in private hands rather than denied. The comparative impulse has, however, been abandoned in recent ethnographies committed to objective representation or theory, or opposed to any form of political advocacy (as if that very stance was not itself political). Among such ethnographers, a commitment to nativism remains strong, and impatience with the influence of Christianity, Classical Music, or electric guitars is hardly disguised. Although they present themselves as friends, such ethnographers are not; they are more concerned to preserve first-level descriptions of indigenous culture than in stressing its contingency or in embracing the contradictions of modern life. This newer discourse slows down the drive to empowerment by clinging to what Africa is—including its ostensible difference from the West—rather than what Africa could be if global resources were differently distributed.

But sameness is liable to leave some people nervous. We surely do not all want to look alike, play the same instruments, listen to the same music, or deploy the same critical language. Sameness carries the threat of hegemonic homogenization analogous to the cultural effects of the movement of global capital. What I am arguing for, however, is not sameness but the *presumption* of sameness—a hypostatized notion whose sweetness lies in the eating. Like Charles Taylor's "presumption of value," a presumption of sameness would precede action and representation. We would not worry about the traces left by acts of representation as long as we could take for granted such presumption. Indeed, such presumption guarantees an ethical motivation.

Those who feel that the presumption of sameness will deprive them of the diversity they cherish in cultural life might consider the grounds from which they are able to hold such a view. And they might consider their own advocacy of sameness in other spheres of life. For example, the view that human rights are for all human beings (and not just for some) is unlikely to be opposed by those who hold that difference and diversity should never be compromised. But why presume the rightness of these rights for all? Why not difference all the way? Such presumption, presumably, represents a strategic embrace of sameness. Like Spivak's notion of "strategic essentialism," strategic sameness declares an interest in political and ethical action by reserving judgment for the end of a proceeding, not its beginning. Nina Auerbach captured this particular sentiment beautifully: "I shun my 'precious specialty' and seek access to the larger, if tarnished, culture that dictates our own and others' differences."[34]

It is time to shun our precious Africanity in order to participate more centrally in the global conversation. It is time, as Paulin Hountondji advocates, "to *impoverish* resolutely the concept of Africa,"[35] free it of dense layers of attributed difference. It is time to restore a notional sameness to our acts of representation.

8
How Not to Analyze
African Music

Analysis, the act of taking apart to see how the thing works, is a vital and potentially empowering practice. No one who has extended our understanding of African musical language has managed without analysis. Studies of rhythm, multipart procedures, melody, and the dynamics of performance are inconceivable without contemplation of events and processes at different levels of structure. Yet analysis remains a contested discipline. Within European musicology, for example, analysts are routinely attacked for their myopia,[1] not attending sufficiently to context, employing anachronistic methods, and imposing "universalizing discourses" on heterogenous musical objects and processes.[2] These matters are equally pertinent to African musicology. But there are others as well. How does one define the object of analysis when there is no score, no written trace for traditional and (most) popular music? What constitutes an appropriate metalanguage? Does a coherent theory emanate from among the people themselves, and if so, should it be given priority over metropolitan theory? What, finally, is the value of analysis? Can it aid performance, listening, composition, history, or is it an autonomous practice?

The battle over analysis stems in part from the peculiar arrangement of the subdisciplines, and so it will be well to begin with a comment on the politics of subdisciplinary interaction. In the (recent) Euro-American academy, division of labor has produced a wide range of specialists, prominent among whom is a triad comprised of historical musicologists, music theorists, and ethnomusicologists. With respect to the analysis of African music, the two relevant disciplines for this discussion are ethnomusicology and music theory. Speaking from the metropolis, composer-theorist David Temperley addresses the ethnomusicology-music theory divide:

> Among the three branches of musicology—historical musicology, theory and ethnomusicology—it is the relationship between the last two that is most distant and tenuous. It is not difficult to see why. In terms of their subject matter, the theorist's domain (mainly Classical, romantic, and twentieth-century art music) is essentially a subdomain of the historical musicologist's (Western art music as a whole); and this, in turn, is non-overlapping with the ethnomusicologist's (everything else). . . . The more serious divide between ethnomusicology and theory, however, is in their philosophy and approach. The theorist's main activity is intensive study of the score of a piece, more or less in isolation from its historical context: the circumstances of its creation, the life and personality of its composer, and its historical milieu. . . . If this approach is troubling to many musicologists, who see the score as but one source of evidence toward the understanding of a work, to ethnomusicologists it is positively anathema. Indeed, to some ethnomusicologists, even the relatively broad perspective of the historical musicologist has seemed too narrow—excessively concerned with limited documentary evidence and factual questions of chronology and authorship, and not enough with larger issues of social context, function, and meaning. From the ethnomusicologist's perspective, confining one's attention to the score alone is simply the extreme of this unhealthy tendency. It represents the ultimate embrace of a dangerous fiction: the autonomy of the musical work.[3]

Temperley's words echo ideas in the popular imagination, according to which the following oppositions seem to hold. Ethnomusicology studies non-Western (unfamiliar, exotic) music while music theory is focused on the core European repertory (familiar music). Ethnomusicology is concerned with the production of differences among world musical cultures, while music theorists tend to produce sameness. Ethnomusicologists take account of the context of a composition; music theorists ignore it. Ethnomusicologists reject the idea of an autonomous musical object; music theorists embrace it. Analysis, when practiced by ethnomusicologists, uses ad hoc, contextually appropriate methods; music theorists strive for systematic methods. Overall, ethnomusicology sails under a pluralistic flag while music theory labors under hegemonic rule.

These oppositions present half-truths at best because even cursory attention to the literatures of both disciplines will reveal exceptions. In terms of domain, for example, some ethnomusicologists have turned their attention to Western art music while music theorists are increasingly interested in noncanonical, popular, and non-Western repertoires. In terms of method, music theorists are now less confident about the autonomy or even relative autonomy of the musical work than they once were. And although ethnomusicology's pluralistic profile is sometimes held up as a shining example,[4] there are centers of power in that subdiscipline that insist on particular methodologies and are propped up by as monistic an attitude as anything one finds among religious zealots. To be useful, therefore, each opposition needs to be examined with proper attention to the historical and material realities that shape scholarly practice.

My task in this chapter, however, is not to discuss the boundaries that separate the musical subdisciplines: that has been accomplished elsewhere by scholars more interested in such developments.[5] I raise the matter of boundaries partly to alert Africa-based readers accustomed to holistic approaches to the fact that things are somewhat different in the metropolis and partly to recognize that all disciplines have their own claims on analysis even if the development of methods has been entrusted primarily to music theorists. Temperley does not stop at a diagnosis; he goes on to prescribe a cure:

> This portrayal of the situation implies that theorists and ethnomusicologists have nothing to talk about (and there are some on both sides . . . who feel this way). But in truth, there is no insurmountable conflict between the two approaches, and indeed, much room for interaction and cooperation. All that is required from ethnomusicologists is the concession that intensive and "autonomous" study of musical objects, represented by scores or in some other way, can be a valuable route to the understanding of music of any kind; and the concession by theorists that this is not the only route to such understanding, and hardly ever a sufficient one. . . . If this much can be agreed, the way would seem clear for a fruitful reconciliation between theory and ethnomusicology, both in philosophy and in subject matter.[6]

The kind of reconciliation sought by Temperley is more easily prescribed than achieved because our disciplinary habits and prejudices are deeply entrenched. I have quoted him at length, however, not (only) because his words were provoked by an analytical project of mine but also because no one is likely to dispute the broad outlines of his characterization. Or, perhaps, I should say "only a few people," because ethnomusicology's built-in heterogeneity makes it possible to contest many generalizations. It is better, then, to turn from generalities to specifics.

The Story of an Analytical Paper

I begin with a story about an attempt to publish an analytical article on African music. I trust that the experience is not peculiar, that others have received and been puzzled by anonymous readers' reports and, although I may be charged with retreating into (intellectual) autobiography, there may well be a communal resonance in this story. In any case, situations of professionally endorsed antagonism are more telling sites for the discovery of our ideological investments than the formal, unprovoked presentation of new knowledge. And because the writing and submitting of articles to journals is so much a part of everyday scholarly life, it may be useful to draw some lessons from a critique of daily practice.

Sometime in 1984, I submitted an article to *Ethnomusicology*, the journal of the Society for Ethnomusicology based in the United States. It was an analytical study of West African drumming. It came about this way: I was teaching an undergraduate class on African music and asked students to transcribe two pieces of music for our next meeting. When I sat up to do my own transcription the night before, I found that one of them ("Gi Dunu") was not as straightforward as I'd imagined. Several cups of coffee, a certain amount of hair tearing, and the prospect of embarrassing myself the next day kept me awake until about 4 A.M., at which point, perhaps as a result of diminishing capacities, I felt that I had cracked it. As you can imagine, the class went very well, because having experienced the students' difficulty, I was in a better position to explain the "solution" to them.

Because the two pieces we worked on were available on a commercially published LP, it occurred to me that publishing my transcriptions together with an analysis might be of interest to other students of African rhythm. Perhaps it might even stimulate debate, I thought, because among the things I missed in Africanist ethnomusicology were competing transcriptions of publicly available compositions that could form the basis of informed, vigorous contestation of appropriate modes of representation. The fact that the analyst of Beethoven's Fifth Symphony could take its familiarity for granted, whereas that of Akan funeral dirges or Igbo *atilogwu* music could not, was a source of frustration. Only later did it dawn on me that the absence of such public documents is in fact preferred by show-and-tell ethnomusicologists whose narrative inclinations are nourished by such conditions. How naive of anyone to think that speaking a common language through dissecting the "same" objects in the process of communal knowledge building was a matter of priority.

I duly wrote up my paper and submitted it to the journal. A response came in three months rejecting the paper. The reasons? Referee 1 pointed out that I was analyzing music I did not record; I "failed to present new data." How could I know the "musical system" of the Malinke people? How could I identify the compositional intention? By "listening to two album cuts"? Worse still, I had used an "etic model whose principal concepts [were] derived from Western individual art music theory." My framework was European because I had used words like periodicity, cadence, down-beat, and meter. "There is no indication," wrote the reviewer, "that the author has first-hand knowledge of African music, for empirical knowledge of an African music theory has not been used to shape the [analytical] model nor has it been evoked to guide the application of the model." In the end, the reviewer recommended "strongly" that the paper be rejected.

Referee 2 was less critical but felt that the analysis lacked "rigour" (I retain the reviewer's spelling). There was confusion between upbeat and off-beat, and I had failed to define improvization. The transcription provided was not acceptable on account of its partiality, and a passing claim that previous scholars had paid little attention to speech rhythm was undermined by his own contributions. I was, however, encouraged to revise and resubmit.

The new version then was sent to referees 3 and 4, not the two whose objections had engendered the revision. Comments were even more vigorous and extensive. Referee 3 was critical of the assumption that there was one main beat in a transcribed measure. This reviewer also felt that the analysis focused too much on the transcription rather than on the music. Nor had I cited the reviewer's own work enough. Referee 4, declining the privilege of anonymity, said that he was sympathetic to the notion of metrical dissonance and the daring but naive claim that the two compositions analyzed were forms of "absolute music." But he disagreed with a metrical modulation that I had (irresponsibly) thrown into the transcription to register a feeling of realignment that I sensed about a third of the way through. And like referees 2 and 3, he lost little time in pointing out that he and others had written about these things before me. As before, I was encouraged to revise again and resubmit.

When it came time to prepare the next set of revisions, I was distinctly aware of the presence of four coauthors, all of them saying somewhat different things. But there was one more surprise. When eventually the article was published in the winter 1986 issue of *Ethnomusicology*, it appeared alongside an article by James Koetting, and both were preceded by a commentary by a senior Africanist, Ruth Stone. She, too, reinforced some of the points made in the earlier reports: that the framework I used was European, that the metaphors used by African musicians (such as "the song going down the road") were not devoid of theoretical content, and that it was "ironic" that I, an African, was enamored of European tools, whereas Koetting, the American, was more sensitive to the African's way of doing things.

One should, I suppose, be grateful for four substantial readers' reports and a published commentary on a not particularly significant article. I tell this story not to parade my incompetence but to draw attention to some of the positions adopted by card-carrying ethnomusicologists. Anonymous readers' reports constitute a rich site for the serious study of ideology, and a thorough published reading of such reports is long overdue. Here, I wish merely to highlight two points: first, that the music I analyzed was, as Stone put it, "recorded by others," and second, that the article's intellectual orientation was overwhelmingly "Western."

Analyzing Music "Recorded by Others"

The idea that you should refrain from analyzing music you did not yourself record is dubious, of course. No doubt being present on location, hearing and seeing the musicians perform, being able to intervene with queries, and later recalling through construction the site of the making of the recording provide you with a visual sense of the occasion that can be helpful to a total understanding of the music. To the extent that no recording is transparent, the person responsible for its creation has access to a series of supplementary texts that may aid interpretation.

But what if we lack access to some of these supplementary texts? What if we do not know the circumstances under which the recording was made? What if we do not know what kind of microphones were used? What if we're not sure whether there were 12 or 15 horns playing? What if we are fooled by a consistent timbral distinction into hearing two drums instead of one? Are we then barred from analyzing aspects of the recording? Why should an all-or-nothing policy obtain here, especially when all is never achievable? Not all of us have the material means to undertake the kind of fieldwork approved by the ethnomusicological guild. Not all of us are able to, or interested in, producing high-quality recordings. Indeed, the process of field recording in Africa sometimes involves so much intervention, trickery, and deception that not everyone is comfortable about thus violating cultures. What about those whose interest is in a certain kind of material, rather than in the superior acoustic quality of a recording? Is it not also the case that some people make recordings essentially to construct a series of documents, having neither the skill nor interest in probing the music for structural secrets? And in cases where detailed and comprehensive description of context is provided in jacket notes, isn't the analyst's task made much easier?

Analysis of music "recorded by others" is not, of course, unheard of in the history of ethnomusicology. In the early twentieth century, comparative musicologists depended on such recordings for analysis. Hornbostel, for example, was able to speculate on various aspects of musical structure and meaning by listening to a variety of recordings. And it is testimony to the strength of some of his insights that they have remained pertinent to

African music research. Blacking in the 1950s pursued some of Hornbostel's ideas about rhythm,[7] Stephen Blum has recently examined Hornbostel's thought through his terminology,[8] and Christopher Waterman, in reviewing the history of conceptualizations of African rhythm, emphasizes Hornbostel's contribution.[9] Imagine saying to Mr. Hornbostel, when he submitted his "African Negro Music" article for publication, that it was based on music "recorded by others," or that it provided "no new data"!

Recall, also, the case of Rose Brandel, who published an entire monograph in 1961 on African music, based not on fieldwork but on close listening to various folkways recordings, music "recorded by others."[10] *The Music of Central Africa* has fallen by the wayside—unjustly, in my view—and mainly, I suspect, because of the suspicion that Brandel did not "really know" the material. Yet, putting aside the impossibility of "really knowing" a musical culture, the idea of the book—an examination of the organizing principles of Central African rhythm—is surely beyond criticism. Brandel's comparativist leanings, her discussion of hemiola patterns, and her attempts to fix pitches and rhythms in notation, made possible a more secure discussion of structure in the modern intellectual economy. Reviewing the book, the young Gerhard Kubik could find little to praise: transcribing from recordings, Brandel lacked knowledge of how the musicians played, and therefore could only represent "paper rhythms," not the true "inherent rhythms" that Kubik was theorizing in his own work of that period.[11] One might disagree with the specific technical means employed by Brandel—such as the Stravinsky-style additive meter criticized in chapter 4. But, as an honest attempt to engage resultant patterns, the book deserves better than to be consigned to the flames. Perhaps recent interest in the building of bridges between subdisciplines may help to revive interest in Brandel's work, which, although far from perfect, is nevertheless suggestive for cross-cultural study. (The question of who owns which bridge is another matter.)

Brandel's example embodies one aspect of the institutional conflict between ethnomusicologists and music theorists. A musician in her own tradition, she developed a curiosity about a body of African music. So, without troubling to weave additional webs of context around her eyes, ears, and brain, she listened to it and wrote her analyses using the metalanguage that was familiar to her. In the process, she conferred a certain identity and status on these musical products. Like the rest of us, she was bound to make mistakes, of course, but her errors were neither total nor uninstructive. Taking a hands-on approach, she availed herself of a moment of authenticity in the analytical act. Ethnomusicological reaction, however, asserts a contrary evaluation. In reaching for folkways recordings, she seemed to have taken an undeserved short cut, jumped some punishing rite of passage, perhaps. Hers was armchair ethnomusicology, not the fieldwork-based ethnomusicology that (alone) guaranteed authoritative knowledge.

However, *all* ethnomusicology is armchair ethnomusicology, because no matter how long you spend in the field, getting out is almost always a condition for producing your ethnography. (Although the contributions of native scholars based on the continent would seem to undermine this claim, we should point out that the more prominent among them have been helped immensely by occasional residency abroad.) Stepping outside the cultural and especially material conditions from which your data was acquired—returning to the armchair, so to speak—is not some unfortunate or inconvenient by-product of the process of ethnographic production. It embodies its very ground of possibility. The difference between a Brandel and others who boast prolonged periods of fieldwork is therefore really a matter of degree, not of kind. Projecting the difference as fundamental reflects not an objective evaluation of the knowledge trace but the enactment of a ritual of dubious value. Nowadays, with the multiplication of sound recordings and visual data, not to mention huge Internet resources, the view that you may analyze only music you yourself recorded seems increasingly absurd.

African Knowledge versus European Knowledge

Referee 1's claim that my essay showed no knowledge of "an African musical theory" set me thinking about what that theory might be, and how and why it might be different from European theory. The idea of an African musical system, propped up by a uniquely African mode of knowledge production, and distinct from a putative European system, is so prevalent that it would seem almost perverse to question it. And yet, when subjected to interrogation, it does not hold up. The truth is that, beyond local inflections deriving from culture-bound linguistic, historical, and materially inflected expressive preferences, there is ultimately no difference between European knowledge and African knowledge. All talk of an insider's point of view, a native point of view, a distinct African mode of hearing, or of knowledge organization is a lie, and a wicked one at that. This idea needs to be thoroughly overhauled if the tasks of understanding and knowledge construction are to proceed in earnest.

The idea that, beyond certain superficial modes of expression, European and African knowledge exist in separate, radically different spheres originated in European thought, not in African thinking. It was (and continues to be) produced in European discourse and sold to Africans, a number of whom have bought it, just as they have internalized the colonizer's image of themselves. Presumption of difference, we have said repeatedly, is the enabling mindset of many musical ethnographers, and one such difference—perhaps the ultimate one—embraces our respective conceptual realms. The history of European thinking since the eighteenth century is replete with such presumption, itself nourished by racist and racialist sentiments. In a valuable recent compilation, Emmanuel Eze presents excerpts from writings by Carl von Linné, Georges-Louis Leclerc, David Hume, James Beattie, Immanuel Kant, Johann Gottfried Herder, Johann Friedrich Blumenbach, Thomas Jefferson, Georges Léopold Cuvier, and, not least, Georg Wilhelm Friedrich Hegel, among others, to exemplify the kind of thinking about race and difference produced during the period of (ostensible) Enlightenment.[12] Throughout there is presumption, an incorrigible will-to-difference sustained by ambitions to dominate at the cognitive and intellectual levels.

Contesting Ethnotheory

Not surprisingly, African philosophy, whose nominal task is to clarify our ways of knowing, has been the scene of a vigorous debate about ethnophilosophy. Chief among debaters is Paulin Hountondji, who argues for philosophy as a scientific discourse of universal standing rather than ethnophilosophy.[13] Hountondji's views have been contested by other philosophers. Olabiyi Yai, for example, describes what he calls "the poverty of speculative thought" in reference to some of Hountondji's propositions.[14] The rejection of ethnophilosophy, some fear, would mean disregarding our languages, our modes of artistic expression, and our religions; it would mean hopping on the bandwagon of some cosmopolitan, "scientific" model. Yet Hountondji is not opposed to imaginative uses of elements of our past in the drive to self-understanding. Rather, it is the specific contours of ethnophilosophy—its implicit embrace of unanimist thought and consequent "oversimplification of Africa's cultural past," its "external designation," and its presupposition of difference—that he feels diminish rather than free our horizons.[15]

How does the prefix "ethno-" arise in connection with African music? Quite simply in an attempt to value the specificity of African musical experience and intellection. Ethnotheory boasts a special sensitivity to the thought schemes of cultural insiders; it probes the metaphors that African musicians use, noting points of nonalignment between them and those of metropolitan languages. To be fair, ethnotheory is at present an implicit rather than explicit discourse in African musicology. Ethnographies that reach into the worlds set in motion by native categories and vocabularies pertaining to the aesthetics of music, speech, and dance prepare the way for a full-fledged ethnotheory.[16]

One should be suspicious of ethnotheory for three preliminary and external reasons. First, and in principle, all theory is ethnotheory because all theory aims at explaining the music produced by specific communities with specific "ethnic" identities. The influential analytical theory of Heinrich Schenker, for example, is not universal theory but an ethnotheory designed to explain a specific aspect of tonal ordering in masterpieces of mostly German and Austrian repertoires of the common practice period. To refer to Schenkerian theory as "theory" and to what the Kpelle do as "ethnotheory" makes no sense, although it may support a political stance that sees European music as the real thing and African music as other, different. Second, ethnotheory seems to be of particular concern to metropolitan scholars, not their colleagues in Africa. African musician-thinkers, while not insensitive to the semantic fields signaled by their own vocabularies and conceptual schemes, treat the schemes as open sets that admit accretions over time. And it matters little whether the accretions result from cultural exchange with Europe, the Middle East, or the Americas, with missionary discourses, or with popular culture. Like all others, African cultures are not frozen in time but are in a constant state of evolution. The tendency to flatten our histories, to stress the synchronic over the diachronic, and to confer on our cultures a certain timelessness epitomized in the dubious word "tradition" has had the very unfortunate consequence of keeping us in another time frame, of denying our contemporaneity (we are, according to a now defunct formulation, the West's "contemporary ancestors"), of underreporting the sometimes dramatic processes of change that dot our (ancient) history.

The study of change in scholarly representation is thus crucial. For example, reconstructing the histories of musical vocabularies found in various African communities would be instructive. Thus, the Ewe, who 200 years ago did not have a word for "conductor," now refer to an *atidala,* "the one who throws the stick." To say that the term emerged in response to a foreign performing practice is to use the matter of origins to deny the Ewe an opportunity to participate in a wider conversation. As far as I know, the term (and there are dozens like it) has not posed any problems for indigenous users, for whom such accretions are a normal part of language evolution. Only the eager ethnotheorist or the nostalgic African, anxious to separate out the "real" Africa from the Africa "spoiled" by Europe, will find uninteresting the terms and practices associated with *atidala.*

The possibility of translation suggests a third reason why we might be skeptical of ethnotheory. The fact that it is expressed in metropolitan language means that a central challenge of ethnotheory making, like that of ethnography making, is that of translation. To translate is to seek imaginative ways of negotiating boundaries and fusing worlds. Translation is a paradoxical act/art, for it is at once possible and ultimately impossible. It is possible because our idiomatic modes, although different, subtend a be-hind-the-scenes sameness in the kinds of forces or drives that animate them. It is impossible, however, because the residue of expressive modes, itself a repository of a history, experience, and worldview, cannot all be conveyed across linguistic divides. Yet the argument for translation's im-possibility harbors a certain amount of mystification. Because it is already verbally mediated, the putative proof of impossibility is itself translatable, at least in principle. We are thus forced, on logical as well as ethical grounds, to concede the translatability of local concepts, no matter how awkward, inelegant, or excessively "poetic." To accept the translatability of all indigenously produced knowledge is to accept the existence of a crucial level of nondifference between the conceptual worlds of any two cultures.

Celebrating Analytical Research

The importance of analysis for African music research cannot be underes-timated. Gone are the days when African music was either reduced to a functional status or endowed with a magical or metaphysical essence that put it beyond analysis. This is not to deny that African music serves func-tional ends—what music does not?—or that some of its practitioners in-vest it with ethical and spiritual powers. But there are other aspects deserving of close scrutiny. The compositional process, for example, re-mains understudied not only because of the normal elusiveness of orally and aurally based composition but also because machines for mystifica-tion abound. And yet, in order to understand the ways in which creative musicians assemble their music, we need to pursue in technical detail the processes of composition. Without analysis, such pursuit is not possible.

There are, of course, many approaches to the analysis of African music. I cannot review that literature here. I will simply draw attention to a handful of the many promising lines of inquiry while countering potential objec-tions to analysis as such. Analysis begins by setting limits, by identifying potential areas for study based on an initial hunch. It rejects the context-multiplying ideology that, if followed to the letter, renders analysis "unbe-ginnable." By reducing the number of a priori requirements for anyone wanting to analyze African music, we make possible a livelier, more rele-vant, ultimately more empowering discourse.

Hornbostel

In his groundbreaking article, "African Negro Music," Hornbostel pro-vided a wide-ranging discussion of the basic organizing principles of

Example 8-1

African music.[17] Basing his analyses on phonograph recordings—incidentally, Hornbostel believed that this approach was superior to taking down melodies directly in the field—he commented on the melodic, harmonic, and rhythmic aspects of African music in terms that have become familiar to later students. Hornbostel's approach is informed by Gestalt psychology, and his method is comparative without denying individual striking features. The article is laced with transcriptions of melodies from different parts of Africa and modest references to the existing literature. Although there are ideas to contest, including claims for drumming's generative role or the theory that African music constitutes a motional system, the author's broad vision, bold theses, and subtle individual perceptions combine to form an important early statement about African music.

One of the more intriguing representations in Hornbostel's article is a set of diagrams labeled "structure" (see illustration in Example 8-1, which is reproduced from page 42 of the article). Employing a form of hierarchic notation, Hornbostel displays the pitch content of each song in compressed form, directing attention to their tonal centers, often heard as the *finalis*. Hornbostel was clearly responding to an intuition that some notes are structural while others are embellishing, and that this basic distinction is operative on immediate as well as less-immediate levels of structure. Notes of different rhythmic value (sixteenth, eighth, quarter, half, and whole in the example) allowed him to display the underlying structure of melody. And given the relatively modest scale of the melodies, some sense of an overall melodic gesture, a concretization of Hornbostel's belief that African music is built on "pure melody," is conveyed.

Whether or not one agrees with the structure that Hornbostel unveils is not the point, although it is hard to see how one can fault his straightforward pitch summary. And the argument that structure might represent ideally moving forces rather than specific pitches, although fully compatible with Hornbostel's thinking, is not given priority in the representation. Although his knowledge of cultural context was second hand (information came from missionaries, colonial officers, and leaders of scientific expeditions), Hornbostel was nonetheless able to penetrate the surface of African music and provide fruitful pointers to further analysis. It may even be that it is precisely because context is downplayed that the analytical discussion can take off. Nowadays, we would do better than Hornbostel in displaying the linear structure of a given African melody, alert as we are to the compound nature of these melodies and to differing models of modal articulation that might dissuade us from treating final pitches as tonal centers. And we might even formulate more dynamic backgrounds that allow for an evolution of musical thought from one pitch (or set of pitches) to another. But these, properly speaking, are refinements, appendages to something that Hornbostel started, not new departures. How irrelevant would be charges that Hornbostel was analyzing music he did not record, that his theories were not shaped by "an African musical theory," that his was "armchair ethnomusicology"! Analysis, as a mode of performance, demands hands-on engagement with the inside of a composition, and this ensures a loss of authenticity because the in-time pressures of performance, which presumably impart some of the pleasure in the activity, force the performer or analyst to re-create structure, style, and meaning on the basis of his or her own (modern) judgment.

Blacking

Hornbostel was not the only scholar who sensed hierarchic organization at the tonal level in African music. In his ethnographically rich work on Venda children's songs, John Blacking includes a chapter entitled "The Structure of the Children's Songs: Patterns of Melody and Tonality."[18] Example 8-2 reproduces part of one diagram, together with a transcription of the second of the five songs analyzed. Reading from left to right, column 1 gives the "tone center" or focal pitch, which is usually found at the end. (Blacking occasionally indicates two rather than one tone center.) Column 2 contains an arhythmic reduction of the sequence of pitches in a given song, eliminating all adjacent repetitions. One can sing the path traced by this sequence of pitches to see how it is activated rhythmically and verbally. Column 3, probably the most interesting for the present discussion, consists of tone-rows. These, too, are pitch summaries, but unlike the presentation in column 2, which preserves the chronology of pitches, column 3

Example 8-2

displays total pitch content in a compressed form. The notes in each display are given different durational values, and this is because Blacking, like
Hornbostel, wishes to convey something of the hierarchic organization of
each melody.[19] He describes these as "weighted tone rows," although the
criteria for weighting are neither comprehensive nor conclusive. Alpha and
omega signs are used to mark the first and last notes of each song to underline their centrality, and a figure at the end of each stave states the total
number of pitch classes in each tone row (2, 4, 6, 6, 6). At a quick glance,
then, one can observe salient aspects of the structure of Venda children's
songs in a comparative setting. Indeed, paradigmatic representations like
these form part of the history of music analysis, having been used by Chant
scholars and music semioticians, among several others.[20]

We should point out that the book from which this demonstration is
taken is a detailed "cultural analysis" of Venda music, one of the major con-

tributions to African music research. Blacking, as is well known, was for a while obsessed with the imbrication of the musical in the social, and he wrote vigorously in *How Musical Is Man?* and elsewhere about their interdependence. But the explanatory potential of the social is limited because music, in order to come into its own as music, must assume a material form that obeys only those laws intrinsic to it. And while Blacking left no stone unturned in investigating the various contexts that impinge on Venda songs, he quickly reached the limits of such contextual thinking. And so he settled on an analytic representation of structure (Example 8-2) that, on the face of it, had little support from the Venda musicians he worked with. The structure he unveiled was his, informed, yes, by sporadic and indirect comments by "informants," but in no way attributable to them as their theory of structure. Should we discount Blacking's analysis because the representational means were borrowed from his European colleague Hornbostel? Should we say that structural analysis of African music is uncool because the Venda do not have a word for "structure"? Obviously not, because analyses are positive violations in the sense that they do not do things to objects; rather, they constitute those objects in the process of doing. And this constant reconstitution is one powerful testimony to the strength and resilience of African art.[21]

"Schenker"

It is likely that the distinction between a structural note and an embellishing one, or between a structural note and its means of prolongation, is widespread, perhaps universal. A definition of music that recognizes fluctuating intensities at the level of articulation of units implicitly recognizes such a distinction without, however, crudely equating strong articulation with structure and weaker articulation with embellishment. While differences are bound to exist among cultures in the specific or idiomatic ways in which people conceptualize such a distinction, the idea itself seems to impose itself wherever music is made. Various African repertoires feature songs in which classical diminutions like passing notes, neighbor notes, and arpeggiations animate the musical surface. Among the Northern Ewe, for instance, notions of embellishment are readily recognized in verbal discourse. The phrase *de atsiã me* means "putting decorations in it," which implies the existence of a structure apart from its decorations. So, although they have not yet produced full-fledged voice-leading graphs in the manner of Schenker, it would not be fanciful to suggest that some aspects of Schenker—or, more broadly, contrapuntal—thinking are fully compatible with Northern Ewe practice.

I have elsewhere borrowed the metalanguage of Schenkerian analysis to demonstrate a pervasive archetype in Northern Ewe song, and to suggest that attention to techniques of variation might aid understanding.[22] It was possible to extract—purely speculatively—a primal or Ur-melody, not un-like Hornbostel's "structure," and to show how individual segments of it are "composed out" using various prolongational techniques. The analysis drew attention to a purely musical residue: the internalized pitch path that guides the more complex negotiation of the music of language. For this repertoire at least, speech tones influence, but they do not determine, melodic contour.

It is this kind of compatibility between conceptual worlds that interests me. If it is valid, then, pursued to its limits, it can facilitate a more even-handed traffic in intellectual capital between musical cultures. Our flow of metalanguages will no longer be the one-way stream that currently ex-ists—essentially from Euro-America to the Third World—but will take on the character and movement potential of an unhierarchized network. Under such conditions, Eurocentric cross-culturalism will be replaced by a dense network of exchanges in which origins and destinations change reg-ularly and swiftly and are accessible to, and at the same time enriching for, all actors.

A Schenkerian approach to African melody, some would argue, is inap-propriate; it represents a form of intellectual imperialism—worse when practiced by native "mimic men" posing as scholars. Symbolically at least—the argument continues—voice-leading graphs carry too much baggage; the surface incompatibility between Africa and Europe is too jar-ring for comfort. As has been suggested repeatedly in this book, to argue in this fashion is to constitute geocultural spaces in oppressively narrow terms and to reveal a dubious ethics and aesthetics. The appropriateness of a representation must be judged by the result of action, not prohibited by fiat. And if the claims made for what a voice-leading graph shows about African melody are indeed supportable, then why deny the appropriate-ness of this metalanguage? Baggage, incompatibility, and symbolic vio-lence must, of course, be understood contextually, because far from representing unfortunate departures from pristine ideals, they are, in fact, perfectly in tune with the ethos of postcolonial experience.

In a 1993 article on the analysis of non-Western music, British scholar Jonathan Stock explores the problems and possibilities of Schenkerian ap-plication:

> In examining more closely the contribution that Schenkerian-inspired forms of analysis could make to ethnomusicology, it is possible to maintain that the reductive analysis of "purely" musical features is a currently underestimated tool, the adoption of which could endow ethnomusicological analysis with a more profound understanding of the creation and performance of sound struc-tures. Such an argument, which presupposes that the musical

analysis of non-Western musics is as valid as the anthropological analysis of non-Western musicians and audiences, may also highlight potential areas of contact between, on the one hand, ethnomusicological study and, on the other, the musicological analysis of pre-tonal, post-tonal and modal musical styles.[23]

Africanist ethnomusicology has yet to benefit from the "more profound understanding of the creation and performance of sound structures" that a Schenkerian perspective brings. To do so, we will need to dismiss as opportunistic the invocations of intellectual imperialism by our metropolitan allies, refuse help from ethnomusicologists seeking to protect Africans from foreign intellectual domination (the outcome will be intellectual isolation and impoverishment), and cunningly appropriate metropolitan techniques not in order to apply them in orthodox fashion—although such application may be strategic—but with a view to inflecting the very makeup of each technique in order to incorporate the imperatives of African structural procedure.

Arom

The search for an underlying model of musical structuring is also a concern of Simha Arom's, whose monumental work *African Polyphony and Polyrhythm* (published first in French in 1985 and in English translation in 1991) provides a systematic and leisurely explication of the organizing principles of the playing of horn ensembles in the Central African Republic.[24] Arom's book provides the most methodologically explicit approach to the analysis of any African music. In order to get at his model, he must set limits. All aesthetic factors are excluded, the words of songs are ignored, and matters of social context are suppressed. More significantly, Arom intrudes mightily in the field, recording and rerecording individual as well as combined horn parts in order to establish each musician's reference points and the overall limits of possibility. As often happens with such grand projects, the essential discovery is rather simple. Example 8-3 displays on a single staff Arom's reconstructed model for a portion of the Banda-Linda horn repertory, distilling the essence of an elaborate ensemble texture of

Example 8-3

some eighteen horn parts. The model provides a cognitive point of reference. Present and absent at the same time, it represents a deep song that gives birth to many surface songs. Arom's analysis gives concrete form to ideas of perpetual variation basic to African music. Others have intuited such structuring, some have even demonstrated processes of variation in other African repertoires, but Arom outdoes them all with the sheer mechanical thoroughness of his method.[25]

Readers of Arom complain about the intrusion of the researcher, the limited amount of contextual information, and the absence of a sound source to test the claims made in the book. But getting inside the music, revealing the bases of musicians' integrity, is not possible without imaginative hypothetical restructuring. Knowing right from wrong means being able to recognize one pattern as well formed, another as defective. And for this to happen, the musical organism must be dissected thoroughly, its parts reassembled in various experimental ways in order to test the stability of the native musician's intuitions. So Arom's intrusions are not only justified but necessary. Only by denying that a right-wrong axis operates among these Central African Republic musicians can one dispense with the strategy implicit in Arom's testing techniques.

As for the relative lack of contextual information, we need, perhaps, to remind ourselves that among Arom's signal contributions to research on African music is a series of recordings of various West and Central African musics, many of them thoroughly annotated. If, in the preparation of his magnum opus, he chose to overlook certain matters, it is surely because such contextual information was not deemed organic to the musical processes themselves, and therefore that suppressing it made possible a sharper focus on the purely musical. And regarding the absence of a correlated sound source, he might have been more generous to the reader. Empiricists searching for one-to-one correspondence between analytical claims and specific performance manifestations may well find this aspect of Arom's work frustrating. Yet in lectures, Arom displays the secret recording that his readers would love to have—a didactic arrangement of sound sources that underpin the method, beginning with a sense of the whole, then returning to reconstitute the ensemble in bits, finally reaching the whole again. Perhaps one day Arom will be persuaded to make this recording available to admirers of his work.

It is just possible, however, that the refusal to facilitate verification retains one advantage, which is that it forces readers to engage with Arom's copious transcriptions by hearing them off the page, so to speak, instead of waiting for the limited corroboration of an actual sound source. Certainly, the aural impression gained from reading these scores communicates ideas of repetition, hocket technique, isorhythm, and isometre. Euro-American composers looking for new ideas about rhythmic organization may well find what they need in Arom's scores; recordings would be superfluous. In that case, Arom's omission may be productively strategic. But it is also just possible that a disjunction exists between the specific performances that Arom recorded and the model that he postulates. Is the model an invention? Is it a laboratory creation that "bears little relation to practice," as Fargion might say?

Jones

One of the names that crops up frequently in Arom's text (and in this one, too) is A. M. Jones, whose *Studies in African Music* (1959) provided transcriptions in extenso of African drum music.[26] Jones's analyses betray the informality and empiricism that one sometimes finds in the work of other British analysts: They are not severely systematic like Arom was in his later work, nor are they explicitly theory-based. They consist, rather, of commonsense observations and insights into how the drum ensemble works rhythmically, whether such things as polymeter and polyrhythm exist, how tone relates to tune, and the impact of the new neofolk music on traditional African expression.

I have often returned to Jones not merely because he is master of the unguarded generalization but because there is hardly an issue in the study of African rhythm that he did not touch upon. And although there is plenty to disagree with, the topics of conversation exposed in his book are rich and diverse, and they have come to dominate subsequent thinking in the field. American writers as diverse as Gunther Schuller, Sam Floyd, Olly Wilson, and Robert Fink have turned to Jones for characterization of traditional African music,[27] as have theorists such as Kubik, Chernoff, and Arom, who have been careful to give Jones credit for certain penetrating insights.[28] Surveys of African music by Myers and Waterman, among others, have not found it possible to ignore Jones.[29] And American composer Steve Reich, some of whose compositions appropriate the devices of Ghanaian drumming, acknowledges Jones as the major influence on the development of his interest in African music.[30] Although the grapevine has it that some leading ethnomusicologists "do not read Jones anymore," there is clearly much to recommend his recognition of, and early attempts to explain, a number of basic features of African rhythm. None of this is to suggest that aspects of Jones have not been superseded. But only the institutional prejudice that targets Jones's ostensibly patronizing tone, grand overgeneralizations, controversial statements, or the informality of his approach will wish to remain deaf to the soundings from his many pages.

The most severe criticism of Jones came, not altogether surprisingly, from a fellow countryman, indeed one of the analysts whose work we are celebrating here: John Blacking.[31] Reviewing Jones's magnum opus for an area studies journal, Blacking offered two sets of criticism. First, the number of people involved in this analytical project was small—specifically two, namely, Jones and his sole informant, Desmond Tay. Second, the transcriptions were problematic. Blacking could not understand "why after twenty-one years' residence in Northern Rhodesia [Zambia], [Jones] should choose to write a book about the music of the Ewe of Ghana, basing his analyses largely on information collected from a single Ghanaian informant in London." But why not? Although as far as we know Jones never made the pilgrimage to Eweland, the fact that he developed an interest in their music hardly needs to be defended. Surely his experience in Zambia, his numerous writings about some of their repertoires, and the familiarity gained through listening to recordings of other African musics could easily have stimulated curiosity about Ewe music. And if good fortune brought him into contact with a knowledgeable and articulate "native informant," so much the better. Blacking's failure to understand Jones's choice is baffling. Did it rest, perhaps, on an uncompromising view that, unless the theorist's data were collected directly from the field and across a spectrum of musical activities, they were finally not admissible? By this reckoning, Jones could theorize Lala music all he wanted, but he had no comparable right with Ewe drumming. Why should Jones be thus confined? Doesn't the "field" migrate?

Blacking was especially troubled by Jones's habit of generalizing for the entire continent on the basis of limited evidence. But the validity of a given generalization is much more than a quantitative measure; it may reflect pragmatic or political ambitions as well. Given the state of written knowledge about African music in the 1950s, it surely could not have been inappropriate, for example, to assemble a map of Black Africa showing what intervals were used by which "tribes" in multipart singing; nor was it inappropriate to point to the wide provenance of a particular rhythm pattern and to enter some hypotheses about musical culture areas. The search for such commonalities had already yielded significant results in language studies, and a few musical precedents promised similar illumination. No doubt Jones's data was far from complete, but to deny the validity of the enterprise seems perverse. It may even be that one pressing project for us today is to update his map in light of ethnographic data accumulated over the last forty years. In the absence of such a synoptic view, some will continue to underestimate the scope of indigenous musical resources.

But to say that Jones's generalizing was premature is to pretend that it could ever be complete. Blacking invokes statistics to undermine Jones's results. According to him, Jones reports data from only 123 out of the 2,400 groups identified by linguists; and he lists only forty-one gramophone records out of presumably thousands known to exist. (Blacking declines to provide a figure.) No doubt these proportions would be greatly improved if one were undertaking a project like that today, but none will ever reach the ideal figure of 1, because the nature of the research enterprise necessitates an infinite deferral of such closure. It is noteworthy that Blacking's own strategy as a scholar was less thoroughly comparative in reference to intraAfrican streams of influence; rather, he milked the Venda for a discourse that would counter that of the hegemonic "West" or "Europe." Talk about generalization!

The statistical argument is even more problematic when applied to informants. "We want to know how the Ewe actually perform their music, not how one Ewe says they should perform it," writes Blacking. But who is this "one Ewe," and how might he differ from others? What if he is especially knowledgeable, talented, and hardworking? More is always better, some would insist. Yet that position already betrays an ideological choice, one that harbors the danger of leveling the knowledge possessed by different African subjects and failing to acknowledge genuine connoisseurs. No, the issue is not how many but *which* informant(s). If this position comes across as elitist, it is nonetheless entirely consistent with the pronounced hierarchies that regulate life in many African societies. Egalitarianism in knowledge construction is still myth, not (yet) reality.

Regarding Jones's transcriptions in volume 2 of his work, Blacking thinks that they are "unnecessarily long" and given in "monotonous detail." He writes:

Nothing is gained by printing page after page of identical drum patterns, and in fact it becomes more difficult for the reader to appreciate the total pattern of the music, because the numerous notes that do not change divert the eyes from those that do.

How long is "long"? The twelve play and fishing songs printed at the beginning of the volume occupy a total of ten pages. Then follow six Ewe dances, which take up, respectively, 30, 36, 16, 19, 53, and 52 pages. Finally, one Lala dance follows, at 19 pages, and the volume ends with a two-page appendix. Placed in the context of other orchestral scores, Jones's volume could hardly be thought of as long. (The print is large, too.) Perhaps the unfamiliarity of the repertoire did not justify such a spread. Perhaps the supplementary knowledge needed by students to bring these scores to life was not easily accessible. Perhaps some were startled by the apparent complexity of what was, after all, folk music from darkest Africa. Whatever the reasons, none could justify a wholesale rejection of this historically significant attempt to reduce significant chunks of African ensemble music to notation.

What about the "monotonous detail" charge, which presumably reflects Blacking's valuation of the extensive use of repetition in Ewe and Lala music? If we wish to probe the meanings—both structural and phenomenological—of repetition, then we need to observe and (silently) hear its material extent. Such an exercise is greatly aided by the availability of detailed scores. Surely, it is not too much to ask of the serious student to study fifty-two pages of the "orchestral" score of *Agbadza*? Granted, not every one is aesthetically drawn to repeated bell patterns, or to the changing rhythm narratives of the master drummer, or to persistent off-beat articulation. But for those who are, Jones's transcriptions make detailed study possible. In time, of course, students for whom repetition signals redundancy or monotony might choose a different analytical path than Jones; but for those who were eager in 1959 and the years following to begin to overcome the temptation to mystify African realities by denying their translatability into standard notation, Jones's work proved enlightening.

One virtue of extensive transcriptions is that they can shed light on musical form. A dance like *Agbadza* displays a cumulative, wavelike form engineered by cycles of repetition. Does Blacking's reticence about endorsing Jones's book reflect, perhaps, a feeling that laying bare such repetitive patterns, foregrounding excess, so to speak, challenges conventional understanding of repetition? Are we perhaps fearful of discovering that repetition is not something that distant others do, but something that all musicians find unavoidable? Confronting the message of Jones's and his followers' scores may prove more destabilizing in the metropolis than has hitherto been granted.

Anku

The work of Ghanaian ethnomusicologist, performer, and composer Willie Anku, although not (yet) widely known (Anku lives in Ghana, teaches in the School of Performing Arts at the University of Ghana, Legon, and has been notably reticent about publishing in institutionally prominent journals), illuminates, in ways not hitherto attempted, the drumming procedures employed by African musicians. He has so far published two booklets of detailed analyses of drum music: *Adowa*, an Akan funeral dance and *Bawa*, a Dagarti (northern Ghana) recreational dance.[32]

Anku describes his approach as "structural set analysis." Invoking certain elementary notions of set complementation, he shows that the lead drummer in the *Adowa* ensemble retains the integrity of his sets throughout, complementing all subsets or compensating for all supersets. A subset is incomplete, and will be completed later, whereas a superset takes more than its due and therefore gives back later. In this way, the drummer, assured that the basic texture is held in place by the bell and supporting drums, can create patterns that push and pull against the 12-beat reference. (Anku writes his transcription in 6/8 in order to convey what he feels is a strong dual feeling in the basic pattern but his referential modes take an implied 12/8 as point of reference.) The analysis is thus informed by a reconstruction of the compositional process. Although the actual motivic surface may lead some listeners to imagine alternative segmentations, Anku's analysis displays the master drummer's high intellectual achievement. Such sophistication is not unknown to students of these musics, of course; even the term "master drummer," which does not originate from among the people, speaks to it indirectly. But unlike those whose response to such ostensibly complicated practices is to shrink from explanation, Anku takes them apart to reveal the creator's method.

Second, by providing a detailed analysis of the master drummer's ostensible improvisations, Anku directs attention toward form in African music, an aspect that remains understudied and underappreciated, for too long eclipsed by the call-response principle. While no one doubts its prevalence or significance, there is more to African form than call and response. Indeed, call and response may function on lower levels of structure while other principles dominate at higher levels. In *Adowa,* the responsorial pattern is evident in the rhythmic work of the support drums while the lead drummer exposes distinct themes interspersed by bridge passages. While the specific order of themes may vary from performance to performance— indeed some may not be used at all—it is the idea of thematic manipulation, held in check by conventional transition, and allowing much repetition in response to specific dancers, that influences the emergence of a dance form. Form is not readily reducible to a formula; it is a procedure, not a mold.

Readers of Anku's work may complain that set theory is not African and therefore should not be used in analyzing African materials. Others will question the status of the artistic objects that Anku analyses, lament the absence of a field recording, and question the authenticity of the dances. These criticisms are irrelevant, of course, for the question is not who invented set theory or for what initial purpose but whether it can be put to intelligent use in areas not initially envisioned by its first users. As regards the complaints of self-appointed guardians of authenticity, Anku is surely following in a distinguished tradition of ethnomusicological analysis by intervening in the definition of the artistic object (Jones and Arom belong firmly to this tradition). The criticism that Anku's *Adowa* is not authentic overlooks the fact that a necessary condition for the production of ethnographic knowledge is a violation of authenticity. Anachronism is not something to be feared but something to be embraced in full awareness of what it leaves out and what it gains as a result. The digital playback recording that accompanies Anku's *Adowa* booklet contains recordings at half speed and quarter speed, which serve as an invitation to readers to experiment with re-creating *Adowa* rhythm—a kind of music-minus-one procedure.

Seeking a one-to-one correspondence between Anku's *Adowa* and a specific performance by a specific group on a specific day is seeking the wrong answer. The relevant issue here, as with Arom's model, is whether the rules of grammar for a given repertoire make possible the particular product that is analyzed. As long as native listeners recognize this as *Adowa*—putting aside for now whether they think it is a good or bad performance—the object is perfectly acceptable. Well-formedness, not preference, is what is at issue here. Insistence on a mystical authenticity robs us of a whole slew of insights stemming from the imaginative capacities of African musicians. It is finally not what is played on a given occasion but what is possible to play that counts. The emancipation of African music begins precisely at the point at which our priorities shift from valuing present realities to constructing future possibilities. Aligning analysis with composition should facilitate such a shift.

Conclusion

I began this chapter by noting the gaps that divide the musical subdisciplines, in particular music theory and ethnomusicology. These gaps originate in certain institutional arrangements, but they are also partly methodological. African musicology must be creatively skeptical toward these boundaries. I went on to relate some publishing experiences of my own, and finished by defending as well as celebrating analyses from different eras of African musicology, including the 1920s (Hornbostel), 1950s (Jones), 1960s (Blacking), 1980s (Arom), and 1990s (Anku). Limitations of space prevented a more extensive celebration, but I hope that what has been said here will be suggestive.

How not to analyze African music? There is obviously no way not to analyze African music. Any and all ways are acceptable. An analysis that lacks value does not yet exist, which is not to deny that, depending on the reasons for a particular adjudication, some approaches may prove more or less useful. We must therefore reject all ethnomusicological cautions about analysis because their aim is not to empower African scholars and musicians but to reinforce certain metropolitan privileges. Analysis matters because, through it, we observe at close range the workings of African musical minds. Given the relative paucity of analyses, erecting barriers against one or another approach seems premature. This is not to discourage critical discussion but to encourage the development of a compendium of analyses—for now, anyway.

Let us, therefore, get away from simple binary divisions of the world, the cultism that wishes to see a categorical difference between Western knowledge and African knowledge. Let us not wait to undertake fieldwork before starting to practice analysis. Music theorists and musicologists should feel at liberty to reach for any of the existing recordings in their libraries and start making transcriptions. Let us strategically overlook arguments about authenticity and embrace the prospect that any worthwhile analysis of an African composition or repertory will, in effect, compromise the authenticity of the artistic object. Finally, let us expose the following secret to our Africa-based colleagues and students: Music analysis, precisely because it minimizes certain forms of cultural knowledge, and because it principally rewards the ability to take apart and discover or invent modes of internal relating, may well be a site at which they can begin to compete favorably with their metropolitan colleagues. Those concerned about leveling academic playing fields could do worse than follow the path of analysis.

9
The Ethics of Representation

We might begin with a definition:

> Ethics is the branch of philosophy which studies the nature and criteria of right and wrong action, obligation, value and the good life, and related principles. Throughout its history it has been a normative and critical discipline, concerned with not only the analysis of concepts but also justifications and principles of how life should be lived. Usually without seeking to supply advice about immediate particularities (in the manner of preachers or agony columns), it has always retained relevance to practical principles, whether at the level of individual action or political policy. Thus principles of ethics necessarily underlie social and political philosophy, disciplines concerned ultimately with the ethics of power and the ethics of social formations and practices.[1]

These are pointed and dicey issues. How is one to determine what is good or bad, right or wrong? Good or bad for whom: the person initiating the action, the one receiving or being affected by it, a third nonparticipating observer, or some combination of these parties? Assuming we can identify a coherent and meaningful "we," in what ways and over what specific issues should we feel obligated to others? Can we agree on what is valuable and what is not? What constitutes the good life?

Granted that ethics, at least as formally defined, is both normative and applied: Is it appropriate "merely" to analyze wrong and right and leave it there, refraining from overt political action? Is it possible to discuss ethics without retreating into the relative security of a particular sociocultural context? And with specific reference to scholarly communities: Are we obliged to lead our lives according to an agreed-upon code of ethics drawn up by a handful of people, or is such a code likely to interfere with the higher goal of knowledge production? Does a code of ethics inhibit or promote intellectual freedom?

This definition of ethics does not refer to musical scholarship, but insofar as it reiterates a standard view that it is "the study of the nature and basis of moral principles and judgments, [one that is] concerned with what is morally good and bad, right and wrong,"[2] it affirms the relevance of ethics to musical practice and scholarship, indeed to any humanistic practice or scholarship that embraces more than one individual. Although music, throughout the ages, has not gone unnoticed by philosophers—its moral effects are acknowledged by European medievalists, Indic musicologists, and African healer-singer-poets, among many others, and the ethics of composing are occasionally mentioned—the issues appear so complex and subjective that they have seemed to resist intensive reflection. The study of music has not, in short, experienced anything like the so-called ethical turn that other humanistic disciplines have experienced recently.[3]

Yet, it is not hard to imagine the kinds of issues that might be of interest to ethically minded musicologists, issues that might form the bases of discussion in lectures and seminars, at professional meetings, and in online discussion groups. When we construct and interpret so-called facts for biographical study, to what extent are we guided by ethical principles? What are the ethics of performing songs whose texts contain anti-Semitic, sexist, or racist sentiments? Do we read such texts as artistic works with a complicated connection to real life; ascribe an intention to their authors; or do the composers who set such texts become secondary authors and thus stand accused of endorsing the original intention? Is it morally right to spend large sums of money on the production of a new edition of, say, Verdi's *Rigoletto,* given the negligible number of substantial changes it might offer, and given the alternative humane causes to which such money and resources might be put? What possible ethical attitude might lie behind the unqualified assertion that "Western music is just too different from other musics"?[4] What is an appropriate ethical perspective on the critical interpretation of a piece of instrumental music, a form of wordless discourse? Is our choice of metaphor governed by an ethical attitude?

Consider also the smaller community of music theorists, some of whose work tends to be systematic and abstract. About the foundations of their discipline, we could ask whether it is morally right to erect a system of relations as universal when only a tiny portion of the world's music uses that system? When analyzing the atonal repertory of the early twentieth century, to what extent are scholars' procedures of segmentation governed by ethical principles? Without confining analysis to that which can be heard, and allowing for a gap between present and future hearing, is it nevertheless morally defensible to propagate certain intramusical relations as hearable when in fact there is no empirical demonstration of their ever having been heard? And would an empirical demonstration be a sufficient condition for passing the ethics test?

And consider, finally, the work of ethnomusicologists, which often involves contact with other cultures: Is it ethical to divide up the musics of the world into two, Western and non-Western, and to use the label "World Music" for the latter? Is the production of an ethnography on the basis of a short period of fieldwork ethically sound? Is it moral, in crafting our ethnographies, to suppress the asymmetries of power that attend the production of knowledge about "others"? What ethical considerations govern a so-called native scholar's construction of images of his or her own people?

These are difficult questions that may not be answered facilely or with an unargued moralist stance. I raise them here partly to suggest that we might profit from seeking answers, and partly to lament the reticence of music scholars. It is true that heated debates have occasionally erupted in musicological circles over such things as the facts of Shostakovich's memoirs, the appropriate forces for performing J. S. Bach's choral works, Stravinsky's setting of texts figured as anti-Semitic, and Schubert's sexual orientation. But none of these has been framed directly as a matter of ethics. Nor is it clear the extent to which members of the American Musicological Society are aware of, or indeed guided in their day-to-day activities by, the "Guidelines for Ethical Conduct" that they receive with each new edition of their *Directory* (pp. xxx–xlii in the 2001 issue).

It is similarly true that some of the most passionate debates in music theory and analysis touch on matters of belief and foundations; one thinks of Ernst Oster's attack on Roy Travis over whether Schenker's theory can be extended to twentieth-century music, Richard Taruskin's exchange with Allen Forte over the explanatory capabilities of set theory,[5] and a far from unanimous response by six music theorists (Patrick McCreless, Scott Burnham, Matthew Brown, Joseph Dubiel, Marion Guck, and myself) to the charge that their discipline remains trapped in formalist ideology.[6] But here, too, no one has been courageous enough to invoke an ethical framework. Indeed, unlike the American Musicological Society or the Society for Ethnomusicology, the Society for Music Theory lacks a published code of ethics. And finally, although ethical matters surface more overtly in ethnomusicology, it is surprising that they do not do so more frequently. Writing in 1992, Mark Slobin found "no self-reflective statements on ethical issues in ethnomusicology until the 1970s."[7] This was not to suggest that ethnomusicology in its first twenty years or so proceeded without moments of ethical doubt or awareness, only that sustained and intense reflection was slow to emerge.

So, why have music scholars avoided ethics? A simple answer might be that ethics is a soft concept that, although pertinent, cannot finally be formulated in a way that can guide practical behavior, professional as well as personal. While we might all agree that as social beings we should be concerned with good and bad, right and wrong, we may not necessarily agree on their concrete expression. Then, too, it might be said that there are no viable *communities* of music scholars—community understood as a unified body of individuals, bound by common characteristics. Many professional associations are merely convenient places to pursue careers; the basis of association rarely touches territory that might extend into a deeper, personal realm. Because ethics is produced in the course of interpersonal exchange, the absence of bona fide communities removes a crucial enabling element. Until such a time in the future that such communities come into existence, an ethical musicology, music theory, or ethnomusicology may continue to elude us.

But this structural absence signals only the tip of the iceberg. What should the content of ethics be? Who decides? How does one correct ethical violation beyond an appeal to the legal code, which, in any case, is not primarily a code of ethics? In situations of intercultural intercourse (Americans working in European libraries, Europeans doing fieldwork in Africa), whose ethics should predominate? Do ethical standards evolve, and if so, how are they regulated? Is ethics finally possible?

It is tempting to declare the impossibility of ethics even before we have begun a formal investigation; but this would be perverse. Highlighting the difficulty at the outset should make us work harder toward defining the conditions of possibility for a relevant ethics. Swimming against a strong tide, we would aim to resist the stubborn skepticism of those who find the status quo perfectly adequate, and for whom talk of ethics threatens to remove some of their privileges. Because ethnomusicology is the subdiscipline that has dealt most directly with ethical questions, and the subject of this book falls in part under its umbrella, we might as well use it as a touchstone. Let us start with two leading practitioners: Barbara Krader and Mark Slobin.

On the Difficulty of Grounding a Discussion of Ethics

In a 1980 article introducing the field of ethnomusicology, Barbara Krader mentions, but does not dwell on, the fact that "ethical considerations are particularly relevant in the study of the music of underdeveloped countries."[8] Putting aside the question whether "ethical considerations" might not be equally relevant to developed countries, we might ask for whom such considerations are relevant. Krader suggests that the ethical issue is an issue for the Westerner or the researcher, not the non-Westerner or researched. According to her, a "trained [Western] researcher" can make a significant contribution to knowledge in collaboration with "native informants." But whose is the resulting knowledge, where is it kept, who benefits from it? Krader does not deal explicitly with these questions, but it is not hard to guess what her answers would be. Just as the non-Westerner or researched is written out of the ethical issue, so the knowledge produced about his or her society is owned by the Westerner; it is housed in their libraries and archives, and consulted most often by them. Krader does not consider the radical possibility that the Western researcher might be irrelevant in the non-West; nor does she entertain the prospect of non-Westerners becoming theorists in their own right, not just "native informants." And she affirms the lingering suspicion that ethnomusicology is a discipline of the West for the West by the West.

The asymmetrical nature of the relationship between researcher and researched is not dramatized in her account, only acknowledged. Even where Krader recommends training "young musicians from underdeveloped countries, and other non-Western cultures" in ethnomusicology, she imagines this to be done *in* the West *with* ethnomusicological tools. The struggles of national governments and ministries of education and the arts to institutionalize music study are thus given short shrift. It would seem that the "special insights" of native specialists have meaning only as supplements to proper ethnomusicological knowledge. Ethics, in short, together with all the factors that inform an ethical environment, becomes an issue for "us," not for "them."

One should not be unduly critical, because Krader's mention of ethics has the virtue of being, according to Mark Slobin, "the first such discussion in a standard reference work."[9] Noteworthy is the fact that in the revised version of the same reference work (*The New Grove Dictionary*) Krader's article has been replaced by a longer, multiauthored one while the subject of ethics has been dropped altogether. Indeed, there is no separate entry for ethics in this twenty-nine-volume reference work. At the very least, then, Krader's remarks of 1980 are commendable.

A more extended discussion of ethics appeared in an introduction to the field of ethnomusicology published in 1992. Written by ethnomusicologist Mark Slobin, the article runs to eight pages, one of the three shortest in the volume, the others being Tilman Seebass's piece on iconography and Kathryn Vaughn's on pitch measurement. Granted that length as measured in pages is not necessarily an indication of the value placed on a subject, it is nevertheless hard not to form the impression that discussion of ethics does not yet hold the highest priority for this group of ethnomusicologists. Slobin's article is significant precisely as an embodiment of a problem.

Frustrated at not being able to isolate "ethical norms" that might then be said to be violated, and sensing the radically contextual nature of ethical considerations, Slobin pitches his article in prospect, not in retrospect. In other words, issues are framed in terms of what might be done—a future, conditional discourse, not-yet but may-happen:

> What if you find a rare instrument in the field, the only one of its kind known to exist, but one likely to be undervalued by the people you are researching? Do you acquire it in the name of science or preservation, perhaps by offering a small sum of money, or do you leave it alone? Is it ethical to record esoteric, secret ceremonies? And what about native musicians who, while on tour abroad, insist on playing stereotypical pieces, instead of those that convey the depth and authenticity of their native cultures? What about writing record jacket notes for recordings whose circumstances of production you do not agree with?[10]

Perhaps it is just as well that these issues are broached with a hypothetical inflection, because whenever Slobin takes a resolute stand, and says something that approaches the condition of an ethical norm, we sense some tension, some equivocation, a difficulty in grounding the discussion. Consider for example the one case that Slobin believes "would probably be universally condemned in the discipline." This is the case in which "roving pseudo- or quasi-Ethnomusicologists . . . produc[e] records after the most casual of contact with local musicians without informing them of the intention to market their music." The word "probably" is crucial. What is the basis for condemnation? Surely not deception, because fieldworkers routinely deceive their subjects. (Indeed, deception, including the withholding of information, may be regarded as a condition for successful fieldwork in Africa.) And what guarantees that recordings made after a longer period of acquaintance with the researched will be better, ethically speaking, than those made by "roving pseudo- or quasi-Ethnomusicologists"? What and whose criteria of value are being invoked here? What if a recording made under ostensibly objectionable circumstances turns out to possess superior (acoustic) quality? What if students find the musical material fascinating? Slobin's surmise that the behavior of these impostors will "probably be universally condemned" may echo the view of his fellow professional ethnomusicologists, a group seeking—understandably—to protect its turf by keeping the uncertified out. But for nonethnomusicologists, condemnation may not necessarily be the automatic response. Indeed, if we excavate the network of factors that have made possible some of our most cherished recordings of, say, traditional African music, we may well find a surprisingly large number of ethical violations. What to do with such recordings in the wake of such revelations?

Grounding a discussion of ethics in explicit ethical norms is thus difficult, perhaps impossible. Many factors hint at the complexity of the issues: who the social actors are and what cements their relationships as members of a community; what the agreed-upon tasks and the community's aspirations are; what corrective or punitive measures exist; what is the community members' view of alterity; and the ethics of inter- or cross-cultural contact, to name a few. It makes sense, then, to approach ethics in African music research not by looking for an abstract grounding principle but by focusing on specific, local situations in which we can better control the necessary constraints.

Ethical Clues in Performing Practice and Song Texts

African ethical thought is the product of various historical and sociocultural circumstances. If we take our orientation from precolonial, preliterate African society, we may, following Appiah,[11] identify the formal features of African ethical thought as follows. First, traditional societies are communitarian or communalistic; rights are essentially "corporate," associated with family, lineage, village, or society. Second, the structure of thought is antiuniversalist. The ethical reach extends only as far as the boundaries of the community, not beyond to some imagined global or universal community. It may be, however, that the impulse is not actively to resist or, indeed, oppose a universalizing reach—as Appiah's prefix "anti" might suggest—but to accept the pragmatic limits of a given cultural landscape. Third, traditional ideas are naturalistic. Gods, spirits, and ancestors regulate life in the natural world. Fourth, "there is often no clearly differentiated and distinctively moral vocabulary. Ethics as a discourse is not differentiated, say, from aesthetics or certain forms of technical language." Fifth and consequently, "African systems of thought are profoundly anthropocentric or humanist." That is to say that they are "centered on the contemporary concerns of human beings (including ancestors) rather than on otherworldly considerations."

Appiah supplements his fivefold characterization of the form of African ethical thought with observations about the contrasts between Africa and Euro-America. First, the focus in Africa is not on individual rights. Second, propriety, reputation, and status are central to practical reasoning, whereas in Europe they are considered superficial. And third, there are "no models of organized reflection [as regards] private moral reflection." Such reflection is collective and based in oral traditions. There are, in other words, no "models of interiority in moral life" in precolonial Africa, in a way that the novel or autobiography in Europe have provided channels for a "private morality."

Not all precolonial African societies exhibit these features in the same ways, but Appiah's characterization is confirmed by a number of ethnographic reports on African religious belief. Yet this is only true of precolonial or traditional society. What happens when we factor in the impact of Christianity? And what about Islam? And what of various Marxist and neo-Marxist ideologies? Clearly, the picture becomes more complicated. Which is why Appiah concludes his concise survey by acknowledging "very substantial ethical crises" produced by the combined forces of modernization, urbanization, literacy, and the imitation of Western artistic modes of expression.

Turning to music, we may identify two related areas that are rich in information about ethics: the site of performance and the content of song texts. In a number of traditional societies, there is a widely shared belief that communal music-making presupposes being at peace with your fellow performers. You do not make music with people with whom you are feuding, or toward whom you harbor wicked intentions. If we are all together and I start making music and I see you standing there but not participating, I will immediately suspect that you hate me or that you are harboring evil thoughts toward me; perhaps, you are planning to kill me. The communalist ethos demands that we drum, sing, or dance *with* others. This does not mean that an element of competition is totally absent. Rather, the deep meaning of my singing is guaranteed only by your participation, your bonding with me. I sing with you and others not so as to win but to affirm mutual investments in belief systems. Thus, when you see drummers drumming, dancers dancing vigorously, singers singing deep words, they mean, among other things, to avow a certain ethical stance.

The site of performance, then, is one at which we uphold the highest ethical standards. Which explains why many performing situations demand an explicit acknowledgment of the presence of gods and ancestors. We pour libation to request their presence and seek their protection. If we do not call on them, and a dancer gets possessed, she may enact uncontrolled or dangerous behavior that may eventually bring trouble; she may not even come out of the possession, or she may lose her mind. So we break a branch over her head, or place a green leaf on her to cool her down. In the process, we signal the presence of those more powerful than us. This is why even the most virtuosic of African drumming, the most athletic of African dancing, or the most elaborate of African singing is never identical with pure virtuosity or mere athleticism or vocal pyrotechnics for their own sake. Virtuosity, athleticism, and vocal pyrotechnics may indeed be on display, but they are effects of a spiritual or ethical performing attitude, not ends in themselves. When African drumming, dancing, and singing are removed from their spiritual homes, reduced to musical forms divested of cultural meaning, they lose the power that they have in traditional society. And this is often what happens when these traditions are enacted outside Africa, indeed, outside their communities of origin and primal enactment. Such transformations are unavoidable, of course, given the vigorous contemporary trade in cultural products. Although it would be a step in the right direction if so-called African drumming groups in Europe, the United States, and Canada sought to inculcate in their members something of this ethical attitude, they should not be denied the privilege of purposeful violation.

This portrait of a thoroughly ethical performance site in traditional society is, of course, an invention. Given an unprecedented degree of interethnic contact, the linguistic and spiritual bases of many repertoires have nowadays been transformed. Without the relative homogeneity of small communities, the communal ethos has proven hard to keep intact. Then also, the commodification of African musics and dances, manifest in staged performances before nonparticipating audiences, poses new challenges to anyone wishing to maintain the highest ethical standards in performance. The result is that African musicians have had to devise ways of paying lip service to "tradition" while responding to newer, modern imperatives. For example, choreographers may retain the morphology of an ancient dance while divesting it of its spiritual and ethical content. The behavior of individual musicians may also embody the conflicting imperatives of tradition and modernity. A well-known lead drummer was notorious for sleeping with the female dancers in his group, a number of whom were other people's wives. (He himself had four.) A wonderfully gifted drummer and inspiring group leader, he could extract whatever form of behavior he desired from his dancers, drummers, and singers. It seemed, in fact, that he could get away with anything. Unfortunately, he died suddenly and under mysterious circumstances. Although the medical people thought they knew what killed him, our people had their own explanation. Had he gone too far in taking what did not belong to him? Had he violated the code of ethics that regulated life in traditional society? We may never know. The fact remains, however, that the idea of performance as a thoroughly ethical set of transactions has become increasingly difficult to maintain in practice. Perhaps contemporary performers are developing new solutions to the problem of performance ethics; but perhaps we have simply crossed over into an era of unethical performing.

A second main repository of traditional wisdom, moral philosophy, and ethics is the content of song texts. This is not to suggest that codifying a society's morals is the primary function of song. Song words are primarily embodiments of certain patterns of play, animated by certain poetic techniques and rhythmic figures. Song words are destined for song, means to an end. Nevertheless, wise composers and ethically motivated singers do not overlook opportunities to edify by projecting shared values or communal beliefs. And it is here that questions of right and wrong, good or bad, are presented directly or, more usually, indirectly. Song words may enjoin us to reflect on the ways we order our lives. This does not mean that the message of song is readily decoded. Song texts may be obscure, counterintuitive, or even meaningless. And imperfections in the mode of transmission ensure that there is no necessary uniformity in the way successive generations read and value the same song.

One Northern Ewe song announces that "Sponge and soap went to the river; soap came back, but not sponge." Now, this is a reversal of the normal situation, because soap should disappear first, not sponge. The fact that sponge finishes before soap gives us pause, reminding us that human knowledge is partial, and that our destinies are not always in our own hands. Hearing this text at the start of a performance inspires participants to adopt an appropriately reverential pose. The listener, too, is stimulated to purely contemplative behavior. The way to create an ethical frame of mind in performers and audiences is to give them something to chew on, a deep or enigmatic thought, perhaps.

Speaking more directly to ethics are those songs designed to correct antisocial behavior. "Yao Kowua," begins a Northern Ewe song, "a real man does not work two jobs." "Yao Kowua" is the name of a man who has been identified as working a second job—in contrast to the rest of us, who only work one. And "one job" means one legitimate job. It turns out that Yaw Kowua's second job was stealing, a mode of behavior frowned upon because it poisoned the community ethos. And so someone composed a song about him. The day the song was sung, Yao Kowua left the village in shame. He never returned. (The song continues to be sung, however, just in case there are other Yao Kowua's out there.)

A special place should be reserved for so-called songs of insult. The idea that verbal insults are sanctioned for community use would seem at first to be antithetical to the spirit of ethics. But good and bad in the genre of insults reside in the same place, making this a rich site for uncovering ethical thought. One famous tradition of insulting is the so-called *haló* tradition of the Anlo-Ewe, now extinct, having flourished between 1912 and 1962 (this according to Daniel Avorgbedor, who has written extensively about the tradition).[12] The word *haló* means "song-proverb" or, in Avorgbedor's gloss, "great song." Proverbs are known to be fruitful sites for the discovery and creation of some of a society's beliefs. A "war of insults and music," *haló* involves rival clans, wards, or villages, who assemble formally to exchange painful and far-reaching insults in the medium of song. The use of insults is not, of course, confined to this specialized repertoire. A broader "insult culture" is present among the Anlo-Ewe, through which a certain amount of moral and ethical instruction takes place. There are, in other words, socially approved ways of insulting people, and one challenge to proper ethical insulting lies in maintaining the appropriate conventions.

In a typology of insults assembled by Avorgbedor, facial and head features, manners, and biography form the loci of insults. I may say of my rival that he has a thin, dry face, or that his face lacks discipline, or it is dirty, or it is unfocused. His head may be round, or he may be twin-headed. About his manners, I may point out that he is useless, empty, too lazy, backward, rotten, untamed, or a bad dancer. And I may describe him as taking someone else's wife, possessing foreign ancestry, or being a thief. If my rival is a woman, I may say of her that she is trading with Mother Earth, or is a prostitute, a gossip, or barren.

When deployed in *hal* songs, these day-to-day insults acquire an added aesthetic dimension. Literal truth is not necessarily the goal of poet-composers. Some songs may indeed be based on historical events; others may deliberately distort historical truth in order to achieve greater rhetorical impact. *Halo* is thus a paradoxical moral practice. By singing insults, performers attain catharsis in a socially approved way. But precisely because the medium is song and not speech, the raw effect of a spoken insult is mediated by memorable melody or polyphony and by the common understanding that we are merely "playing." And this apparently contradictory practice of teaching morality by ostensibly violating it models an ethics of Ewe society at large, a society in which varieties of musicoverbal genres are used in the daily teaching of good and bad, virtue and vice, right and wrong. (Violent clashes have been known to erupt as a result of *halo* performance—testimony to the fact that the boundaries between life and art are not always comfortably maintained.)

Are there clues to the practice of scholarship in the kinds of ethical thought discussed so far? Suppose, for example, that we import the Anlo-Ewe insult culture into Africanist ethnomusicology, and perhaps even find imaginative ways of assimilating it into our code of ethics. Imagine describing an ethnomusicologist as having a crooked penis, or referring to another as lazy, or telling a senior colleague that his face is bony, or saying to another that she is an empty shell on account of her barrenness. These may be provocative and perhaps extreme examples, but it surely will be a long time before music scholars feel comfortable about trading insults in the process of community building. And despite all the talk about globalization nowadays, it may take a while before the trade in ethical norms extends to the relinquishing of one's individuality, or letting status determine in advance the value of what is spoken. Behind the roughly relativistic liberal position lies an ethical absolutism manifest in the metropolitan rejection of others' ethics. Once again, we are reminded that researcher and researched inhabit different spheres, that the discontinuities between our worlds are highly marked. Proceeding in full awareness of these discontinuities may in some ways be far more desirable—and ethical—than pious and premature efforts to close the gap.

Fieldwork Ethics: Some Personal Reflections

In July of 1986, during fieldwork in Ghana, I went to the village of Akpafu-Odomi to record some music. I am myself an Akpafu, but I come from the Akpafu on the hilltop, Todzi. In spite of enduring rivalries and tensions between the Akpafu villages, I was, together with a group of American volunteers, welcomed with open arms. In a number of prayers offered that day, I was described as the son of my father. (My father's name was Onaiyere, which means "he has no name"; he was named as nameless in order to deceive the spirits that had taken all but one of his siblings away in infancy.) It was claimed that he did what was good to do at the time I was born by sending me to school. Book knowledge—but not necessarily wisdom—then made it possible for me to go abroad, where I saw and heard things. Now I had decided that I should bring the people I work with to my home. And so the ancestors should bless the occasion, make me rich with money and cloth, so that others might benefit from my wealth. (Prayers accompanying the pouring of libation are invitations to skilled individuals to indulge a narrative habit. Some of the people who held forth about me on that occasion knew little or nothing about me prior to that, but this did not stop them from supplying their own texts. "Facts" were made up as we went along. A pedantic analysis of the truth value of statements made in these prayers would be very much beside the point, as would any attempt to track the outcome of the prayers.)

At one point during the recording of drumming, dancing, and singing, the chief of the village, Nana Ntiamoah II, called me aside and told me in a somewhat stern voice that when I take my recordings over there (i.e., to America), I should not go and say that they represent the music of the Akpafu people as a whole; rather, I should identify them specifically as coming from Akpafu-Odomi. I told Nana I had heard, that I would do as he had requested, and went back to work.

However, when I came to write up my research, years later, I saw no need to make the particular distinction Nana Ntiamoah had asked me to make. Working within a structuralist framework dedicated to explicating general principles, I ignored specific features and favored shared ones. My aim was to define a musical grammar. To have insisted on identifying all my Akpafu-Odomi material in the way that Nana Ntiamoah demanded would have produced an even more awkward and inelegant text. Nor was it clear to me that the chief was in a position to appreciate a grammar of Akpafu music, or to understand the institutional constraints under which I was operating. So I ignored what he said. In effect, it might be claimed, I broke my word to him.

Did I act ethically? I don't know, but I'm quite certain that I did not act unethically. The constraints imposed on us during fieldwork are often different from those imposed during the production of our ethnographies. The proof of one's attentiveness and sensitivities to the local environment lie in the text one makes afterwards. And that is where we have to contend with the inescapable fact that writing and representation, mediated by thick layers of convention, are irreducibly intertextual. So if the various texts and intertexts implicated in our cross-cultural effort are not assembled comprehensively and with great care, questions of ethics cannot be properly understood. Not that the conventions of scholarly representation are fixed and unalterable. But because I was not persuaded that Nana Ntiamoah's request was motivated by honorable concerns, and because it was not clear what we had finally agreed on in our brief exchange, a radical revision of academic practice on my part did not seem called for.

Well, there is (at least until I wrote this) no external record of my exchange with Nana Ntiamoah; nor is it possible to confer with him fifteen years later, for he left to join our ancestors three years ago. But for those inclined toward the view that something unethical has transpired, let me propose that we not underestimate the complexities of cross-cultural translation. Remember that systematic deception—understood and recognized as deception—is so much a part of day-to-day living in this part of the world that assumptions about the transparency of certain pronouncements may prove hazardous. Could it in fact be that Nana understood the expression on my face, sensed the quiver in my voice, and suspected that I had not half an intention of making the particular distinction that he was so anxious that I make? Were not the very circumstances in which this command was delivered such that no answer except "yes" was possible? (To say "no" to the chief in public would amount to a serious violation of etiquette, but this is not the same thing as saying that subjects have no way of registering difference from the big man.) It is further possible that Nana Ntiamoah understood that, as an Akpafu, I was conversant with the saying, "The time that you're in, its thing is what is done." This saying, the temporal equivalent, perhaps, of "When in Rome do as the Romans do," sanctions pragmaticism, wisdom, opportunism, cunning. So, by "lying," I was actually speaking the truth of the Akpafu tradition, the truth that required me to embrace the challenge of contemporaneity as I encountered it, for example, in the viciously competitive academic world of the United States. An analysis of this incident—or rather my account of this incident—that maintained that I said one thing and did another is likely to be flawed, because what I "said" may not be what I said. To seek to cut through the maze by means of a naive-realist view of "truth" is to approach this African culture with the wrong tools. Indeed, if this experience is generalizable, it may reinforce the point—made often enough in this book—that deception is necessary for successful fieldwork. If deception is judged to be unethical, then the construction of an ethnography can never be an ethical process.

On another occasion in 1986, I went with a different group of American volunteers to record sacred and recreational music in the village of Avenui-Awudome. We had overlooked the fact that one of the Awudome towns had recently been at war with its neighbors to the west, the people of Peki, over disputed land. We thought nothing, therefore, of including in our entourage a native of Peki. At one point, I adopted a deliberately naive manner (another mode of deception!) and inquired about their most sacred drum. We noticed that the drum formed part of the ensemble of drums, rattles, and bells we were recording, but seemed to be hidden from view. "May we photograph this drum?" I asked. Everything rapidly came to a halt. Photograph their most sacred drum, the drum that accompanies warrior groups into battle? Some people seemed not to mind (I was assured that nothing would register on the camera's film!), but a very vocal group was implacably opposed. Although I made a feeble attempt to withdraw my request (studied feebleness indexes another act of deception), the cat was now out of the bag: The matter would be settled in the chief's house. So we abandoned the recording, trekked there, and after an elaborate exchange of greetings, (re)presented a formal request to photograph the drum. By now, I had played up the fact that I was a student of culture, that I was only there to learn. Before permission could be granted, the chief demanded to know *who* was in our entourage and where they came from. My heart missed several beats as I thought of our man from Peki. You see, it would have been dangerous in the extreme to let on that he was from enemy territory because this would have aroused suspicion that he had been smuggled in as a spy to collect war secrets. Our request to photograph their most sacred drum would have taken on added significance. We had no moral choice, it seemed, than to replace our coworker's Peki identity with another. We even insisted that he knew none of our local languages. Assured that our purposes were not exploitative or intrusive, or politically or militarily motivated, the chief gave us permission to photograph the sacred drum.

I do not exaggerate when I say that our man could have been killed if we had spoken the truth about his origins and identity. Did we act unethically in lying? In retrospect, it is hard to imagine that we did. Of course, speaking the truth may have had other consequences because it was not Avenui that was at war with Peki but Tsito, one of its neighbors. Still, we erred on the side of caution. The situation was precarious. Had our friend been killed and his testicles removed—as was said to have happened only a few weeks earlier to a member of the Peki royal family who strayed onto a farm in Tsito—blame would very likely have been placed on me. And knowing how inventive our people can be when it comes to narrating such events, basic questions about my claim to be there to learn about culture would have been raised. Dare one conclude, then, that there is virtue in deception, in hiding the truth? Does not the unveiling of a certain form of truth qualify as unethical if it is likely to produce a tragic outcome?

To choose a third example: when I came to write *African Rhythm: A Northern Ewe Perspective,* I was faced with the challenge of fashioning a plausible and informative ethnography.[13] I had neither the skill nor the data to provide a scientific account of Northern Ewe culture. Nor had I spent the time in the field collecting numbers and names, which, it ought to be said, are no more than culturally specific modes of knowledge organization. I recalled a framework that I knew intimately as a child, namely, that of the folktale. At the end of a typical performance, the narrator would say, "I have come to deceive you with this tale," or "This tale was given to me by an old lady down the road to come and deceive you with it." The idea was that, unlike the real world, which imposes all kinds of constraints on permissible utterance, the fictional world constructed in folktale performance allows the imagination free rein, making possible any and all utterances without fear of offending someone or violating the ethics of narration. Fiction is free, realism restricted. So I went the fictional ethnography route: I reported some events, and made up several others on the basis of things I remembered as a child and stories told to me by family, relatives, and friends.

How ethical is a fictional ethnography? A lot depends on the claims made for it, of course, because there can be nothing wrong with an ethnography that concedes its fictional status. Did I violate some ethical norm by writing about things that never happened during fieldwork? Perhaps so, perhaps not. The medium of language, with its multiple resonance and conceptual slipperiness, has always seemed to me incapable of conveying "real" truths. To go the way of realist ethnography, one based ostensibly on truth, I would have to adopt a naive pose about the way language signifies. So why not accept the artificial and constructed status of any ethnographic report? Why not allow the imagination to do ethnographic work? Why resist the writerly urge, the urge to write in the style of, rather than to write about? Is it not unethical to assume the transparency of language, press it into service in the construction of an ethnography that ostensibly presents only the "facts" of a given culture? Should it not be our aim, in crafting a fictional ethnography, to achieve an uncanny fusion of real and imagined worlds? Are we not, in fact, being ethical precisely by encouraging rather than suppressing the role of the imagination in ethnographic construction?

It is possible that some of these experiences are specific to so-called native scholars. And some may deny that the stories I tell have value for a more normative understanding of ethics. Because ethnography classically involves non-native scholars, such experiences as I might have are at best of tangential relevance to the issue at hand. So let me return to metropolitan scholars and ask about the ethics of their ethnographic work.

The Ethics of Self-Reflexivity

In a recent book, American ethnomusicologist Michelle Kisliuk provides an ethnography of performance of the BaAka of the Central African Republic (CAR).[14] This elegant book stands out among recent ethnographies of African music for its deep investment in first-person narrative. Earlier ethnographies by John Chernoff and Paul Berliner, which, incidentally, number among her "dearest models for ethnography of African musics,"[15] had exploited this voice to report experiences as apprentices to master musicians, but Kisliuk outdoes them all.[16] We learn about her upbringing in a Jewish home in suburban Boston, the books she read (including Carlos Castaneda's *The Teachings of Don Juan* at the age of ten), study of African dance with ethnomusicologist David Locke, and restless years in college. Kisliuk mentions a preparatory visit to the Central African Republic, intensive listening to recordings of pygmy music, and intense engagement with Colin Turnbull's material. The core of the book then rehearses her attempt to live and learn from the BaAka. Hers was "participatory fieldwork." Accordingly, she took part in performances of dance and song, involved herself in women's affairs, fought with missionaries on behalf of the BaAka, and had a couple of near-death experiences.

It is hard to finish *Seize the Dance* without knowing a great deal about its author; whether one finishes the book knowing a great deal about the musical practices of the BaAka is a separate issue. Kisliuk declares greater interest in the dynamics of performance than in musical structure. And although the book includes brief transcriptions and two compact discs, there is less than full commitment to exploring the nature of such sonic data. Kisliuk is, in fact, critical of certain forms of structural analysis, reluctant to reduce things to numbers, and eager to avoid the distorting prism of European notational conventions. Readers who had expected to gain a deeper understanding of the notes and rhythms that BaAka perform, not as an end but as a means to an end, may need to supplement Kisliuk's account with others, for example, that of Simha Arom.

There is more to music than notes and rhythms, however, and this is in part what Kisliuk means to convey by focusing on the network of social intercourse that produces dance. Her strength lies in evocative and sometimes moving description not so much of BaAka musical life but of her role in it. This is a subject-oriented as opposed to an object-oriented ethnography; agency is never confined to the margins. We meet real people doing real dances in specific places at specific times and in specific ways. Nor is her report confined to positive or happy experiences. Moments of anger, frustration, fear, disappointment, and ideological conflict over a wide range of happenings also are vividly conveyed. She succeeds in disrupting the tendency to idealize the BaAka and other pygmy groups even as she reveals her own biases as a cultural being.

It is precisely because of this person-orientation that the issue of ethics looms large in Kisliuk's account. The disappearance of an author behind a stance of objectivity and a mass of facts tends to hide the extent to which our ethnographies are inflected. Better to bare it all, thematize conflicts and ambiguities, and convey an unsettled or precarious picture. Kisliuk is keenly aware of the difference between self-indulgence and reflexivity, and although she naturally positions her work in the more respectable reflexivity camp, her brief attempt to distinguish between the two remains vague. One woman's reflexivity, it turns out, is another's self-indulgence. In any case, reflexivity has no a priori good or ethical status, any more than self-indulgence is bad or unethical. But even if we grant Kisliuk the benefit of the doubt, we might still want to ask what things are proper to be said, and what not. Are there limits to acceptable discourse? Who sets such limits? Are we obliged to incorporate the canons of indigenous intellectual expression into our ethnographic writing, or is representation the prerogative of the metropolitan scholar? And although we can never control how others read our thoughts, to what extent should we be concerned about the different reactions of different interpretive communities?

As an indication of the kinds of ethical issues raised by Kisliuk's absorbing account, consider the following trivial incidents. Early on, we meet Dominique, a deaf man who helped the author fend off a green mamba. Kisliuk conjectures that Dominique "could sympathize . . . with how it feels to be a foreigner."[17] Some might read this as a shade patronizing, a self-indulgent appropriation of another's tragedy, or insensitive. The ethnographer chose her particular situation in the CAR in order to advance a personal quest; the deaf man, in contrast, did not (presumably) choose his condition. (That he might have been chosen—speaking at the level of system—is a possibility.) Not that one cannot see the formal similarity that Kisliuk is talking about. But from Dominique's point of view, perhaps, it may even seem cruel to tender such a comparison. Imagine asking him which of the two kinds of tragedy—being deaf or being a foreigner—he would prefer if given a choice, and you will immediately see how inappropriate the comparison is.

On one occasion, Kisliuk celebrates her victory in refusing to succumb to the pressure of offering cigarettes as gifts to the BaAka in exchange for knowledge. Cigarettes are harmful, she reasons, and although she did offer them during an earlier visit, she was now determined not to be seen nurturing such a harmful habit. And when faced with the prospect of not getting the knowledge that she was seeking unless cigarettes were made available, she claimed that she did not wish to "buy an understanding of the world of the pygmies" but to "earn" it. There is an earnestness here mixed with naivete that some postcolonial critics associate with American fieldworkers. Having ridden on the coat tails of symbolic power into this region of the world—having, in other words, endorsed the a priori power relations involved in her, a white American, entering an African world— the ethnographer now turns around and insists that she wants to be like the natives, she wishes to interact with them on an equal footing. Are we not on the verge of buying egalitarianism? Perhaps, then, it is true what they say: There's nothing money can't buy.

On another occasion, Kisliuk offered a tiny slice of tomato to Banditt, a BaAka boy. Instead of eating it, he took a knife and cut it into sixteen pieces, which he then shared with other children. Apparently, the BaAka had never seen a tomato before. This particular sample was grown by Kisliuk in a friend's garden. Touched by Banditt's selflessness, perhaps, Kisliuk comments: "I felt like a pig, sitting there with the whole rest of the tomato." Perhaps this is indeed a story about egalitarianism, as the author intends, but what does it say about these "primitive" peoples that they had not seen a tomato before? Why is the absence of tomatoes from their plants worth remarking? Overly sensitive African readers may accuse Kisliuk of casting herself in a superior light with incidents like this.

And finally, how are we to read Kisliuk's report about her clash with missionaries of the Grace Brethren Church? By this time during her stay, she knows enough about the indigenous culture to be able to report its virtues and confront the harmful effects of missionization. She is even perceived on occasion as a spokesperson for the BaAka, and this pleases her enormously. But what if one adopted a pragmatic approach, rejected the essentialism of cultures, and accepted the inevitable erosion of traditional cultures in the face of foreign influences? What if the BaAka decided that what they want is power at all costs, and therefore that investing in reading and writing, in going to school and church, are the things that will eventually transform their society from a traditional one into one that is fully competitive within the larger capitalist economy? Do we dare deny them participation in that world, even if it takes a long time to achieve full participation? Could it be that protecting the BaAka (by encouraging them to retain their songs, myths, and dances) is a way of protecting our research? Do we want the BaAka to remain "different" so that we can continue to thematize them in our writing, exploit them intellectually? Perhaps it is the ethics of *this* kind of investment in difference to which we need to give priority, not whether BaAka smoke cigarettes, believe in Satan, or stop dancing their traditional dances.

Kisliuk's willingness to give voice to experience confers an honest aura on her ethnography. Those who share her background will empathize with her; they will find meaningful the cultural terms that she employs to distinguish "us" from the BaAka. But as we move beyond this cultural group, as we speculate on the responses of, say, other Africans, what seems honest and ethical may come across as narcissistic. Indeed, one might go so far as to suggest that the adoption of an apparently ethical frame, the effort to be superethical from one cultural point of view, produces the opposite effect in one's ethnography. To say that in her ethnography Kisliuk reveals the humanity of the BaAka is to hint at a dark assumption, namely, that they possessed a different humanity. It is at the level of such assumptions that the most frightening workings of ideology may be found. Whether Kisliuk's book will help to counter such assumptions is not clear.

There is one surprising understatement in the book, and this concerns the author's relationship to her chief informant. Mongosso Justin Serge is described as "research partner, host, teacher, and dearest friend."[18] He is not credited with great knowledge of music and musical traditions, but of culture in general, the local ecology, and language in particular. A picture of him "at home with daughters Bibi and Mandazo" appears early on; later we are introduced to one of his wives; in due course we meet a rich uncle. We encounter Mongosso's wisdom and knowledge throughout the book. We read of moped rides with Kisliuk, camping, and arguing about strategy. Then, almost out of nowhere, in the closing pages of the book, Kisliuk tells the BaAka, in response to a question about what her home looks like, that "even Mongosso (Justin) had not yet visited [her] home," even though they knew that the two frequently visited the capital. A footnote then directs us to the last page of the book where we learn: "In 1993 Justin did travel to the United States to visit for six months. And as of May 1998 he lives with the author in Charlottesville, Virginia."[19]

Jonathan Stock, who drew attention to this footnote in his review of *Seize the Dance*, questions Kisliuk's exclusion of certain kinds of information:

[T]he nature of the author's growing personal relationship with her research assistant Justin is barely hinted at until a sudden, dramatic endnote. . . . My point here is not that Kisliuk should be expected to tell us any or all of these things, or that there is something to be hidden about parental visits or growing relationships. Rather, I would suggest that if one wishes to write a narrative, experiential work that bases its authority partly on being an account of significant events as they actually happened—the performance of life, as it were—then the inclusion of some of these topics might indeed be required.[20]

Marrying your chief informant (divulged in a subsequently published video to accompany *Seize the Dance*) is not necessarily an issue of ethics in itself. As Stock notes, Kisliuk is at liberty to tell us as little or as much as she desires. The confusion that arose for me in making sense of this part of Kisliuk's book is that the personal space has already been opened up and exploited so extensively in this biography/ethnography that one is simply not prepared for any such "major" disclosure. Kisliuk is not above mentioning marital infidelity among the BaAka, or tensions arising from male-female performance of domestic roles, or the thematization of sex in BaAka myth. It is thus surprising that a crucial aspect of her relationship with Mongosso is strategically underreported. Some might wonder how the dynamics of this particular relationship affected the kinds of data collected. Did they enhance or disrupt fieldwork or, later, the writing of the book? What are the ethics of such involvement in the field, and what ethical attitude governs their translation into narrative? Should the author be "required" to include certain topics, as Stock implies?

I bring up these matters about Kisliuk's fascinating book to point in part to the ultimate irony enshrined in her project. At first blush, a reflexive ethnography, complete with various disclosures about field experience, comes across as more ethical than one that gives no hints of behind-the-scenes tensions. Yet, as we have seen, reporting experience also entails choosing some incidents over others. What are the ethics of choice? Whom does one seek to influence by playing down (or up) certain field experiences? Self-reflexivity as a public and publicized discourse is challenging and contradictory, making huge ethical demands on producers and consumers alike. Kisliuk's book has the great virtue of making possible a more informed discussion.

A Note about the Ethics of Copyright

In oral traditions, where composers are not always named, and works circulate as communal property, issues of copyright do not normally arise. But in the age of recording and writing, when composers are named, their works given titles, and copyright is written into the law, ownership becomes an important issue. Sometimes the letter of the law comes into conflict with the prescriptions of a normative ethics. Consider the following story, told by Steven Feld.[21]

Madonna's 1994 album, *Bedtime Stories,* includes a track labeled "Sanctuary" that, according to Jon Pareles, uses "pygmy-like hoots." These hoots were taken from Herbie Hancock's 1973 album, *Headhunters,* specifically from a remake of the song "Watermelon Man," with which Hancock had made a splash on his *Takin' Off* album of 1962. Where did Hancock get the pygmy sounds from? Bill Summers, percussionist on the 1992 reissue of *Headhunters,* is said to have created those sounds by blowing on a beer bottle in imitation of the pygmy whistle, *hindewhu.* Hancock and Summers presumably heard this music on an ethnographic recording of 1966 by Simha Arom and Geneviève Taurelle, *The Music of the Ba-Benzele Pygmies,* and were struck by it.[22] Summers thus used a different medium to replicate the effect of the pygmy whistle. Had Hancock lifted this material, plagiarized it, appropriated it without acknowledging its source?

Enter ethnomusicologist Steven Feld, who picks up the phone, calls Herbie Hancock, and asks him about "the *hindewhu* copy on Headhunters." Hancock replies,

> You see, you've got to understand, this is a brothers kind of thing, you know, a thing for brothers to work out. I mean, I don't actually need to go over there and talk to them. I could do it but I know that it's OK 'cause it's just a brothers kinds of thing.[23]

And with that remark Hancock constructs a favorable genealogy to explain his appropriation of the pygmy sound, calling on a public with its copyright stringencies to overlook an African American's appropriation of African music. Pygmy music is, after all, the music of Hancock's ancestors; it embodies his musical heritage, albeit a distant one. And given how much other people have plundered Africa's traditions of music, Hancock's appropriation is hardly a matter to be broadcasted.

While Feld acknowledges that Hancock's comments "are now routine grounds for political attack," his own concern is different; it is with

> how such standard polemics might be held aside for a moment so that we might more subtly scrutinize the complexity of Hancock's subject position. In other words, how else might we inquire about the musical-political-industrial habitus in which particular acts of schizophonic mimesis take place, how might we locate and interpret discourses which surround their circulation?[24]

Feld accordingly embarks on a discussion of African-American citational practices, other appropriations of pygmy music by jazz musicians, and Afro-centricism in jazz. Among other things, Feld scrutinizes recordings— who owns them, what royalty agreements are made—and speculates on the frequent appropriation of only the most superficial aspect of the pygmy legacy. All of this is in service to a theorization of mimesis.

Some readers may be disappointed that, after raising the issue of ethics, Feld withholds judgment on the Hancock affair. He is more interested, if you like, in providing as rich and informed a context as possible for making sense of the rightness or wrongness of what Hancock did. It is a matter for discussion whether this entirely salutary resistance to premature judgment finally conveys an ethical attitude. Some critics will argue that Feld understates the radically different positions occupied by Pygmies, jazz musicians (like Hancock), scholars (like Feld), and record producers in this elaborate shell game. To manipulate these elements analytically without stressing the fact that they are also relational sites of radically different power and status is to mute the ethical issues.

Feld's strategic reticence may be instructive, however. In the article by Mark Slobin discussed near the beginning of this chapter, Slobin raises the question whether it is ethical to discuss ethics. Talk of ethics may lead to a lowering of morale among members of a professional association. Passing judgment produces a negative effect. Indeed, by raising the issue of ethics in connection with certain publications in this chapter, I have already risked passing judgment. Would it not be better, then, to be silent about ethics, to fold it into broader discussions—like aesthetics?

If we elect to choose the way of silence, it should be because of what is perhaps the biggest obstacle to a productive discussion of ethics, namely, finding an overarching principle to anchor the entire discussion. To the extent that there is such a principle, it resides in something we might call an *ethical attitude,* a disposition toward frameworks and styles of reasoning that finally seek—actively, rather than passively—to promote the common good. An ethical attitude cannot be defined in terms of praxis, as a set of prescriptions for social action. Concrete prescriptions risk betraying their own thorough imbrication in the intricacies of local context; they risk undercomplicating the historical, social, political, and ideological factors that must attend any worthwhile development of an ethical environment. To the extent that knowledge-producing subdisciplines remain aggregations of individuals rather than genuine communities, an ethical study of African music will continue to elude us. Perhaps, then, our best bet is simply to enjoin all actors to pursue, in as intense a fashion as they can manage, the said ethical attitude.

Epilogue

At the close of these journeys, it is well to remind ourselves that the background against which specific arguments have been made is vast, diverse, and complex. Africa, as we all know or should know, is the second largest continent, its population is upward of 800 million (a tenth of the world's), more than 2,000 languages are spoken there (roughly a third of the world's living languages, not counting dialects), its ethnic groups number over 3,000, and human genetic contrasts exceed those found anywhere else. This structural assortment—the poetics of which I do not explore—is, in turn, reflected, though not always directly, in several cultural spheres. In musical life, for example, instruments are numerous and strikingly differentiated both physically and symbolically, compositional styles and aesthetic ideals reproduce something of Africa's larger linguistic and oral-literary plurality, while emergent critical discourses range from the narrowly technical and descriptive to the broadly metaphorical and interpretive.

Out of thousands of books, articles, videos, sound recordings, and oral texts, I have chosen only a handful for critique in this book. And I have tended to simplify the histories of theoretical practice in order to keep certain concerns before the reader. It would be a limited analysis, however, that did not pursue the programmatic arguments begun here into specific and more intricate contexts; it would be a limited analysis that failed to broach the politics of choosing what to critique, the challenge of achieving comprehensiveness in covering a continent this large, and the ethics of the double talk that shapes postcolonial notions of truth.

What kind of summary, last word, or parting thought is possible for so eclectic and contradictory a project like this? Or, as my American students sometimes say when I give out an assignment, "What do you want?" Although it appears innocent at first, the invitation to spell out what you want is a trap. My students invoke it in order to influence the evaluation

221

process because if they have done not what I want but what I said I wanted—no one is more keenly aware that the gap is not subject to closure, the said being always already a diminished form of the imagined—how can I justify giving them anything less than an "A"? Here, however, no comparable power differential exists. The stakes are very much lower because an individual's polemical reflections on the canons of African music scholarship are merely that: thoughts, ideas, speculation. They may resonate with others, grate against some sensibilities, or seem personal. Moreover, the positions taken here are vulnerable because what seems to me ethically self-evident, namely, that Africans should be, if not primary, then at least equal beneficiaries of research into African music, apparently still needs to be argued.

These chapters are, in any case, dotted with assertions intended as material for debate rather than historically validated prescriptions for how to conduct our theoretical lives. Proceeding from last to first: I sought to encourage an open discussion of ethics (chapter 9) and to endorse conventional approaches to the analysis of African music (chapter 8). I urged an understanding of difference as a fictional construct that is sometimes deployed at others' expense (chapter 7), and a revaluation of popular music based on what is played and sung, and how it resonates with or shapes the actions of individual listeners (chapter 6). Music and language were drawn into a mutually reinforcing interpretive effort (chapter 5), and I rejected constructions of African rhythm as different in an *a priori* sense; I suggested that an eagerness to produce difference leads to distortions and inaccuracies in technical as well as non-technical writing (chapters 4 and 3). Finally, I drew attention to the inequities between African subjects/scholars and their metropolitan colleagues and how the asymmetry influences the shape of the archive (chapter 2) and showed the pervasive impact of colonialism on the theory and practice of music in both traditional and modern idioms (chapter 1).

Do these positions present a coherent or unified program? The question itself is suspect, of course, because the will to empower has never depended on the coherence of its supporting worldview, only on the availability of the material means to turn thought into action, fantasy into reality. Such are the workings of power, and such is what metropolitan ethnomusicologists have long enjoyed. Refusing the stricture that our agenda must meet the normative requirements of metropolitan logic may seem evasive—a facile way of deflecting criticism, a defense of incoherence, perhaps. But such resistance may prove advantageous if it highlights the contradictions, incongruities, anachronisms, and antinomies that animate postcolonial life and thought.

Recall, for instance, my shifting stances toward ethnotheory. In rejecting it, I seemed to place a great deal of confidence in metropolitan regimes of knowledge and representation. Yet, aspects of my analysis of African song took valuable clues from indigenous aesthetics, pedagogy, and critical expression. If there is a contradiction, it is more apparent than real because the deployment of critical categories is most effective when it is strategic. Depending on context and immediate goals, the "same" strategy may be put to different but equally effective uses. Opportunistic pragmatism of this sort is absolutely essential to postcolonial music criticism. Such pragmatism surely accounts, in part, for the metropolis' own hegemony. Positing essential distinctions between things African and Western (which, incidentally, often originates from Western discourses) all too often disuades African scholars from adopting the pragmatic stances that I feel are our only option for permanently achieving a truly emancipated discourse.

What is easily forgotten is that metropolitan theory rules not because of its intrinsic superiority, not because it got there first (the massive literature on the Afro-Asiatic roots of European thinking should make us think twice, even if some diehards continue to quibble with particular readings of archival and archaeological sources), but because, having appropriated certain intellectual traditions, it proceeded to dictate the terms of subsequent discussion. Given that we nowadays share these theoretical spaces, albeit in a somewhat tense configuration, African musicologists must fiercely resist being presented with an either-or option. Which way they choose will be determined by their collective ambition. If knowledge systems are in principle translatable, then it ultimately does not matter whether we refer to a particular moment in a song as a "cadence" or as a "throwing-away place." Both index closure or punctuation and are therefore interchangeable at a certain level of discourse. But what if one wishes to address other levels? Here we confront the fact that the creation of levels or horizons of understanding is as much an *interested* undertaking as it is an abstractly logical exercise.

One could argue that "cadence" and "throwing-away place" are complementary, not opposed, that they enrich as well as diversify our economy of expressive terms. To argue in this fashion, when all the signs are that the two terms exist in an undisguised hierarchy in sociocultural use, is to adopt a mode of deception that metropolitan scholars have often used to consolidate their positions of mastery. It is easy to be enamored of diversity—indeed to promote and celebrate it—if you are not required to yield a square inch of intellectual or cognitive territory. But if you believe, in more than a token way, that translation is possible, then we ought, for example, to hear you proclaim the virtues of African knowledge systems, not as decorative supplements to your own but as genuine and desirable alternatives, the adoption of which becomes increasingly urgent in our ostensibly global village. Alas, such radical reversal is put into practice by only a few nonconformists and outcasts; it remains no more than an abstract idea for metropolitan theorists who are, in truth, terrified at the prospect of inhabiting the very African worlds they embrace in their theoretical work.

Other contradictions in these essays may be understood as products of a similar intellectual-activist impulse. For example, while questioning the metropolitan appropriation of the autobiographical mode in ethnographic reportage, I nevertheless turned to personal experience in order to substantiate aspects of my own critique (as in the discussion of ethics, or the analysis of readers' reports sent out by journal editors). The status of this action as contradictory rather than ambivalent rests on one's valuation of agency. To insist that the autobiographical mode mean the same no matter where or by whom it is employed is surely excessive. Meaning is further complicated in the case of scholars whose sense of intellectual location is frequently in flux. Critics may complain that the strategy emerging here is designed to ensure that one eats one's cake and has it too. But why not? Only blind adherence to the dubious truth of a conventional saying originating in a dominant culture would discourage us from seeking to have it both ways.

It is easy to forget that our subject is music, one of Africa's richest media for group as well as individual expression. Apparently contradictory tendencies within the domains of gesture and affect, the heard and the imagined, the played and the sung enshrine tremendous potential not only for ongoing, socially relevant "musicking" but also for culturally appropriate and ultimately empowering development. Helpful clues abound in the practices of our traditional musicians who have innovated and experimented for centuries, who have maintained deep associations with language and religion, and for whom the sheer joy in play has enabled the formation of powerful bonds among dancers, singers, orators, and drummers. We need to revisit these sites frequently even while vigilantly sifting through and appropriating representational strategies nominally marked "metropolitan." Challenging though it may be, such a two-pronged approach will almost certainly facilitate efforts to reclaim what is said and thought about African music in the future.

Notes

Introduction

1. Hountondji (1992), 238.
2. von Hornbostel (1928), 30–62.
3. Kirby (1934).
4. Rahn (1987); Pressing (1983); and Anku (1992).
5. See the film "Africa Come Back: The Popular Music of West Africa," Program 7 of *Repercussions: A Celebration of African-American Music* series. Directed by Geoffrey Haydon and Dennis Marks (RM Arts and Channel Four Television, 1984).
6. Mudimbe (1988).
7. Ekwueme (1975–1976), 5.
8. Scherzinger (2000).
9. Nzewi (1997).
10. Tagg (1994), 285–98.
11. Wachsmann (1969), 164.
12. Euba (2001), 137, 139.
13. A thoughtful introduction to postcolonial theory is Moore-Gilbert (1997). Representative texts by leading figures include: Ahmad (1992); Spivak (1999); Said (1978); Bhabha (1990); and Gilroy (1993). With specific reference to Africa, see Mudimbe (1988); Appiah (1992); Wiredu (1980); Miller, (1990); Mbembe, (2001); and Hountondji (1983). Also of interest is Young (1990).
14. Waterman (1991), 179.
15. What ethnomusicologists do is lucidly and engagingly presented in Nettl (1983); an earlier classic is Merriam (1964). A fresh and optimistic account is given by Pegg, Myers, Bohlman, and Stokes (2001).

Chapter 1

1. For a straightforward introduction to Africa's history, to which my own digest here is indebted, see Shillington (1989). The colonial period is discussed by African historians in Boahen (1990).

2. Basil Davidson, *Africa: A Voyage of Discovery*, Program 5 "The Bible and the Gun" (RM Arts, 1984); Boahen, (1987), 111. Not everyone agrees that periodizing our history within a precolonial-colonial-postcolonial framework is desirable. Doing so amounts to overrating European influence on Africa. Such a periodization in effect denies the possibility of an African history that is not on some level mediated by European frames or conceptualizations. Insofar as the scholarship discussed in this book dates from a very recent African past, a past entirely coeval with European colonialism in Africa, I have chosen, for purely pragmatic reasons, to overlook the ostensible overvaluing of the colonial determination of African musical history.

3. For an excellent introduction to the epistemology of music history, see Dahlhaus (1983). Among more recent contributions, Tomlinson (1993) and Taruskin (1997) are widely read. None of these authors refers to African music, however, although Tomlinson and Taruskin have things to say about "others." Of immediate relevance are Wachsmann (1971) and Djedje (1992).

4. Kubik (1994), 23.

5. Davidson (1966), 50.

6. Kirby (1934).

7. Kubik (1997), 85–97.

8. Charry (2000).

9. See also the two iconographic volumes edited by Kubik and others (1982) and (1989), as well as a third, Gansemans, Schmidt-Wrenger, et al. (1986).

10. Hunwick (1991).

11. McCall (1998).

12. Jones (1971). Jones's theories are not universally accepted, however. See, for example, Blench (1982).

13. There is no shortage of information on African musical instruments, although the emphasis has been on traditional rather than modern (i.e. Western, imported) ones. Two classics from the early twentieth century are Kirby (1934) and Ankermann (1976; orig. 1901). A beautiful and informative recent catalogue, complete with eighteen essays in organology, is Djedje (1999).

14. The history of the Evangelical Presbyterian Church may be read in Ansre (1997). Neither here nor in other accounts of the development of the church is particular attention given to the place of music. We await a full-scale musical history of the Evangelical Presbyterian Church.

15. For a valuable account, see Boonzajer-Flaes and Gales (n.d.). Robert Rumbolz (2000) has recently written an equally valuable musicological study, complete with detailed ethnographies of specific bands, their repertories and aesthetic concerns. Rumbolz also includes transcriptions of selected compositions.

16. This hypothetical account echoes habits reported elsewhere about Christian hymn singing among African congregations. See, among numerous examples, Weman (1960) and Ekwueme (1973–1974). Also of interest for its insights into African reception of European music is the chapter "Neo-folk Music" in Jones (1959), 232–75. Although this particular chapter is not the most frequently read—attention is often focused on the transcriptions and technical discussion of Ewe (Ghanaian) and Lala (Zambian) drumming in earlier chapters—it provides a provocative and highly essentialist account of what Africans supposedly like and are able to do within the limits of European harmonic idioms.

17. A concise introduction to composers of African art music may be found in the series of entries on individual composers written by Daniel Avorgbedor and published recently in Sadie and Tyrrell (2001). Among composers represented are Fela Sowande (1905–1987), Theophilus K. Ekundayo Phillips (1884–1969), Ephraim Amu (1895–1995), Ayo Bankole (1935–1976), Akin Euba (b. 1935), Kenneth Kafui (b. 1951), Mzilikazi Khumalo (b. 1932), Emmanuel Gyimah Labi (b. 1950), Okechukwu Ndubusi (b. 1936), Ato Turkson (1937–1993), Joshua Uzoigwe (b. 1946), and Nicholas Zinzendorf Nayo (1922–1993). A valuable earlier study is Omojola (1995). Analytically oriented discussion may be found in Mensah (1998) and Agawu (2001). For a critical discussion of the conditions of possibility for the practice of art music in Africa, see Irele (1993), to which Nick Nesbitt (2001) has provided one answer. Euba (1989) offers a composer-critic's perspective; Martin Scherzinger (forthcoming) considers cross-cultural reverberations.

18. On the procedures of multipart singing in traditional music, see, among others, Kubik, (1968); England (1967); Euba (1967); Nketia (1967); Tsukada (1990); and Agawu (1990). Of special interest is the "strategic analysis" of harmonic patterning by Martin Scherzinger (2001).

19. Ward (1927), 223.

20. Operas, cantatas, and other music-theatrical genres are more common throughout Africa than is commonly supposed. Euba (1993) lists numerous operas, dance dramas, and plays with music. On the concert party tradition, see Barber, Collins, and Ricard (1997).

21. Echeruo (1977).

22. For a history of Achimota School up to 1977, see Agbodeka (1977). Also of interest are the scattered recollections of music-making in Achimota during the late 1920s and 1930s by Ward (1991).

23. For more on music education, see Akrofi (1982) and Kwami (1989). A concise introduction is Kwami (1994). Kwami's bibliography will be helpful to those who wish to pursue the subject further.

24. John Collins has written extensively about highlife. See, among numerous publications, Collins (1994), (1986), and (1992). On highlife song texts see, among others, Brempong, (1986), Yankah (1984), and Van der Geest (1982). An excellent introduction to highlife may be heard on the CD *Giants of Danceband Highlife* (Original Music OMCDO11). I will have more to say about highlife in chapter 7.

25. For an outstanding study of popular music that lays great store by "deeply grounded Yoruba practices" (14), see Waterman (1990).
26. Euba (1993).
27. Echeruo, (1977), 68–69.
28. Readers unfamiliar with the distinctive sound of the Pan-African Orchestra may hear it on the 1995 CD, *The Pan-African Orchestra, op. 1* (Real World Records, CAR2350). For a brief introduction, see Avorgbedor (2001).
29. For an excellent discussion of the colonial impact on discourses about Africa, see Mudimbe (1988), 1–23. See also the strategy for overcoming certain dilemmas mapped out in Ekpo (1995).
30. On the concept of *pêle*, see Stone (1982). On *agora*, see Nketia (1991). And on *egwu*, see Nzewi (1991), 24–44.

Chapter 2

1. *Longmann Dictionary of the English Language* (Harlow, England: Longman Group, 1984), s.v. "Archive," 74.
2. The concept of archive plays a major role in Foucault's (1972) archaeology, in which it designates "systems that establish statements as events (with their own conditions and domain of appearance) and as things (with their own possibility and field of use" [128]). Foucault's emphasis on "discursive practices," conditions, and possibilities is germane to my argument here.
3. The literature on orality versus literacy is huge, of course. An early classic is Vansina (1985; orig. 1961). Two recent literary studies are Miller (1990), 68–113 and Irele (2001), 23–38. Of particular relevance to music study is Ong (1977).
4. Desmond Tay is featured in A. M. Jones (1959), Alhaji Abdulai Ibrahim in Chernoff 1979), and Godwin Agbeli in Locke (1992). Chernoff (forthcoming) will feature Abdulai Ibrahim even more magnificently.
5. Schneider (1957).
6. Koetting (1985).
7. Rouget (1980).
8. Kubik (1998).
9. See, among numerous publications, Capo (1986) and (1991).
10. Kubik (1983), 27, quoted in Waterman (1992), 240.
11. Nzewi (1997), 31.
12. Bebey (1975); Nketia (1974); Brandily (1997).
13. Landmarks include Waterman (1991); Euba (1991); Kubik (1996); Friedson (1996); and Charry (1996). See also Charry's brisk guide to studies of African music at www.fitzroydearborn.com/Samples/MusRGsamp.htm.
14. Lomax (1968), xvi.
15. Information about the African Music Archive at Mainz is on the web at www.unimainz.de.
16. Locke (1992).
17. See, also, Christopher Waterman's (1994) review of Gray for a concise and sympathetic evaluation.

18. See Dakubu (1988).
19. Kubik (1994), 9.
20. Westermann (1928). Westermann's numerous publications on the Ewe language include articles on technical-linguistic aspects, word lists, a grammar, translations of Bible stories, and essays on witchcraft, slavery, and mission life in Africa. For a full listing, see Zielnica (1976).
21. Ashcroft, Griffiths, and Tiffin (1998), 85.
22. See, for example, the absorbing collection of essays, Barz and Cooley (1997).
23. Blacking (1967), 3.
24. Blacking (1973), 118.
25. Blacking (1995), 75.
26. Kisliuk (1998), 16.
27. Locke (1982), 245. This citation and much of the following discussion are lifted from Agawu (1992), 245–66.
28. See Kartomi (1990), 241–53 for discussion of "the personification of instruments in some West African classifications."
29. The linguistic turn in anthropology, associated with books like Geertz (1988) and Clifford and Marcus (1986), has been underway for some time now. A comparable turn in Africanist ethnomusicology is not yet in evidence, although Kisliuk (1997) suggests that it may not be long in coming.
30. Fabian (1983), 31.
31. A stimulating collection of essays on this subject is Okely and Callaway (1992).
32. For a historical sketch, see Ellingson (1992). On specifically Africa related practices, see Shelemay (1998).
33. Ellingson (1992), 110.
34. Silsbee (1986), 7.
35. Hornbostel (1928).

Chapter 3

1. Butlan (1979), 160. See also John Hunwick's rendition of (presumably) the same phrase as quoted in chapter 1.
2. This history is yet to be written, but some of its materials may be gleaned from, among other sources, Gansemans et al. (1986); Kubik et al. (1989); Jones (1957); Hirschberg (1969); and Charry (2000). In an unpublished paper, Stephen Blum, citing Lewis (1990), notes that "the Medieval Arabic literature on racial stereotypes provided many of the images that were subsequently deployed by European and American writers." See also Hunwick (1991).
3. Ogilby (1670), 466; quoted in Jones (1957), 7.
4. Adanson (1759), 111; quoted in Jones (1957), 5.
5. Bowdich (1819), 278.
6. Freeman (1898), 257–61; quoted in Nketia (1970), 13.
7. Northcott (1899); quoted in Nketia (1970), 12.
8. For a related argument about the emergence of a "black rhythmic construct" in discourse about African-American music, see Radano and Bohlman (2001),

459–480. See also Radano (forthcoming) for a comprehensive historical and critical study of the emergence of various discourses about black American music.

9. Hornbostel (1928), 52.
10. Ward (1927), 203–04, 222.
11. Waterman (1948), 24.
12. Jones (1949), 13, 8–9.
13. Merriam (1959); reprinted in Merriam (1982), 84.
14. Myers (1983), 28.
15. Nettl (1986), 18.
16. Bebey (1975), 17; and Gbeho (1957), 63.
17. Weman (1960), 58.
18. Senghor (1956), 37, 30.
19. Anon. (1958), 62.
20. Kingslake (1959), 85.
21. Nketia (1974), 125.
22. Introducing a set of recordings of music from French Africa, André Schaeffner, although careful to dissuade us from thinking that Africa is all drum music, and that no other world cultures exhibit rhythmic mastery, nevertheless maintains that "perhaps . . . rhythm in African music is more persuasive and more subtle than in any other music" (Lomax [1955–56]). Willie Anku (1995) writes that "the root of sub Saharan music lies deep in its rhythmic complexion" (167). And David Temperley (2000) describes the view that "rhythm is of paramount importance in African music" as "widespread" and "popular," and as having "received a good deal of scholarly affirmation" (65). And the list goes on. Such remarks are rife in popular sources as well. Thus Martin Scherzinger (unpublished paper) quotes Jon Pareles as saying in a *New York Times* article of May 3, 1998, on the subject of Global Pop that there has been a "rise of rhythm," and that this may be attributed to "the receding influence of European culture in a global mix, as the Western emphasis on melody and harmony gives way to the beat." Pareles's conclusion is breathtaking: "Africa, where rhythm rules, has paid back its conquerors and slave traders by colonizing the world's music" (47). Two films that exemplify African rhythmic life are *Listening to the Silence: African Cross Rhythms as Seen through Ghanaian Music* (Princeton: Films for the Humanities, 1996; orig. 1994) and *When the Moment Sings* (with Jon-Roar Bjorkvold) (Visions TV: Oslo, Norway, 1995).
23. Koetting (1984), 66; and Wachsmann (1969), 187.
24. Rycroft (1981), 209.
25. Mudimbe (1988).
26. Appiah (1992), 62.
27. Jones (1954), 84.
28. Nketia (1974), 125. The theoretical idea that mutually interacting dimensions in some sense compensate for one another did not originate with Nketia. Benjamin I. Gilman (1909), for example, noted that "for its jejune structure in tone non-

European music [Hindu and African] makes amends by a rhythmic richness beside which that of European music seems in its turn poverty" (534). Similarly, Wachsmann and Cooke (1981) write: "It seems almost to be an axiom of the economy of musical devices in Africa, at least to the foreign observer, that the preference for an elaborate polyphony goes hand in hand with moderation in rhythmical variety, and vice versa" (147).

29. Chernoff (1979), 41–42.

30. Hobsbawn and Ranger (1983); Ranger (1985); Mudimbe (1988); Appiah (1992; the opening chapter is entitled "The Invention of Africa"); Oyewumi (1997); and Waterman (1991), 179. Similarly Achille Mbembe (2001) aligns the West's imaginary significations with invention: "Africa, because it was and remains that fissure between what the West is, what it thinks it represents, and what it thinks it signifies, is not simply *part of* its imaginary significations, it is *one* of those significations. By imaginary significations, we mean 'that something invented' [following C. Castoriadis] that, paradoxically, becomes necessary because 'that something' plays a key role, both in the world the West constitutes for itself and in the West's apologetic concerns and exclusionary and brutal practices towards others" (2).

31. Jones (1959).

32. Westermann (1930).

33. Keil (1979), 47; Monts (1990), 90; Ames and King (1971); and Charry (1992), 210.

34. Agawu (1995), 5–7.

35. Jones (1949), 11.

36. A fuller account of Jones's work would recognize a latent, largely undeveloped comparative framework in his writings. His would therefore not be the most spectacular instance of a retreat from comparison. Nevertheless, Jones tends to underdevelop one term of his binary structure: the West.

37. Hornbostel (1928); Jones (1959); Weman (1960); Blacking (1973); Monts (1990); Nketia (1974); Chernoff (1997).

38. Koetting (1970) and Pantaleoni (1972).

39. Koetting (1970), 126.

40. Ibid., 120.

41. See, for example, the discussion in Zuckerkandl (1973) or in Lerdahl and Jackendoff (1983). Although both of these works postdate Koetting's study, the phenomena they discuss go back to the earliest theorizing about musical rhythm.

42. Serwadda and Pantaleoni (1968).

43. Rycroft (1967).

44. Green (1977), 149–67.

45. "Cross rhythms," according to Jones (1949), "make every muscle in [the African's] body clamour for dancing" (21). Jones is not the only writer who has taken note of this polyrhythmic behavior. Ward (1927) refers to "a native dancer keeping with different sets of muscles five different rhythms at once" (222).

46. See Locke (1982), among many publications, and Arom (1991).
47. I have provided alternatives to Jones's transcriptions in the "Epilogue" of Agawu (1995).
48. Pressing (1983), 5.
49. See Feld (1987).

Chapter 4

1. For an overview of competing views of African rhythm up until 1980, see Kauffman (1980). More interesting and authoritative, although somewhat dated by now, is Kubik (1985). Of interest as critique is Waterman (1991). Arom (1991) reviews and engages with a broad range of theories.
2. The term "time line," invented by Kwabena Nketia, appears for the first time in his *African Music in Ghana* (1962), in which it is defined as "a constant point of reference by which the phrase structure of a song as well as the linear metrical organization of phrases are guided" (78). "Bell pattern" is widely used, as in Jones (1959). Nzewi (1997) prefers "phrasing referent" but insists that it is "*not* a structural referent in African musical thought and ensemble composition" (35).
3. Echezona (1966), 43.
4. The term appears in Kubik (1985), and is attributed to Cameroonian musician and scholar, Eno Belinga.
5. Kubik (1994), 44–46.
6. Kubik (1999), 52–62, and also (1972). For a concise statement, see Kubik (2001), 201–02.
7. Pressing (1983). But see London (2001).
8. Rahn (1987).
9. Lehmann (2000).
10. See Lehmann (2000) and Rahn (1987).
11. Locke (1987), 78.
12. Nketia (1974), 132, line 3 of Example XII-11a.
13. Temperley (2000).
14. Jones (1954), 27; quoted in Chernoff (1979), 47.
15. See Nzewi (1997) for further discussion.
16. Waterman (1967 [c1952]).
17. Although "polymeter" is sometimes used to indicate a succession of different meters rather than their simultaneous occurrence, I will confine my usage here to the latter sense.
18. This designation of Jones is by Fabrice Marandola; see Marandola (1997), 139.
19. Nzewi (1997), 41.
20. Locke (1987), 78.
21. Chernoff (1979), 45–47.
22. Locke (1982), 235.
23. Powers (1986).
24. Merriam (1959), 85.

25. Ward (1927), 214.
26. Merriam (1959), 78.
27. Merriam (1982).
28. Ward (1927), 217.
29. Merriam (1959), 78.
30. Wachsmann and Cooke (1980), 146.
31. Myers (1983), 28. See also Norma McCleod's (1980) extraordinary claim that "true polymetre occurs [in the music of the Malagasy Republic] when, for example, a song is in 27/9 and its accompaniment in 24/12" (549).
32. Keil (1979) would disagree, however. About the Tiv of Eastern Nigeria, he says: "The term [*tsorogh*] can also be used to compliment an excellent dancer who is moving different parts of his or her body in different meters simultaneously. *A viven a tsorogh* might be translated, 'She is dancing polymetrically'" (40, 52). Unfortunately, Keil does not pursue this lead into any actual music analysis.
33. Waterman (1948), 25.
34. Lerdahl and Jackendoff (1983), 17.
35. See Agawu (1995), 185–95, for further discussion.
36. Arom (1991), 205.
37. Anku (1995), 170.
38. Nzewi (1997), 41.
39. The evidence against polymeter seems to have been advanced by scholars working on West and Central African music. East and southern Africa seem to represent a different ball game. According to Kubik (1994), "[the] phenomenon of an 'individual beat' in instrumental ensembles is frequently encountered in musical traditions of Bantu language speakers of east and east-central Africa (e.g. among the Baganda, Basoga, Wagogo, Anyanja, Wayao, Ashirima, Vamakonde, Babemba, etc., to mention a few "ethnic groups") while in the musical cultures of west-central Africa and the Guinea Coast it seems to be less frequent" (43). Elsewhere, Kubik credits Jones with the discovery that musicians performing interlocking patterns on xylophones play with different pulses, which may also entail a multiplicity of meters. Trevor Wiggins (1999), too, has found "multiple pulses" in various Ghanaian repertoires (63). Arom (1991), however, remarks that we would be "unwise to suppose that two different pulsations can be conjoined in a single piece of traditional African music" (210). Clearly, then, more research is needed to shed light on the issue.
40. I'm echoing here Gary Tomlinson's (1993) exhortation to his fellow musicologists: "we might begin to interrogate our love for the music we study" (24).
41. Brandel (1961), 74.
42. Jones (1959), 8.
43. Nketia (1974), 131.
44. See Pantaleoni (1972); Kauffman (1980); Locke (1997); Wiggins (1999); Kubik (1994); Walker (1983); Pressing (1983), 11; Rycroft (1954), 20. See also the discussion in Rahn (1996).

45. See, for example, Fabrice Marandola's (1997) remark that the rhythmic figure 3+3+2 "est courant dans le plupart des musiques d'Afrique subsaharienne" (138). It is possible that an original divisive conception has evolved into an additive conception in places like Cuba, Brazil, Haiti, and Jamaica. And this may have something to do with the tempo at which the pattern unfolds. At relatively fast tempos, the divisive conception is more meaningful than an additive one. African traditional music retains this divisive feel. When heard in dance halls at considerably slower tempi, however, as in Cuban clave or in the "returned" diasporic music of, say, Kinshasa, the additive feel begins to seem real. This matter could be investigated further.

46. Nzewi (1997), 39.

47. C. K. Ladzekpo, *Foundation Course in African Dance Drumming*. On the web at www.bmrc.berkeley.edu/people/ladzekpo/Foundation.html

48. Jones (1959), vol. 2, 3.

49. Wängler (1983), 63.

50. Nketia (1974), 150. Presumably, this particular transcription was made by Nissio Fiagbedzi. Some of the confusion evident in transcriptions of African song stems from the failure to distinguish properly between word accents and metrical accents. There are performances of Ghanaian song—the Adzewa group in Cape Coast, for example—in which a minimal ensemble (of, say, drum and bell) "accompanies" (in this case) all-female singing. Such accompaniment is more often a fixed, recurring background rather than one that is organically woven into the song. The compositional intention seems to represent two separate musical bodies that sometimes reinforce one another, at other times do not. Factoring this element of caprice into the analysis may help eliminate some unintended complexities in representation.

51. Said (1978).

52. Herskovits (1941). See also Maultsby (1990).

53. Mudimbe (1988).

Chapter 5

1. Colapietro (1993), s.v. "Text."

2. Quoted in Todorov (1981), 17. For a concise introduction to issues raised by music's textuality, see Dahlhaus (1982).

3. Dehoux (1986). A sampling of the repertoire may be heard on *Centrafrique: Musique Gbáyá. Chants à penser,* CD C560079 (Paris: Ocora, 1995).

4. Nketia (1962), 118. An arrangement of this song, described as "a Ga cradle song with rhythmic accompaniment," appears in Amoaku (1971), 32, and may be heard on Side B of Amoaku (1978). For another performance, listen to track 3 of the CD *Legendary Wulomei.*

5. Monts (1982).

6. On some of the intellectual processes found in children's music, see Blacking (1967); Johnston (1973); Addo (1995); Kubik (1994), 330–48, and Agawu (1995),

62–73. It goes without saying that the literature on African children's music is extensive.

7. For a comprehensive study of techniques of verbal art found among the Ewe, see Anyidoho (1983). An excellent analytical work is Haring (1992).
8. Kivy (1990).
9. Hornbostel (1928), 53, 62.
10. Blacking (1955).
11. Baily (1985).
12. Kubik (1994), 37–46.
13. Baily (1985), 239.
14. Ibid., 242.
15. Chernoff (1979), 33.
16. Quoted in Jakobson (1971), 696.
17. Benveniste (1985), 239. The language-music nexus lies at the heart of Nattiez (1990). See also Agawu (1999).
18. Blacking (1981) argues for music as a primary modelling system.
19. Klaus P. Wachsmann (1969), 187.
20. Chernoff (1979), 75.
21. Kubik (1994), 9.
22. Bebey (1975), 115.
23. Locke (1980), 128.
24. Fiagbedzi (1977), 10.
25. See also Agawu (1995), 1–5.
26. Keil (1995).
27. For another comment on the recognition and transformation of performance errors, see Nzewi (1981), 391–92.
28. See Nketia (1988).
29. See Richards (1972) for a rigorous approach. See also Agawu (1988), 127–46 for another approach, as well as citations of other studies.
30. Kramer (1984), 129.
31. Nketia (1963), 17–31.
32. The literature on talking drums is extensive but variable. A good introduction is Carrington (1949), which may be supplemented directly by Walter Ong (1977).
33. Nketia (1971), 711.
34. Cf. this juicy anecdote: "During my first day practicing with Gideon, I was following him well until he suddenly performed a rather complicated series of rhythms and then went back to the basic rhythm he was showing me. A few minutes later a man who had passed at that moment returned with two bottles of beer" (Chernoff [1979], 75).

Chapter 6

1. Nketia (1974).
2. Bebey (1975; orig. 1969).

3. Stone (1998). There are three essays on popular music: Angela Impey writes about "Popular Music in Africa"; David Coplan surveys "Popular Music in South Africa"; while Christopher Waterman introduces "Yoruba Popular Music." In addition, three articles address popular music indirectly: Andrew L. Kaye's "The Guitar in Africa"; Cynthia Schmidt's "Kru Mariners and Migrants of the West African Coast"; and Kazadi wa Mukuna's "Latin American Influences in Zaïre." Finally, comments on popular music may be found in surveys of various regions (e.g., "Musical Life in the Central African Republic").

4. See Coplan (1985); Waterman (1990); Mukuna (1992) Collins (1992); Graham (1988); Mensah (1971–1972); Ballantine (1993); Erlmann (1991); Chernoff (1985); Meintjes (1990); Bender (1991); Olaniyan (2001); and Veal (2000).

5. Graham (1988), 10.

6. Barber (1997), 1.

7. Adorno (1941). For critical responses to Adorno, see Sandner (1979); Paddison (1982); Gendron (1986); and Robinson (1994).

8. Austin (1975); Hamm (1979).

9. Adorno (1967). Laurence Dreyfus (1983) before me appropriated Adorno's title in his "Early Music Defended against Its Devotees."

10. See Bareis (1991) and Kubik (1974).

11. Barber (1987), 19.

12. See especially Collins (1986) and (1994).

13. Some of the generalizations entered below may seem puzzling to readers who have different highlife repertoires in mind. Therefore, although the approach outlined here may be more widely applicable, I offer the classic highlife of E. T. Mensah and the Tempos from the 1950s as the main point of reference in the following discussion. More specifically, the first four tracks on the CD *African Music: The Glory Years* (Original Music OMCDO11)—"Yei Ngbewoh," "School Girl," "Makoma," and "You Call Me Roko"—may serve as a point of aural reference.

14. Leech-Wilkinson (March 16–22, 1990), 185.

15. Discussion of some of these views is implicit in Agawu (1992). The musicological literature on words and music is vast, of course, and cannot be summarized in a footnote. Nor is such a summary called for in the context of this brief passing reference.

16. Frith (1988, 118–20) reports some of these in "Why Do Songs Have Words?"

17. Manuel (1988, 91) credits James Koetting with this observation.

18. Cited in Mitchell (1985), 62.

19. Readers unfamiliar with the sound of the one-stringed fiddle may wish to listen to Track 7, "Gonje," on the CD *Ghana: Rhythms of the People: Traditional Music and Dance of the Ewe, Dagbamba, Fante, and Ga People* (Montpelier, Vt.: Multicultural Media, 2000, MCM 3018) and Track 4 "*Kusasi* (Muslim)" of *Ghana: Music of the Northern Tribes* (New York: Lyrichord Discs, 1976 LYRCD 7321).

20. Anku (1992); Zabana (August 2001).

21. *West African Music: The Rough Guide* (London: World Music Network, 1995, RGNET 1002), Track 8, "205."
22. Roger Vetter, *Rhythms of Life, Songs of Wisdom: Akan Music from Ghana, West Africa* CD (Washington, D.C.: Smithsonian Folkways [SF CD 40463], 1996).
23. Schenker (1979), 129. "With the arrival of 1," Schenker writes, "the work is at an end. Whatever follows this can only be a reinforcement of the close—a coda—no matter what its extent or purpose may be."
24. A more extensive and interesting discussion of the meaning(s) of repetition may be found throughout Chernoff (1979).
25. See, for example, Ratner's (1995) discussion of the "popular style."
26. Although not framed in terms of a Creole language, the analysis of Beethoven op. 132, first movement, which appears in Agawu (1991), 110–26, identifies a variety of stylistic references that would support such an interpretation.
27. Hanslick, *On the Musically Beautiful,* excerpted and trans. in Bujic (1988), 19.
28. Sprigge (1961); Collins and Richards (1982); Coplan (1978); Yankah (1984); Geest (1982); Brempong (1986); Sackey (1989); and Mensah (1980).
29. Kubik (1974); Waterman (1990).
30. Forte (1995); Walser (1993); Brackett (1995); Middleton (1990); Frith (1996); Taylor (1997); and Adorno (1941).

Chapter 7

1. Spivak with Rooney (1989), 146.
2. Solie (1993).
3. Brett, Wood, and Thomas (1994).
4. Radano and Bohlman (2001).
5. While a comprehensive guide to the literature is neither possible nor desirable here, a few important titles might be mentioned. A collection of essays that speaks to many of this book's concerns is Born and Hesmondhalgh (2000). Mention should also be made of the fruits of Gary Tomlinson's (1995) engagement of anthropology and postmodernism, Martin Scherzinger's (2000) bold postcolonial forays, and Erlmann's (1999) domestication of a great deal of contemporary social, cultural, anthropological, and historical theory for readers. A long reading list awaits those who would venture into other fields in search of difference. For one among several points of departure, see Minow (1990).
6. Stokes et al. (2001), 388.
7. For two valuable accounts of the history, theory, and practice of ethnomusicology, neither of which is couched in terms of the production of difference, see Krader (1980) and Myers (1992). See also Gourlay's (1982) thoughtful and challenging essay. "Our ultimate concern," writes Gourlay, "is with ourselves and our own culture. . . . At bottom we are in it to save our souls or at least, to find them" (411, 412).
8. Nettl (1986).
9. Cited in Myers (1992), 8.

10. Ibid., 16.
11. Ibid., 8.
12. Ahmad (1995), 17.
13. Spivak with Rooney (1989), 133.
14. "Musicology," in Randel (1986).
15. For critiques of "world music," see Rouget (1996), 339–51; Erlmann (1996); and Feld (1994).
16. On different subdisciplinary turfs, see Kerman (1985) and Cook (1998). Stock (1998) offers a cogent account of ethnomusicology vis-à-vis a changing musicology. See also Cook and Everist (1998) and Clayton, Middleton, and Herbert (2003).
17. Fabian (1983), 17, 32, 95–96.
18. Hornbostel (1928), 30.
19. Excerpted in Eze (1997), 126. Hegel's rough treatment of Africa is widely discussed. See, for example, Olufemi Taiwo, "Exorcising Hegel's Ghost: Africa's Challenge to Philosophy," on the web at web.africa.ufl.edu/asq/v1/4/2.htm.
20. Jones (1959), 1.
21. Tracey (1954), 8.
22. Chernoff (1997).
23. Chernoff (1979).
24. Hornbostel (1928), 30.
25. Cooke (1999), 73.
26. For an excellent introduction to issues of race and interpretation, see Gates (1986).
27. Waterman (1993).
28. For a related argument, see Scherzinger (2001).
29. Taylor (1994).
30. Ibid., 67.
31. See Henrotte (1985) for a brief discussion of the translatability of gestures.
32. See also the discussion in Bhabha (1994).
33. On this view, see Spivak with Rooney (1989); pertinent, too, is Spivak (1999).
34. Auerbach (1985), 232; cited in Solie (1993), 14.
35. Hountondji (1983), xii.

Chapter 8

1. Kerman (1985), 63.
2. In her excellent introduction, Solie (1993) credits Gary Tomlinson with the view that "traditional musical analysis is one of the most aggressively universalizing discourses still in common use" (8, n.24).
3. Temperley (1998), 69.
4. See, for example, musicologist Philip Brett's (1997–1998, 158) praise song for ethnomusicological pluralism.
5. See, for example, Cook and Everist (1998) for essays covering the different branches of musicology.

6. Temperley (1998), 69–70.
7. Blacking (1955).
8. Blum (1991).
9. Waterman (1991).
10. Brandel (1961).
11. Kubik (1962).
12. Eze (1997).
13. See especially Hountondji (1983).
14. Yai (1977).
15. See the preface to Hountondji (1996).
16. Ethnographies employing African-language concepts include Zemp (1971), Stone (1982), and Keil (1979), to cite only three influential examples.
17. Hornbostel (1928).
18. Blacking (1967).
19. For use of a similar analytic notation, see Merriam (1957).
20. See Powers (1980). Of interest in the history of African music analysis is Sprigge's (1968) brief but suggestive "paradigmatic" analysis of a song from Eweland's Adangbe. The most thoroughgoing paradigmatic analyses of African music are found in Arom (1991).
21. According to Arom, "African taxonomies, while adequate from a social and/or religious perspective, throw no light whatsoever on the systematic structure of the *musical techniques* employed" (1991, 215). Reviewing Igbo conceptual categories, however, Nzewi mentions the use of words like *udi* for "how a thing is constructed/shaped" and *ngwakota* for "how the structural components come together to give wholeness" (1991, 19; 56). It is possible, then, that a less absolute view of structure than Arom's might find indigenous conceptions suggestive.
22. Agawu (1990).
23. Stock (1993), 225.
24. Arom (1991). For two authoritative assessments, one Africanist, the other methodological, see, respectively, Locke (1992) and Nattiez (1993).
25. Variation processes are studied in Erlmann (1985) and Jones (1975–1976). Of special interest in aligning technical procedure and native conceptualization is Uzoigwe (1998), 90–128.
26. Jones (1959).
27. See Schuller (1968); Floyd (1995); Wilson (1974); and Fink (1998).
28. Kubik (1994); Chernoff (1979); and Arom (1991).
29. Myers (1983); Waterman (1992).
30. Reich (2002), 55.
31. Blacking (1960).
32. Anku (1992) and (1993). See also Anku (1995), (1997), and (2000).

Chapter 9

1. Attfield and Gibson (1996), 178.
2. Gewirth (1974), 976.

3. See, for example, Garber, Hanssen, and Walkowitz (2000).

4. Kerman (1985), 174.

5. See Taruskin (1986) and Forte (1986).

6. McCreless, et al. (1997).

7. Slobin (1992), 329.

8. Krader (1980).

9. Slobin (1992), 329.

10. Slobin (1992) lists these among "sample cases illustrating standard areas of ethical concern" (332). I have turned his statements into questions for rhetorical effect.

11. Appiah (1992).

12. Avorgbedor (2001).

13. Agawu (1995).

14. Kisliuk (1998).

15. Ibid., 106.

16. Chernoff (1979); Berliner (1978); Locke (1987).

17. Kisliuk (1998), 20.

18. Ibid., x.

19. Ibid., 217.

20. Stock (2000).

21. Feld (2000).

22. *Music of the Ba-Benzélé Pygmies,* Bärenreiter Musicaphon BM 30 L 2303 (1966).

23. Feld (2000), 257.

24. Ibid., 258.

References

Achebe, Chinua. *Things Fall Apart.* London: Heinemann, 1958.

Addo, Akosua Obuo. "Ghanaian Children's Music Cultures: A Video Ethnography of Selected Singing Games." Ph.D. diss., University of British Columbia, 1995.

Adanson, Michel. *A Voyage to Senegal, the Isle of Gorée, and the River Gambia.* London: J. Nourse and W. Johnston, 1759.

Adorno, Theodor, with George Simpson, "On Popular Music." *Studies in Philosophy and Social Sciences* 9 (1941): 17–48.

———. "Bach Defended against His Devotees." In *Prisms.* Translated by Samuel and Shierry Weber, 133–46. Cambridge, Mass.: MIT Press, 1967.

Agawu, Kofi. "Tone and Tune: The Evidence for Northern Ewe Music." *Africa* 58 (1988): 127–46.

———. "Variation Procedures in Northern Ewe Song." *Ethnomusicology* 34 (1990): 221–43.

———. *Playing with Signs: A Semiotic Interpretation of Classic Music.* Princeton, N.J.: Princeton University Press, 1991.

———. "Representing African Music." *Critical Inquiry* 18 (1992): 245–66.

———. "Theory and Practice in the Analysis of the Nineteenth-Century Lied." *Music Analysis* 11 (1992): 3–36.

———. "The Invention of 'African Rhythm.'" *Journal of the American Musicological Society* 48 (1995): 380–95.

———. *African Rhythm: A Northern Ewe Perspective.* Cambridge: Cambridge University Press, 1995.

———. "The Challenge of Semiotics." In *Rethinking Music.* Edited by Nicholas Cook and Mark Everist, 138–60. Oxford: Oxford University Press, 1999.

———. "Analytical Issues Raised by Contemporary Art Music." In *Intercultural Music 3.* Edited by Cynthia Tse Kimberlin and Akin Euba, 135–47. Richmond, Calif.: MRI Press, 2001.

241

Agbodeka, Francis. *Achimota in the National Setting: A Unique Experiment in West Africa.* Accra: Afram Publications, 1977.

Ahmad, Aijaz. *In Theory: Classes, Nations, Literatures.* London: Verso, 1992.

———. "The Politics of Literary Postcoloniality." *Race and Class* 36 (1995): 1–20.

Akrofi, Eric A. "The Status of Music Education Programs in Ghanaian Public Schools." Ed.D. diss., University of Illinois at Urbana-Champaign, 1982.

Ames, David W., and Anthony V. King. *Glossary of Hausa Music and Its Social Contexts.* Evanston, Ill.: Northwestern University Press, 1971.

Amoaku, William K. *African Songs and Rhythms for Children: A Selection from Ghana.* Mainz: Schott, 1971.

———. *African Songs and Rhythms for Children.* Washington, D.C.: Smithsonian/ Folkways Records, 1989. Sound cassette. Originally issued as Folkways FC 7844, 1978.

Ankermann, Bernhard. *Die afrikanischen Musikinstrumente.* Leipzig: Zentralantiquar-iat der Dt. Demokrat, 1976. Originally published in 1901.

Anku, Willie. "Towards a Cross-Cultural Theory of Rhythm in African In Drumming." *Intercultural Music.* Vol. 1. Edited by Cynthia Tse Kimberlin and Akin Euba, 167–202. London: Centre for Intercultural Music Arts and Bayreuth, 1995.

———. *Structural Set Analysis of African Music 1: Adowa.* Legon, Ghana: Soundstage Production, 1992.

———. *Structural Set Analysis of African Music 2: Bawa.* Legon, Ghana: Soundstage Production, 1993.

———. "Principles of Rhythm Integration in African Drumming." *Black Music Research Journal* 17 (1997): 211–38.

———. "Circles and Time." *Music Theory Online* 6 (2000). Website at www.smt.ucsb. edu/mto/issues/mto.00.6.1/mto.00.6.1.anku.html

Anon. "Music Festivals in Africa: Notes for the Guidance of Adjudicators." *African Music* 2 (1958): 61–62.

Ansre, Gilbert, ed. *The Evangelical Presbyterian Church: 150 Years of Evangelization and Development, 1847–1997.* Ho, Ghana: Evangelical Presbyterian Church, 1997.

Anyidoho, Kofi. "Oral Poetics and Traditions of Verbal Art in Africa." Ph.D. diss., University of Texas at Austin, 1983.

Appiah, Kwame Anthony. *In My Father's House: Africa in the Philosophy of Culture.* New York: Oxford University Press, 1992.

———. "Africa." In *Encyclopedia of Ethics.* Edited by Lawrence C. Becker and Charlotte B. Becker, 25–28. New York: Garland Publishing, 1992.

Arom, Simha. *African Polyphony and Polyrhythm: Musical Structure and Methodology.* Translated by Martin Thom, Barbara Tuckett and Raymond Boyd. Cambridge: Cambridge University Press, 1991. Originally pub. 1985.

Ashcroft, Bill, Gareth Griffiths, and Helen Tiffin. *Key Concepts in Post Colonial Studies.* London: Routledge, 1998.

Attfield, Robert, and Susanne Gibson. "Ethics." In *A Dictionary of Cultural and Critical Theory,* 178–182. Edited by Michael Payne. Oxford: Blackwell, 1996.

Austin, William. *'Susanna', 'Jeanie', and 'The Old Folks at Home': The Songs of Stephen C. Foster from His Time to Ours.* New York: Macmillan, 1975.

Avorgbedor, Daniel K. "Pan-African Orchestra." In *The New Grove Dictionary of Music and Musicians,* volume 19, 23–24 2d ed. Edited by Stanley Sadie and John Tyrell. New York: Macmillan, 2001.

———. "It's a Great Song!" *Halo* Performance as Literary Production." *Research in African Literatures* 32 (2001): 17–43.

Baily, John. "Music Structure and Human Movement." In *Musical Structure and Cognition.* Edited by Peter Howell, Ian Cross, and Robert West, 237–58. London: Academic Press, 1985.

Ballantine, Christopher. *Marabi Nights: Early South African Jazz and Vaudeville.* Johannesburg: Raven Press, 1993.

Barber, Karin. "Popular Arts in Africa." *African Studies Review* 30 (1987): 1–78, 105–32.

———, ed. *Readings in African Popular Theatre.* Bloomington: Indiana University Press, 1997.

———, John Collins, and Alain Ricard. *West African Popular Theatre.* Bloomington: Indiana University Press, 1997.

Bareis, Urban. "Formen neo-traditioneller Musik in Kpando, Ghana." In *Populäre Musik in Afrika.* Edited by Veit Erlmann, 59–108. Berlin: Staatliche Museen Preussischer Kulturbesitz, 1991.

Barz, Gregory F., and Timothy J. Cooley, eds. *Shadows in the Field: New Perspectives for Fieldwork in Ethnomusicology.* New York: Oxford University Press, 1997.

Bebey, Francis. *African Music: A People's Art.* Translated by Josephine Bennett. New York: Lawrence Hill, 1975. Originally pub. 1969.

Bender, Wolfgang. *Sweet Mother: Modern African Music.* Chicago: University of Chicago Press, 1991.

Benveniste, Émile. "The Semiology of Language." *Semiotica.* Special Supplement, 1981, 5–23. Reprinted in *Semiotics: An Introductory Reader.* Edited by Robert E. Innis, 226–46. Bloomington: Indiana University Press, 1985.

Berliner, Paul. *The Soul of Mbira.* Berkeley: University of California Press, 1978.

Bhabha, Homi. *Nation and Narration.* London and New York: Routledge, 1990.

———. *The Location of Culture.* London and New York: Routledge, 1994.

Bischoff, Peter. *Listen to the Silence: African Cross Rhythms as Seen through Ghanaian Music.* Princeton, N.J.: Films for the Humanities and Sciences, 1996.

Blacking, John. "Some Notes on a Theory of Rhythm Advanced by Erich von Hornbostel." *African Music* 1 (1955): 12–20.

———. "Review of *Studies in African Music* by A. M. Jones." *African Studies* 19 (1960): 98–101.

———. *Venda Children's Songs: A Study in Ethnomusicological Analysis.* Johannesburg: Witwatersrand University Press, 1967.

———. *How Musical Is Man?* Seattle: University of Washington Press, 1973.

———. "The Problem of 'Ethnic' Perceptions in the Semiotics of Music." In *The Sign in Music and Literature.* Edited by Wendy Steiner, 184–94. Austin: University of Texas Press, 1981.

————. *Music, Culture and Experience.* Chicago: University of Chicago Press, 1995.

Blench, Roger. "Evidence for the Indonesian Origins of Certain Elements of African Culture: A Review, with Special Reference to the Arguments of A. M. Jones." *African Music* 6 (1982): 81–93.

Blum, Stephen. "European Musical Terminology and the Music of Africa." In *Comparative Musicology and Anthropology of Music.* Edited by Bruno Nettl and Philip Bohlman, 3–36. Chicago: University of Chicago Press, 1991.

Boahen, A. Adu. *African Perspectives on Colonialism.* Baltimore: Johns Hopkins University Press, 1987.

————, ed. *General History of Africa. VII. Africa under Colonial Domination 1880–1935.* Paris: UNESCO, 1990.

Boonzajer-Flaes, Robert M., and Fred Gales. *Brass Bands in Ghana.* Unpublished paper, University of Amsterdam.

Born, Georgina and David Hesmondhalgh, eds. *Western Music and Its Others: Difference, Representation, and Appropriation in Music.* Berkeley: University of California Press, 2000.

Bowdich, Thomas E. *Mission from Cape Coast to Ashantee.* London: J. Murray, 1819.

Brackett, David. *Interpreting Popular Music.* Cambridge: Cambridge University Press, 1995. 2d ed. Berkeley: University of California Press, 2000.

Branda-Lacerda, Marcos. *Kultische Trommelmusik der Yoruba in der Volksrepublik Benin: Bata-Sango und Bata-Egungun in den Städten Pobè und Sakété.* Hamburg: Verlag der Musikalienhandlung K. D. Wagner, 1988.

Brandel, Rose. *The Music of Central Africa: An Ethnomusicological Study.* The Hague: Martinus Nijhoff, 1961.

Brandily, Monique. *Introduction aux musiques Africaines.* Arles: Cité de la musique/ Actes Sud, 1997.

Brempong, Owusu. "Akan Highlife in Ghana: Songs of Cultural Transition." Ph.D. diss., Indiana University, 1986.

Brett, Philip. "Piano Four-Hands: Schubert and the Performance of Gay Male Desire." *19th-Century Music* 21 (1997–1998): 149–76.

————, Elizabeth Wood, and Gary C. Thomas. *Queering the Pitch: The New Gay and Lesbian Musicology.* New York and London: Routledge, 1994.

Bujic, Bojan. *Music in European Thought 1851–1912.* Cambridge: Cambridge University Press, 1988.

Capo, Hounkpati B. C. *Renaissance du Gbe.* Lomé: Université du Benin, 1986.

————. *A Comparative Phonology of Gbe.* New York: Foris Publication, 1991.

Carrington, John. *Talking Drums of Africa.* London: Carey Kingsgate Press, 1949.

Centrafrique: Musique Gbáyá. Chants à penser. CD (C560079). Paris: Ocora, 1995.

Charry, Eric. "Musical Thought, History, and Practice." Ph.D. diss., Princeton University, 1992.

————. *Mande Music: Traditional and Modern Music of Maninka and Mandinka of Western Africa.* Chicago: University of Chicago Press, 2000.

————. "Guide to African Music." Website at www.fitzroydearborn.com/Samples/ MusRGsamp.htm.

Chernoff, John Miller. *African Rhythm and African Sensibility: Aesthetics and Social Action in African Musical Idioms*. Chicago: University of Chicago Press, 1979.

———. "Africa Come Back: The Popular Music of West Africa." In *Repercussions: A Celebration of African-American Music*. Edited by Geoffrey Haydon and Dennis Marks, 152–78. London: Century Publishing, 1985.

———. "'Hearing' in West African Idioms." *The World of Music* 39 (1997): 19–26.

———. *A Drummer's Testament*. Chicago: University of Chicago Press, forthcoming.

Clayton, Martin, Richard Middleton, and Trevor Herbert, eds. *The Cultural Study of Music*. New York: Routledge, 2003.

Clifford, James and George Marcus, eds. *Writing Culture: The Poetics and Politics of Ethnography*. Berkeley: University of California Press, 1986.

Colapietro, Vincent M. *Glossary of Semiotics*. New York: Paragon House, 1993, s.v. "Text."

Collins, John. *E. T. Mensah, King of Highlife*. London: Off the Record Press, 1986.

———. *West African Pop Roots*. Philadelphia: Temple University Press, 1992.

———. *Highlife Time*. Accra, Ghana: Anansesem Publications, 1994.

——— and Paul Richards. "Popular Music in West Africa: Suggestions for an Interpretative Framework." In *Popular Music Perspectives*. Edited by David Horn and Philip Tagg, 111–41. Göteborg and Exeter: International Association for the Study of Popular Music, 1982.

Cook, Nicholas. *Music: A Very Short Introduction*. Oxford: Oxford University Press, 1998.

———, and Mark Everist, eds. *Rethinking Music*. Oxford: Oxford University Press, 1998.

Cooke, Peter. "Was Ssempeke Just Being Kind? Listening to Instrumental Music in Africa South of the Sahara." *The World of Music* 41 (1999): 73–83.

Coplan, David. "Go To My Town, Cape Coast! The Social History of Ghanaian Highlife." In *Eight Urban Musical Cultures*. Edited by Bruno Nettl, 96–114. Urbana: University of Illinois Press, 1978.

———. *In Township Tonight!: South Africa's Black City Music and Theatre*. Johannesburg: Ravan Press and London/New York: Longman, 1985.

Dahlhaus, Carl. *Foundations of Music History*. Translated by J. B. Robinson. Cambridge: Cambridge University Press, 1983.

———. "Music as Text and Work of Art." In *Esthetics of Music*. Translated by William Austin, 9–15. Cambridge: Cambridge University Press, 1982.

Dakubu, M. E. Kropp. *The Languages of Ghana*. London: Kegan Paul International, 1988.

Davidson, Basil. *Africa: A Voyage of Discovery*. 4 videocassettes. London: RM Arts, 1984.

———. *African Kingdoms*. London: Time-Life, 1966.

Dehoux, Vincent. *Les "chants à penser" des Gbaya (Centrafrique)*. Paris: SELAF, 1986.

Djedje, Jacqueline Cogdell. "The Present State of African Music Historiography and Sources of Historical Data." Paper read at the International Conference on African Music and Dance. Bellagio Study and Conference Centere, October 12–16, 1992.

————, ed. *Turn Up the Volume! A Celebration of African Music*. Los Angeles: UCLA Fowler Museum of Cultural History, 1999.

Dreyfus, Laurence. "Early Music Defended against its Devotees." *Musical Quarterly* 69 (1983): 297–322.

Echeruo, Michael J. C. *Victorian Lagos: Aspects of Nineteenth-Century Lagos Life*. London: Macmillan Education Limited, 1977.

Echezona, William, W. C. "Compositional Techniques of Nigerian Traditional Music." *Composer* 19 (1966): 41–49.

Ekpo, Dennis. "Towards a Post-Africanism: Contemporary African Thought and Postmodernism." *Textual Practice* 9 (1995): 121–35.

Ekwueme, Lazarus N. "African Music in Christian Liturgy: The Igbo Experiment." *African Music* 5 (1973–1974): 12–33.

————. "Guest Editorial: African Musicological Investigation in a Culture Conscious Era." *African Music* 4 (1975–1976): 4–5.

Ellingson, Ter. "Transcription." In *Ethnomusicology: An Introduction*. Edited by Helen Myers, 153–64. New York: Norton, 1992.

England, Nicholas. "Bushman Counterpoint." *Journal of the International Folk Music Council* 19 (1967): 58–66.

Erlmann, Veit. "Model, Variation and Performance: Fulbe Praise Song in Northern Cameroon." *Yearbook for Traditional Music* 17 (1985): 88–112.

————, ed. *Populäre Musik in Afrika*. Berlin: Staatliche Museen Preussischer Kulturbesitz, 1991.

————. "The Aesthetics of the Global Imagination: Reflections on 'World Music' in the 1990s." *Public Culture* 8 (1996): 467–87.

————. *Music, Modernity and the Global Imagination: South Africa and the West*. Oxford: Oxford University Press, 1999.

Euba, Akin. "Multiple Pitch Lines in Yoruba Choral Music." *Journal of the International Folk Music Council* 19 (1967): 66–71.

————. "Do We Need Ethnomusicology in Africa?" *Proceedings of the Forum for Revitalizing African Music Studies in Higher Education*. Edited by Frank Gunderson, 137–39. Ann Arbor, Michigan: U.S. Secretariat of the International Center for African Music and Dance, 2001.

————. *Essays on Music in Africa 2: Intercultural Perspectives*. Elekoto and Bayreuth: Iwalewa-Haus, 1989.

————. *Yoruba Drumming: The Dùndún Tradition*. Lagos and Bayreuth: Elekoto Music Centre and Bayreuth African Studies Series, 1991.

————. *Modern African Music: A Catalogue of Selected Archival Materials at Iwalewa-Haus, University of Bayreuth, Germany*. Bayreuth: Iwalewa House, 1993.

Eze, Emmanuel Chukwudi, ed. *Race and the Enlightenment: A Reader*. Oxford: Blackwell, 1997.

Fabian, Johannes. *Time and the Other: How Anthropology Makes Its Object*. New York: Columbia University Press, 1983.

Fargion, Janet Topp. "Ewe and Yours." Review of *African Rhythm: A Northern Ewe Perspective* by K. Agawu. *The Times Higher Education Supplement* (April 4, 1997), 26.

Feld, Steven. "Dialogic Editing: Interpreting How Kaluli Read *Sound and Sentiment.*" *Cultural Anthropology* 2 (1987): 190–210.

———. "Ethnomusicology and Visual Communication," *Ethnomusicology* 20 (1976): 293–325.

———. "From Schizophonia to Schismogenesis: On the Discourses and Commodification Practices of 'World Music' and 'World Beat.'" In *Music Grooves* by Charles Keil and Steven Feld, 257–89. Chicago: University of Chicago Press, 1994.

———. "The Poetics and Politics of Pygmy Pop." In *Western Music and Its Others: Difference, Representation, and Appropriation in Music.* Edited by Georgina Born and David Hesmondhalgh, 254–79. Berkeley: University of California Press, 2000.

Fiagbedzi, Nissio. "The Music of the Anlo: Its Historical Background, Cultural Matrix and Style." Ph.D. diss., University of California at Los Angeles, 1977.

Fink, Robert. "Elvis Everywhere." *American Music* 16 (1998): 135–79.

Floyd, Malcom, ed. *Composing the Music of Africa: Composition, Interpretation and Realisation.* Aldershot, U.K.: Ashgate, 1999.

Floyd, Sam. *The Power of Black Music: Interpreting its History from Africa to the United States.* Oxford: Oxford University Press, 1995.

Forte, Allen. "Letter to the Editor in Reply to Richard Taruskin." *Music Analysis* 5 (1986): 321–37.

———. *The American Popular Ballad of the Golden Era, 1924–50.* Princeton, N.J.: Princeton University Press, 1995.

Foucault, Michel. *The Archaeology of Knowledge.* Translated by A. Sheridan. New York: Pantheon, 1972.

Freeman, Richard A. *Travels and Life in Ashanti and Jaman.* London: A. Constable, 1898.

Friedson, Steven. *Dancing Prophets: Musical Experience in Tumbuka Healing.* Chicago: University of Chicago Press, 1996.

Frith, Simon. *Performing Rites: On the Value of Popular Music.* Cambridge, Mass.: Harvard University Press, 1996.

———. "Why Do Songs Have Words?" In *Music for Pleasure: Essays in the Sociology of Pop,* 118–20. Cambridge: Polity Press, 1988.

Frozen Brass: Africa and Latin America: Anthology of Brass Music. CD. Pan Records 2026C.

Gansemans, Jos, and Barbara Schmidt-Wrenger. *Zentralafrika.* Leipzig: Deutscher Verlag für Musik, 1986.

Garber, Marjorie, Beatrice Hanssen, and Rebecca L. Walkowitz, eds. *The Turn to Ethics.* New York and London: Routledge, 2000.

Gates, Henry Louis, Jr. III, ed. *'Race', Writing, and Difference.* Chicago: University of Chicago Press, 1986.

Gbeho, Philip. "Music of the Gold Coast." *African Music* 1 (1957): 62–64.

Geertz, Clifford. *Works and Lives: The Anthropologist as Writer.* Stanford, Calif.: Stanford University Press, 1988.

Geest, Sjaak Van der. "The Political Meaning of Highlife Songs in Ghana." *African Studies Review* 25 (1982): 27–35.

Gendron, Bernard. "Theodor Adorno Meets the Cadillacs." In *Studies in Entertainment: Critical Approaches to Mass Culture*. Edited by Tania Modleski, 18–38. Bloomington: Indiana University Press, 1986.

Gewirth, Alan. "Ethics." In *The New Encyclopedia Brittanica*. 15th ed. Chicago: University of Chicago Press, 1974.

Ghana: Music of the Northern Tribes CD. New York: Lyrichord Discs, 1976 LYRCD 7321.

Ghana: Rhythms of the People: Traditional Music and Dance of the Ewe, Dagbamba, Fante, and Ga People CD. Montpelier, Vt.: Multicultural Media, 2000, MCM 3018.

Giants of Ghanaian Danceband Highlife: 1950s–1970s. CD [OMCD011]. Tivoli, N.Y. : Original Music, 1990.

Gilman, Benjamin I. "The Science of Exotic Music." *Science* 30 (1909): 532–35. Reprinted in *Ethnomusicology: History, Definitions and Scope*. Edited by Kay Kauffman Shelemay, 2–5. New York: Garland, 1992.

Gilroy, Paul. *The Black Atlantic: Modernity and Double Consciousness*. London: Verso, 1993.

Gourlay, Kenneth A. "Towards a Humanizing Ethnomusicology." *Ethnomusicology* 26 (1982): 411–20.

Graham, Ronnie. *Stern's Guide to Contemporary African Music*. London: Zwan Publications and Off the Record Press, 1988.

Gray, John. *African Music: A Bibliographical Guide to the Traditional, Popular, Art, and Liturgical Musics of Sub-Saharan Africa*. Westport, Conn.: Greenwood Press, 1991.

Green, Doris. "The Liberation of African Music." *Journal of Black Studies* 8 (1977): 149–67.

Hamm, Charles. *Yesterdays: Popular Song in America*. New York: W. W. Norton, 1979.

Hanslick, Eduard. *On the Musically Beautiful*. Excerpted in *Music in European Thought 1851–1912*. Edited by Bojan Bujic, 11–39. Cambridge: Cambridge University Press, 1988.

Haring, Lee. *Verbal Arts in Madagascar: Performance in Historical Perspective*. Philadelphia: University of Pennsylvania Press, 1992.

Haydon, Geoffrey, and Dennis Marks (directors). *Repercussions: A Celebration of African-American Music*. Program 7, "Africa Come Back: The Popular Music of West Africa."

Hegel, Georg Wilhelm Friedrich. *Lectures on the Philosophy of World History*. Translated by H. B. Nisbet. Cambridge: Cambridge University Press, orig. pub 1822–28. Rep. 1975.

Henrotte, Gayle. "Music as Language: A Semiotic Paradigm?" In *Semiotics 1984*. Edited by John Deely, 163–70. New York: University Press of America, 1985.

Herskovits, Melville J. *The Myth of the Negro Past*. Boston: Beacon Press, 1941.

Hirschberg, Walter. "Early Historical Illustrations of West and Central African Music." *African Music* 4 (1969): 6–18.

Hobsbawn, Eric, and Terence Ranger. *The Invention of Tradition*. Cambridge: Cambridge University Press, 1983.

Hornbostel, Erich M. Von. "African Negro Music." *Africa* 1 (1928): 30–62.

Hountondji, Paulin J. "Recapturing." In *The Surreptitious Speech: Présence Africaine and the Politics of Otherness 1947–1987*. Edited by V. Y. Mudimbe, 238–48. Chicago: University of Chicago Press, 1992.

———. *African Philosophy: Myth and Reality*. Translated by Henri Evans with the collaboration of Jonathan Rée. Bloomington: Indiana University Press, 1983.

———. "Preface to the Second Edition" In *African Philosophy: Myth and Reality*, vii–xxviii, second edition. Translated by Henri Evans with the collaboration of Jonathan Rée. Blooming: Indiana University Press, 1996.

Hunwick, John Owen. *West Africa and the Arab World: Historical and Contemporary Perspectives*. The J. B. Danquah Memorial Lectures. Twenty third Series—February 1990. Accra, Ghana: Ghana Academy of Arts and Sciences, 1991.

Irele, Abiola. "Is African Music Possible?" *Transition* 61 (1993): 56–71.

———. *The African Imagination: Literature in Africa and the Black Diaspora*. New York: Oxford University Press, 2001.

Jakobson, Roman. "Language in Relation to Other Communication Systems." In *Selected Writings*. Vol. 2, 697–708. The Hague: Mouton, 1971.

Johnston, Thomas F. "Tsonga Children's Folksongs." *Journal of American Folklore* 86 (1973): 225–40.

Jones, A. M. *African Music in Northern Rhodesia and Some Other Places*. The Occasional Papers of the Rhodes-Livingstone Museum. Livingstone, Northern Rhodesia: Rhodes-Livingstone Museum, 1949.

———. "African Rhythm." *Africa* 24 (1954): 26–47.

———. "Drums Down the Centuries." *African Music* 1 (1957): 4–10.

———. *Studies in African Music*. 2 vols. Oxford: Oxford University Press, 1959.

——— –. *Africa and Indonesia: The Evidence of the Xylophone and Other Musical and Cultural Factors*. Leiden: E. J. Brill, 1971.

———. "Swahili Epic Poetry: A Musical Study." *African Music* 5 (1975–1976): 105–29.

Kartomi, Margaret. *On Concepts and Classifications of Musical Instruments*. Chicago: University of Chicago Press, 1990.

Kauffman, Robert. "African Rhythm: A Reassessment." *Ethnomusicology* 24 (1980): 393–415.

Keil, Charles. *Tiv Song: The Sociology of Art in a Classless Society*. Chicago: University of Chicago Press, 1979.

———. "The Theory of Participatory Discrepancies." *Ethnomusicology* 39 (1995): 1–20.

Kerman, Joseph. *Musicology*. London: Fontana, 1985.

Keuken, Johan van der. *Bewogen Koper* (Brass Unbound). Videocassette. Amsterdam: IDTV, 1993.

Kingslake, Brian. "Review of *Studies in African Music* by A. M. Jones." *African Music* 2 (1959): 84–86.

Kirby, Percival Robson. *The Musical Instruments of the Native Races of South Africa*. London: Oxford University Press, 1934.

Kisliuk, Michelle, "(Un)doing Fieldwork: Sharing Songs, Sharing Lives." In *Shadows in the Field: New Perspectives for Fieldwork in Ethnomusicology*. Edited by Gregory Barz and Timothy J. Cooley, 23–44. New York: Oxford University Press, 1997.

————. *Seize the Dance: BaAka Musical Life and the Ethnography of Performance.* New York: Oxford University Press, 1998.

Kivy, Peter. *Music Alone: Philosophical Reflections on the Purely Musical Experience.* Ithaca, N.Y.: Cornell University Press, 1990.

Koetting, James T. "Africa/Ghana." In *Worlds of Music: An Introduction to the Music of the World's Peoples.* Edited by Jeff Todd Titon, 64–104. New York: Schirmer, 1984.

————. "The *New Grove*: Sub-Saharan Africa." *Ethnomusicology* 29 (1985): 314–17.

————. "Analysis and Notation of West African Drum Ensemble Music." *Selected Reports in Ethnomusicology* 1 (1970): 115–46.

Krader, Barbara. "Ethnomusicology." In *The New Grove Dictionary of Music and Musicians.* Volume 6, 275–282. Edited by Stanley Sadie. London: Macmillan, 1980.

Kramer, Lawrence. *Music and Poetry: The Nineteenth Century and After.* Berkeley: University of California Press, 1984.

Kubik, Gerhard. "Review of Rose Brandel, *The Music of Central Africa.*" *African Music* 3 (1962): 116–18.

————. *Mehrstimmigkeit und Tonsysteme in Zentral- und Ostafrika.* Österreische Akademie der Wissenschaften. Vienna: Herman Böhlaus Nachfolger, 1968.

————. "Oral Notation of Some West and Central African Time-Line Patterns." *Review of Ethnology* 3 (1972): 169–76.

————. *The Kachamba Brothers' Band: A Study of Neo-Traditional Music in Malawi.* Lusaka: Institute for African Studies, University of Zambia, 1974.

————. "Musikgestaltung in Afrika." In *Musik in Afrika: 20 Beiträge zur Kenntnis traditioneller afrikanischer Musikkulturen.* Edited by Artur Simon, 27–40. Berlin: Staatliche Museen Preussicher Kulturbesitz, 1983.

————. "The Emics of African Musical Rhythm." In *Cross Rhythms 2.* Edited by Daniel Avorgbedor and Kwesi Yankah, 26–66. Bloomington, Ind.: Trickster Press, 1985.

————. *Theory of African Music.* Vol. 1. Wilhelmshaven: Florian Noetzel Verlag, 1994.

————. "Multipart Singing in Sub-Saharan Africa: Remote and Recent Histories Unravelled." In *Papers Presented at the Symposium on Ethnomusicology: Number 13 University of Zululand 1995 and at the Symposium Number 14 Rhodes University 1996.* Edited by Andrew Tracey, 85–97. Grahamstown, South Africa: International Library of African Music, 1997.

————. "Intra-African Streams of Influence." In *The Garland Encyclopedia of World Music: Africa.* Edited by Ruth Stone, 293–326. New York: Garland, 1998.

————. *Africa and the Blues.* Jackson: University Press of Mississippi, 1999.

————. "Africa." In *The New Grove Dictionary of Music and Musicians.* 2d. ed. Edited by Stanley Sadie and John Tyrell. Volume 1, 190–210. London: Macmillan, 2001.

————, et al., eds. *Musikgeschichte in Bildern: Ostafrika.* Band I: Musikethnologie Lieferung 10. Leipzig: VEB Deutscher Verlag für Musik, 1982.

————, et al., eds. *Musikgeschichte in Bildern: Westafrika.* Band II: Musikethnologie Lieferung 10. Leipzig: VEB Deutscher Verlag für Musik, 1989.

Kwami, Robert M. "African Music Education and the School Curriculum." 2 vols. Ph.D. Diss., University of London Institute of Education, 1989.

———. "Music Education in Ghana and Nigeria: A Brief Summary." *Africa* 64 (1994): 544–60.

Kyagambiddwa, Joseph. *African Music from the Source of the Nile*. London: Atlantic Press, 1956.

Lacerda, Marcos. "Yoruba Sacred Music and the *Barform*." *Sonus* 23 (2002): 32–55.

Ladzekpo, C. K. *Foundation Course in African Dance Drumming*. Website at www.bmrc. berkeley.edu/people/ladzekpo/Foundation.html

Lehmann, Bertram. "Timeline Database." Unpublished paper for the seminar, "Theories of African Rhythm," Harvard University, Spring 2000.

Leech-Wilkinson, Daniel. "Right at the Wrong Time" (review of Don Harrán, *In Defense of Music: The Case of Music as Argued by a Singer and Scholar of the Late Fifteenth Century*). *Times Literary Supplement* (March 16–22, 1990), 185.

Legendary Wulomei: Maa Amanua. CD (SRCD 019). Accra, Ghana: Sam Records, 2000.

Lerdahl, Fred, and Ray Jackendoff. *A Generative Theory of Tonal Music*. Cambridge, Mass.: MIT Press, 1983.

Lewis, Bernard. *Race and Slavery in the Middle East: An Historical Inquiry*. London: Oxford University Press, 1990.

Locke, David. "Improvisation in West African Musics." *Music Educators' Journal* 66 (1980): 125–32.

———. "Principles of Offbeat Timing and Cross-Rhythm in Southern Ewe Dance Drumming." *Ethnomusicology* 26 (1982): 217–46.

———. *Drum Gahu: A Systematic Method for an African Percussion Piece*. Crown Point, Ind.: White Cliffs Media Company, 1987.

———. *Kpegisu: A War Drum of the Ewe*. Crown Point, Ind.: White Cliffs Media, 1992.

———. "Review of *African Polyphony and Polyrhythm* by Simha Arom." *Notes* 48 (1992): 501–07.

Lomax, Alan, ed. *African Music from French Colonies*. The Columbia World Library of Folk and Primitive Music. Vol. 2. New York: Columbia Records, 1955–1956.

———. *Folk Song Style and Culture*. Washington: American Association for the Advancement of Science, 1968.

London, Justin. "Some Non-Isomorphisms between Pitch and Time." Paper read at a meeting of Music Theory Mid-West, April 2001. Website at www.acad.carleton. edu/curricular/MUSC/faculty/jlondon/somenonisomorphisms.htm.

Longmann Dictionary of the English Language. Harlow, U.K.: Longman Group Limited, 1984.

Manuel, Peter. *Popular Musics of the Non-Western World*. New York: Oxford University Press, 1988.

Marandola, Fabrice. "Review of *African Rhythm: A Northern Ewe Perspective* by K. Agawu." *Revue de Musicologie* 83 (1997): 137–39.

Maultsby, Portia K. "Africanisms in African-American Music." In *Africanisms in American Culture*, 185. Edited by Joseph E. Holloway. Bloomington: Indiana University Press, 1990.

Mbembe, Achille. *On the Postcolony.* Berkeley: University of California Press, 2001.

McCall, John. "The Representation of African Music in Early Documents." In *The Garland Encyclopedia of World Music: Africa.* Edited by Ruth M. Stone, 74–99. New York and London: Garland Publishing, 1998.

McCleod, Norma. "Malagasy Republic." In *The New Grove Dictionary of Music and Musicians.* Volume 11, 547–549. Edited by Stanley Sadie. London: Macmillan, 1980.

McCreless, Patrick, et. al. "Contemporary Music Theory and the New Musicology." *Journal of Musicology* 15 (1997): 291–352.

Meintjes, Louise. "Paul Simon's *Graceland,* South Africa, and the Mediation of Musical Meaning." *Ethnomusicology* 34 (1990): 37–73.

Mensah, Atta Annan. "Jazz—The Round Trip." *Jazzforschung/Jazz Research* 3 (1971–1972): 124–37.

———. "Highlife." In *The New Grove Dictionary of Music and Musicians.* Edited by Stanley Sadie. London: Macmillan Press, 1980.

———. "Art-Composed Music in Africa." In *The Garland Encyclopedia of World Music: Africa.* Edited by Ruth M. Stone, 208–31. New York: Garland, 1998.

Merriam, Alan P. "Songs of the Ketu of Bahia." *African Music* 1 (1957): 73–80.

———. "African Music." In *Continuity and Change in African Cultures.* Edited by William Bascom and Melville J. Herskovits, 49–86. Chicago: University of Chicago Press, 1959. Reprinted in Merriam, *African Music in Perspective.* New York: Garland, 1982.

———. *The Anthropology of Music.* Evanston: Northwestern University Press, 1964.

———. "Concepts of Time Reckoning." In *African Music in Perspective.* New York: Garland, 1982.

Middleton, Richard. *Studying Popular Music.* Milton Keynes: Open University Press, 1990.

———, ed. *Reading Pop: Approaches to Textual Analysis in Popular Music.* Oxford: Oxford University Press, 2000.

———, and David Horn, eds. *Popular Music 2: Theory and Method.* Cambridge: Cambridge University Press, 1982.

Miller, Christopher L. *Theories of Africans: Francophone Literature and Anthropology in Africa.* Chicago: University of Chicago Press, 1990.

Minow, Martha. *Making All the Difference: Inclusion, Exclusion, and American Law.* Ithaca, N.Y.: Cornell University Press, 1990.

Mitchell, Donald. *Gustav Mahler: Songs and Symphonies of Life and Death: Interpretations and Annotations.* London: Faber, 1985.

Monts, Lester P. *An Annotated Glossary of Vai Musical Language and Its Social Contexts.* Paris: Peters-SELAF, 1990.

———. LP *Music of the Vai of Liberia.* New York: Folkways, 1982.

Moore-Gilbert, Bart. *Postcolonial Theory: Contexts, Practices, Politics.* London: Verso, 1997.

Mudimbe, Valentin Y. *The Invention of Africa: Gnosis, Philosophy, and the Order of Knowledge.* Bloomington: Indiana University Press, 1988.

Mukuna, Kazadi wa. "The Genesis of Urban Music in Zaïre." *African Music* 7 (1992): 72–84.

Music of the Ba-Benzélé Pygmies. Bärenreiter Musicaphon BM 30 L 2303, 1966.

Myers, Helen. "African Music." In *The New Oxford Companion to Music.* Vol. 1. Edited by Denis Arnold, 25–38. Oxford: Oxford University Press, 1983.

———, ed. *Ethnomusicology: An Introduction.* London: Macmillan, 1992.

Nattiez, Jean-Jacques. *Music and Discourse: Toward a Semiology of Music.* Translated by Carolyn Abbate. Princeton, N.J.: Princeton University Press, 1990.

———. "Simha Arom and the Return of Analysis to Ethnomusicology." *Music Analysis* 12 (1993): 241–65.

Nesbitt, Nick. "African Music, Ideology, and Utopia." *Research in African Literatures* 32 (2001): 175–86.

Nettl, Bruno. "Africa." In *The New Harvard Dictionary of Music.* Edited by Don Randel. Cambridge, Mass., and London: The Belknap Press of Harvard University Press, 1986.

———. *The Study of Ethnomusicology: Twenty-Nine Issues and Concepts.* Urbana: University of Illinois Press, 1983.

Nketia, J. H. Kwabena. *African Music in Ghana.* Evanston, Ill.: Northwestern University Press, 1962.

———. *Drumming in the Akan Communities of Ghana.* Edinburgh: Thomas Nelson and Sons Ltd., 1963.

———. "Multi-Part Organization in the Music of the Gogo of Tanzania." *Journal of the International Folk Music Council* 19 (1967): 79–88.

———. *Ethnomusicology in Ghana.* Accra: Ghana Universities Press, 1970.

———. "Surrogate Languages of Africa." In *Current Trends in Linguistics: Linguistics in Sub-Saharan Africa.* Edited by Thomas A. Sebeok. The Hague: Mouton, 1971.

———. *The Music of Africa.* New York: Norton, 1974.

———. "The Intensity Factor in African Music." *Journal of Folklore Research* 25 (1988): 53–86.

———. *The Play-Concept in African Music.* Laura Boulton Lectures. Edited by Tom Vennum. Tempe, Ariz.: Hurd Museum, 1991.

Northcott, Lieutenant-Colonel H. P. *Report on the Northern Territories of the Gold Coast.* London, 1899.

Nzewi, Meki. "Social-Dramatic Implications of Performance-Composition in Igbo Music." In *International Musicological Society: Report of the Twelfth Congress Berkeley 1977.* Edited by Daniel Heartz and Bonnie Wade, 391–92. Kassel: Bärenreiter, 1981.

———. *Musical Practice and Creativity: An African Traditional Perspective.* Bayreuth: Iwalewa-Haus, University of Bayreuth, 1991.

———. *African Music: Theoretical Content and Creative Continuum: The Culture-Exponent's Definitions.* Olderhausen, Germany: Institut für populärer Musik, 1997.

Ogilby, John. *Africa.* London: T. Johnson, 1670.

Okely, Judith, and Helen Callaway, eds. *Anthropology and Autobiography*. London: Routledge, 1992.

Olaniyan, Tejunmola. "The Cosmopolitan Nativist: Fela Anikulapo Kuti and the Antinomies of Postcolonial Modernity." *Research in African Literatures* 32 (2001): 76–89.

Omojola, Bode. *Nigerian Art Music, with an Introductory Study of Ghanaian Art Music*. Ibadan: Institut français de Recherche en Afrique, University of Ibadan, 1995.

Ong, Walter. "African Talking Drums and Oral Noetics." In *Interfaces of the Word: Studies in the Evolution of Consciousness and Culture*, 92–120. Ithaca, N.Y.: Cornell University Press, 1977.

Oyewumi, Oyeronke. *The Invention of Women: Making an African Sense of Western Gender Discourses*. Minneapolis: University of Minnesota Press, 1997.

Paddison, Max. *Adorno's Aesthetics of Music*. Cambridge: Cambridge University Press, 1993.

———. "The Critique Criticised: Adorno and Popular Music." In *Popular Music 2: Theory and Method*. Edited by Richard Middleton and David Horn, 201–18. Cambridge: Cambridge University Press, 1982.

The Pan-African Orchestra, op. 1. CD. Real World Records, CAR2350, 1995.

Pantaleoni, Hewitt. "Toward Understanding the Play of Sogo in Atsia." *Ethnomusicology* 16 (1972): 1–37.

———. "Three Principles of Timing in Anlo Dance Drumming." *African Music* 5 (1972): 50–63.

Pareles, Jon. "The Rhythm Century: The Unstoppable Beat." *New York Times*, May 3 1998, 1.

Pegg, Carole, Helen Myers, et. al. "Ethnomusicology." In *The New Grove Dictionary of Music and Musicians*. Volume 8, 367–403. 2d ed. Edited by Stanley Sadie and John Tyrell, London: Macmillan, 2001.

Powers, Harold. "Language Models and Music Analysis." *Ethnomusicology* 25 (1980): 1–60.

———. "Rhythm." In *The New Harvard Dictionary of Music*. 700–706. Edited by Don Randel. Cambridge, Mass.: Harvard University Press, 1986.

Pressing, Jeff. "Cognitive Isomorphisms between Pitch and Rhythm in World Musics: West Africa, the Balkans and Western Tonality." *Studies in Music* 17 (1983): 38–61.

———. "Rhythmic Design in the Support Drums of Agbadza." *African Music* 6 (1983): 4–15.

Radano, Ronald. "Hot Fantasies: American Modernism and the Idea of Black Rhythm." In *Music and the Racial Imagination*. Edited by Ronald Radano and Philip V. Bohlman, 459–80. Chicago: University of Chicago Press, 2001.

———. *Lying Up a Nation: Race and the Origins of Black Music*. Chicago: University of Chicago Press, forthcoming.

———, and Philip Bohlman, eds. *Music and the Racial Imagination*. Chicago: University of Chicago Press, 2001.

Rahn, Jay. "Asymmetrical Ostinatos in Sub-Saharan Music: Time, Pitch and Cycles Reconsidered." *In Theory Only* 9 (1987): 23–37.

———. "Turning the Analysis Around: Africa-Derived Rhythms and Europe-Derived Music Theory." *Black Music Research Journal* 16 (1996): 71–89.

Randel, Don Michael, ed. *The New Harvard Dictionary of Music.* Cambridge, Mass.: Harvard University Press, 1986.

Ranger, Terence. *The Invention of Tribalism in Zimbabwe.* Gweru, Harare, Gokomere, Zimbabwe: Mambo Press, 1985.

Ratner, Leonard. *The Beethoven String Quartets: Compositional Strategies and Rhetoric.* Stanford, Calif.: Stanford Bookstore, 1995.

Reader, John. *Africa: A Biography of the Continent.* New York: Alfred A. Knopf, 1998.

Repercussions: A Celebration of African-American Music. Directed by Geoffrey Haydon and Dennis Marks. RM Arts and Channel Four TV, 1984.

Reich, Steve. Writings on Music, 1865–2000. Edited with an introduction by Paul Hillier. New York: Oxford University Press, 2002.

Richards, Paul. "A Quantitative Analysis of the Relationship between Language Tone and Melody in a Hausa Song." *African Language Studies* 13 (1972): 137–61.

Roberts, John Storm. *Black Music of Two Worlds.* New York: Praeger, 1972.

Robinson, J. Bradford. "The Jazz Essays of Theodor Adorno." *Popular Music* 13 (1994): 1–25.

Rouget, Gilbert. "Benin." In *The New Grove Dictionary of Music and Musicians.* Volume 2, 487–493. Edited by Stanley Sadie. London: Macmillan, 1980.

———. *Un roi Africain et sa musique de cour: Chants et danses du palais à Porto-Novo sous le régne de Gbèfa (1948–76).* Paris: CNRS Editions, 1996.

Rumbolz, Robert Charles. "'A Vessel for Many Things': Brass Bands in Ghana." Ph. D. diss, Wesleyan University, 2000.

Rycroft, David. Review of *African Rhythm and African Sensibility* by John Chernoff. *Popular Music 1.* Edited by Richard Middleton and David Horn, 208–10. Cambridge: Cambridge University Press, 1981.

———. "Tribal Style and Free Expression." *African Music* 1 (1954): 16–27.

———. "Nguni Vocal Polyphony." *Journal of the International Folk Music Council* 19 (1967): 88–103.

Sackey, Chrys. *Konkoma: Eine Musikform der Fanti-Jungfischer in den 40er and 50er Jahren (Ghana, Westafrika).* Berlin: D. Reimer, 1989.

Sadie, Stanley and John Tyrell, eds. *The New Grove Dictionary of Music.* 2d edition. 29 vols. London: Macmillan, 2001.

Said, Edward. *Orientalism.* New York: Pantheon Books, 1978.

Sallée, Pierre. *Deux études sur la musique du Gabon.* Paris: O.R.S.T.O.M, 1978.

Sandner, Wolfgang. "Popularmusik als somatisches Stimulans: Adornos Kritik der 'leichten Musik.'" In *Adorno und die Musik.* Edited by Otto Koleritsch, 125–32. Graz: Universal Edition, 1979.

Schenker, Heinrich. *Free Composition.* Translated by Ernst Oster. New York: Longmann, 1979. Orig. pub. as *Der freie Satz,* 1935.

Scherzinger, Martin Rudolf. "Notes on a Postcolonial Musicology: The Case of Inventing African Rhythm." Unpublished paper.

———. "Musical Formalism as Radical Political Critique: From European Modernism
to African Spirit Possession." Ph.D. diss., Columbia University, 2000.

———. "Negotiating the Music-Theory/African-Music Nexus: A Political Critique of
Ethnomusicological Anti-Formalism and a Strategic Analysis of the Harmonic
Patterning of the Shona Mbira Song *Nyamaropa.*" *Perspectives of New Music* 39
(2001): 5–118.

———. "Review of *Music, Modernity and the Global Imagination* by Veit Erlmann."
Journal of the Royal Musical Association 126 (2001): 117–41.

———. "Art Music in a Cross-Cultural Context: The Case of Africa," forthcoming.

Schneider, Marius. "Primitive Music." In *The New Oxford History of Music. Volume 1:
Ancient and Oriental Music,* 1–82. Edited by Egon Wellesz. London: Oxford University Press, 1957.

Schuller, Gunther. *Early Jazz: Its Roots and Musical Development.* New York: Oxford
University Press, 1968.

Senghor, Léopold. "Africa-Negro Aesthetics." *Diogenes* 16 (1956): 23–38.

Serwadda, Moses, and Hewitt Pantaleoni. "Possible Notation for African Dance Drumming." *African Music* 4 (1968): 47–52.

Shelemay, Kay Kauffman. "Notation and Oral Tradition." In *The Garland Encyclopedia of
World Music: Africa.* Edited by Ruth M. Stone, 156–63. New York: Garland, 1998.

Shillington, Kevin. *History of Africa.* New York: St. Martin's Press, 1989.

Shiloah, Amnon. *The Theory of Music in Arabic Writings (c. 900–1900): Descriptive Catalogue of Manuscripts in Libraries of Europe and the USA.* Munich, 1979.

Silsbee, Robert H. "Acoustics." In *The New Harvard Dictionary of Music.* Edited by Don
M. Randel, 7–13. Cambridge, Mass.: Harvard University Press, 1986.

Slobin, Mark. "Ethical Issues." In *Ethnomusicology: An Introduction.* Edited by Helen
Myers, 329–36. London: Macmillan Press, 1992.

Solie, Ruth. "Introduction: On Difference." In *Musicology and Difference: Gender and
Sexuality in Music Scholarship.* Edited by Ruth Solie, 1–20. Berkeley: University of
California Press, 1993.

Soyinka, Wole. "African Traditions at Home in the Opera House." *New York Times,* April
25, 1999, Arts and Leisure, 25–26.

Spivak, Gayatri Chakravorty, with Ellen Rooney. "In a Word [Interview]." *Differences*
1(1989): 124–56.

———. *A Critique of Postcolonial Reason: Toward a History of the Vanishing Present.*
Cambridge, Mass.: Harvard University Press, 1999.

Sprigge, R. G. S. "The Ghanaian Highlife: Notation and Sources." *Music in Ghana* 2
(1961): 70–94.

———. "A Song from Eweland's Adangbe: Notes and Queries." *Ghana Notes and
Queries* 10 (1968): 23–28.

Stock, Jonathan. "The Application of Schenkerian Analysis to Ethnomusicology: Problems and Possibilities." *Music Analysis* 12 (1993): 215–40.

———. "New Musicologies, Old Musicologies: Ethnomusicology and the Study of Western Music." *Current Musicology* 62 (1998): 40–68.

———. Review of *Seize the Dance* by M. Kisliuk. *Music and Letters* 81 (2000): 479–84.

Stokes, Martin, et al. "Ethnomusicology." In *The New Grove Dictionary of Music and Musicians.* 2nd ed. Edited by Stanley Sadie and John Tyrell. London: Macmillan, 2001.

Stone, Ruth M. *Let the Inside Be Sweet: The Interpretation of Music Event among the Kpelle of Liberia.* Bloomington: Indiana University Press, 1982.

———, ed. *The Garland Encyclopedia of World Music: Africa.* New York: Garland, 1998.

Tagg, Philip. "Analysing Popular Music: Theory, Method and Practice." In *Popular Music 2: Theory and Method.* Edited by Richard Middleton and David Horn, 37–67. Cambridge: Cambridge University Press, 1982.

———. "Letter to the Editor." *Popular Music* 8 (1994): 285–98.

Taiwo, Olufemi. "Exorcising Hegel's Ghost: Africa's Challenge to Philosophy." Website at www.web.africa.ufl.edu/asq/v1/4/2.htm

Taruskin, Richard. "Letter to the Editor." *Music Analysis* 5 (1986): 313–20.

———. *Defining Russia Musically.* Princeton, N.J.: Princeton University Press, 1997.

Taylor, Charles. *Multiculturalism: Examining the Politics of Recognition.* Edited by Amy Gutman. Princeton, N.J.: Princeton University Press, 1994.

Taylor, Timothy D. *Global Pop: World Music, World Markets.* New York: Routledge, 1997.

Tempels, Placide. *Bantu Philosophy.* Paris: Présence Africaine, 1959. Originally published as *La philosophie bantoue.* Elisabethville, Belgian Congo: Lovania, 1945.

Temperley, David. Review of *African Rhythm: A Northern Ewe Perspective* by K. Agawu. *Current Musicology* 62 (1998): 69–83.

———. "Meter and Grouping in African Music: A View from Music Theory." *Ethnomusicology* 44 (2000): 65–96.

Todorov, Tzvetan. *Mikhail Bakhtin: The Dialogical Principle.* Minneapolis: University of Minnesota Press, 1981.

Tomlinson, Gary. *Music in Renaissance Magic: Toward a Historiography of Others.* Chicago: University of Chicago Press, 1993.

———. "Ideologies of Aztec Song." *Journal of the American Musicological Society* 48 (1995): 343–79.

———. "Musical Pasts and Postmodern Musicologies: A Response to Lawrence Kramer." *Current Musicology* 53 (1993): 18–24.

Tracey, Hugh. "The State of Folk Music in Bantu Africa." *African Music* 1 (1954): 8–11.

Tsukada, Kenichi. "Variation and Unity in African Harmony: A Study of Mukanda Songs of the Luvale in Zambia." In *Florilegio Musicale. Festschrift für Professor Dr. Kataoka Gido zu seinem siebzigsten Geburtstag.* Edited by Usaburo Mabuchi et al., 157–97. Tokyo: Onagaku no Tomo, 1990.

Uzoigwe, Joshua. *Ukom: A Study of African Craftsmanship.* Okigwe, Nigeria: Fasmen Educational and Research Publications, 1998.

Vansina, Jan. *Oral Tradition as History.* Madison: University of Wisconsin Press, 1985. Orig. pub. 1961.

Veal, Michael. *Fela: The Life and Times of an African Musical Icon.* Philadelphia: Temple University Press, 2000.

Vogel, Joseph O., ed. *Encyclopedia of Pre-colonial Africa.* London: Sage Publications, 1997.

Wachsmann, Klaus P. "Music." *Journal of the Folklore Institute* (Indiana University) 6 (1969): 164–91.

———, ed. *Essays on Music and History in Africa.* Evanston, Ill.: Northwestern University Press, 1971.

———, and Peter Cooke. "Africa." In *The New Grove Dictionary of Music and Musicians.* Edited by Stanley Sadie. Volume 1, 144–153. London: Macmillan, 1980.

Walker, Judith Ann. "Rhythmic Non-Alignment in Aboriginal Australian, West African, and Twentieth-Century Art Musics." Ph.D. diss., University of Wisconsin at Madison, 1983.

Walser, Robert. *Running with the Devil: Power, Gender, and Madness in Heavy Metal Music.* Middletown, Conn.: Wesleyan University Press, 1993.

Wängler, Hans-Heinrich. "Über Beziehungen zwischen gesprochenen und gesungenen Tonhöhen in afrikanischen Tonsprachen." In *Musik in Afrika.* Edited by Artur Simon, 58–65. Berlin: Museum für Völkerkunde, 1983.

Ward, William E. F. "Music in the Gold Coast." *Gold Coast Review* 3 (1927): 199–223.

———. *My Africa.* Accra: Ghana Universities Press, 1991.

Waterman, Christopher. *Jùjú: A Social History and Ethnography of an African Popular Music.* Chicago: University of Chicago Press, 1990.

———. "The Uneven Development of Africanist Ethnomusicology: Three Issues and a Critique." In *Comparative Musicology and Anthropology of Music: Essays on the History of Ethnomusicology.* Edited by Bruno Nettl and Philip V. Bohlman, 169–86. Chicago: University of Chicago Press, 1991.

———. "Africa." In *Ethnomusicology: Historical and Regional Studies.* Edited by Helen Myers, 240–59. London: Macmillan, 1992.

———. "'Racial Imagination' and Yorubá Popular Music." Paper delivered at the Annual Meeting of the Society for Ethnomusicology, 1993.

———. "Review of John Gray, *African Music: A Bibliographical Guide.*" *Notes* 51 (1994): 213–15.

Waterman, Richard A. "'Hot' Rhythm in Negro Music." *Journal of the American Musicological Society* 1 (1948): 24–37.

———. "African Influence on the Music of the Americas." In *Acculturation in the Americas. Proceedings and Selected Papers.* Edited by Sol Tax, 207–18. New York: Cooper Square Publishers, 1967 [c1952].

Weman, Henry. *African Music and the Church in Africa.* Translated by Eric J. Sharpe. Uppsala: Svenska Institutet för Missionsforskning, 1960.

West African Music: The Rough Guide. CD. London: World Music Network, 1995.

Westermann, Diedrich. *Evefiala or Ewe-English Dictionary.* Berlin: Reimer, 1928.

———. *Gbesela yeye or English-Ewe Dictionary.* Berlin: Reimer, 1930.

When the Moment Sings (with Jon-Roar Bjorkvold). Oslo, Norway: Visions TV, 1995.

Wiggins, Trevor. "Drumming in Ghana." In *Composing the Music of Africa: Composition, Interpretation and Realisation.* Edited by Malcolm Floyd, 45–66. Aldershot, U.K.: Ashgate, 1999.

Wilson, Olly. "On the Significance of the Relationship between African and Afro-American Music." *The Black Perspective in Music* 2 (1974): 3–22.

Wiredu, Kwasi. *Philosophy and an African Culture.* Cambridge: Cambridge University Press, 1980.

———. *Cultural Particulars and Universals: An African Perspective.* Bloomington: Indiana University Press, 1996.

Yai, Olabiyi Babalola. "Theory and Practice in African Philosophy: The Poverty of Speculative Philosophy. A Review of the Work of P. Hountondji, M. Towa, et al." *Second Order* 2, no. 2 (1977): 3–20.

Yankah, Kwesi. "The Akan Highlife Song: A Medium of Cultural Reflection or Deflection?" *Research in African Literatures* 15 (1984): 568–82.

Young, Robert. *White Mythologies: Writing History and the West.* London: Routledge, 1990.

Zabana, Kongo. *African Drum Music: Adowa.* Accra, Ghana: Afram Publications, 1997.

———. *African Drum Music: Slow Agbekor.* Accra, Ghana: Afram Publications, 1997.

———. *African Drum Music: Kpanlogo.* Accra, Ghana: Afram Publications, 1997.

———. "Form in African Music." Paper Presented at the Center for Intercultural Music Conference, Cambridge, August 2001.

Zemp, Hugo. *Musique Dan: La Musique dans la pensée et la vie sociale d'une société africaine.* Paris: La Haye, Mouton, 1971.

Zielnica, Krzysztof. "Biliographie der Ewe in Westafrika." *Acta Ethnologica et Linguistica* 38 (1976): 1–177.

Zuckerkandl, Victor. *Sound and Symbol. Vol. 2: Man the Musician.* Translated by Norbert Guterman. Princeton, N.J.: Princeton University Press, 1973.

Index